THE Clothes BOOK

THE Clothes BOOK

Charmian Watkins

DORLING KINDERSLEY · LONDON

Editors Bridget Harris, Melanie Miller
Art Editor Denise Brown
Designer Debbie Lee
Managing Editor Amy Carroll

First published in Great Britain in 1984 by
Dorling Kindersley Limited
9 Henrietta Street
Covent Garden, London WC2E 8PS

Second impression 1984

British Library Cataloguing in Publication Data
Watkins, Charmian
   The clothes book
   1. Dressmaking
   I. Title
   646.4′3204   TT515

   ISBN 0-86318-030-2

Printed in Italy by A. Mondadori, Verona

Contents

In *The Clothes Book* I have set out to present a completely new and original approach to home dressmaking, offering a unique opportunity to make your own complete wardrobe of co-ordinated original designer clothes. Dressing is an important part of our daily lives, and vanity apart, most of us like to feel we look our best on every occasion. However, despite our continuing efforts, few of us are totally satisfied with the clothes we have and the way we look. Whilst mass-produced, chain-store garments lack the individuality most of us like to express through our clothes, designer originals tend to be financially beyond our reach.

In an attempt to solve this dilemma, after looking closely at the needs and budgets of most women today, I decided to create an extensive and versatile collection of interrelated designs for women of all ages and lifestyles – all of which can be made at home. The resulting fifty garment collection includes clothes for every occasion and season: day or evening, winter or summer, work or leisure. At the same time, I have tried to incorporate different slants in each of the outfits so that you can choose the particular image you desire, be it classical, directional, casual or youthful.

At a more practical level, I have tried to present the dressmaking aspect of *The Clothes Book* in a new and exciting way. It is frustrating that many commercial paper patterns offer little opportunity to see the actual texture, fabric and finer details of a garment. By including large, full-colour photographs of every article in the collection, I hope you will be able to picture and understand just what it is you are aiming at before you even choose your fabric. At the back of the book I have provided a complete "how-to" sewing course, explaining all the common dressmaking techniques required for making the garments, so that you always have a reference at hand. Moreover, by making up each of the designs myself, I hit upon specific techniques and methods which became common to all the garments. This proved invaluable as it served to hold the entire collection together not only through its themes but also through the finish and final line. Once you become familiar with these techniques, which I have described fully in the text, you'll find they become a time-saving routine, which cuts out many of the complexities encountered when following individual dressmaking patterns and which can be applied to all your sewing projects.

Although I have separated the garments thematically into sections, I hope you will not feel restricted by them. I have intentionally designed the collection with a "mix-and-match" element in mind, in the hope that you will feel encouraged to create outfits as well as individual garments. I have added suggestions for alternative fabrics and colourways and for different ways of wearing and combining outfits. Once you have made your basic patterns you will undoubtedly discover a variety of ways of interpreting particular shapes. Additionally, at the back of the book you will find a chart suggesting alternative combinations for each of the designs. Use it to explore different ways of combining garments within the collection and to experiment with alternative fabrics, so that ultimately you evolve a wardrobe which exactly matches your lifestyle.

The Clothes Book is about dressing creatively, about making the most of your time and money to produce clothes that are fashionable, wearable, well-made and inexpensive. Use it to produce a year by year collection which is unique and entirely your own!

HOW TO USE THIS BOOK

FIRST OF ALL . . .

Choose a pattern – flip through the book to find a garment or outfit you like the look of, or consult the mix-and-match chart at the back of the book to co-ordinate your own outfit. The outlines on pp. 132–3 give a clear impression of the front and back views of the different garments. The way outfits have been put together is not definitive – mix and match the designs as illustrated opposite to produce individual looks to suit your particular needs.

Also take into account your own sewing skills and the time available to you before embarking on a project. The colour coding (p. 132) indicates the degree of expertise required to make up the various garments. *Very easy* garments are quick to sew and are ideal for beginners as they are based on simple shapes and have few extra details. *Easy* garments are also based on simple shapes, but tend to have a few additional features such as fastenings, pockets and collars. *Moderate* garments require a little extra time but not necessarily greater expertise; they are made up from several pattern pieces which give a more stylised finish. *Advanced* patterns require special materials and techniques, such as linings, bound buttonholes and simple tailoring; however, time spent on these will be rewarded by the thoroughly professional look of the finished garment.

THEN . . .

Choose your fabric. The amount of fabric you need is given at the beginning of each pattern. Each garment has been made up in a suitable fabric, and alternative suggestions have been given. Many of the lightweight separates and dresses work just as well made up in heavier weight fabrics, and vice versa. Where a garment is made with features in contrasting fabric, separate allowances for the "contrast" fabric have been given alongside the "main" (or "self") fabric of the main body of the garment. The pattern pieces are referred to accordingly on the pattern charts.

Having decided on your pattern and bought the fabric, read through the entire pattern instructions. Use the photograph, the pattern chart (found at the end of each section) and the outlines to help clarify features, and refer to the sewing techniques in the back of the book if you don't understand any of the terms used.

NEXT . . .

Decide your size. Most of the pattern charts are graded for sizes 10, 12 and 14 (see p. 141 for breakdown of measurements), but a few of the patterns are designed as one-size garments. When deciding on your size, take into account the cut of the garment: some are intentionally loose-fitting, or have emphasized features (e.g. shoulders), while others are close-fitting. Consult the introduction for each garment. It is always possible to alter a pattern to fit your particular shape.

Seam and hem allowances are included on the pattern pieces and the outline given on the chart is the cutting line. Seam allowances are 1.5cm unless otherwise stated – always consult the instructions on the chart. Hemlines are indicated, but check the overall measurements are suitable for your height and taste before cutting the pattern. Try on the finished garment before hemming.

NOW . . .

Cut out your pattern. Transferring the patterns to the pattern paper is very easy – however if you need it, a full step-by-step guide is given in the sewing techniques section, as are helpful tips for cutting out. Each pattern piece carries its own cutting out instruction.

For example:

Cut two opposite but identically shaped pieces, right or wrong sides together, depending on your fabric.

Cut two identical pieces, on separate, folded pieces of fabric.

Cut one piece, with the fabric facing uppermost, as this is the way it will appear in the garment.

A more extensive key to the marks on the patterns appears on p. 144. Where a pair of collar pieces, yoke pieces, placket pieces or cuff pieces are to be cut, the two resulting pieces will become the "top" and "under" pieces to distinguish them, and are referred to as such throughout the main body of the text.

FINALLY . . .

Start assembling your garment. Follow the instructions carefully, and refer to the diagrams and the sewing techniques when necessary. Right and wrong sides of the fabric are indicated in the diagrams with different shades. Remember to try on your garment at all stages, and press after completing each stage. We have included a small ⊒ symbol as a guide.

HAVE FUN . . .

Creating your own designer wardrobe – the possibilities are endless!

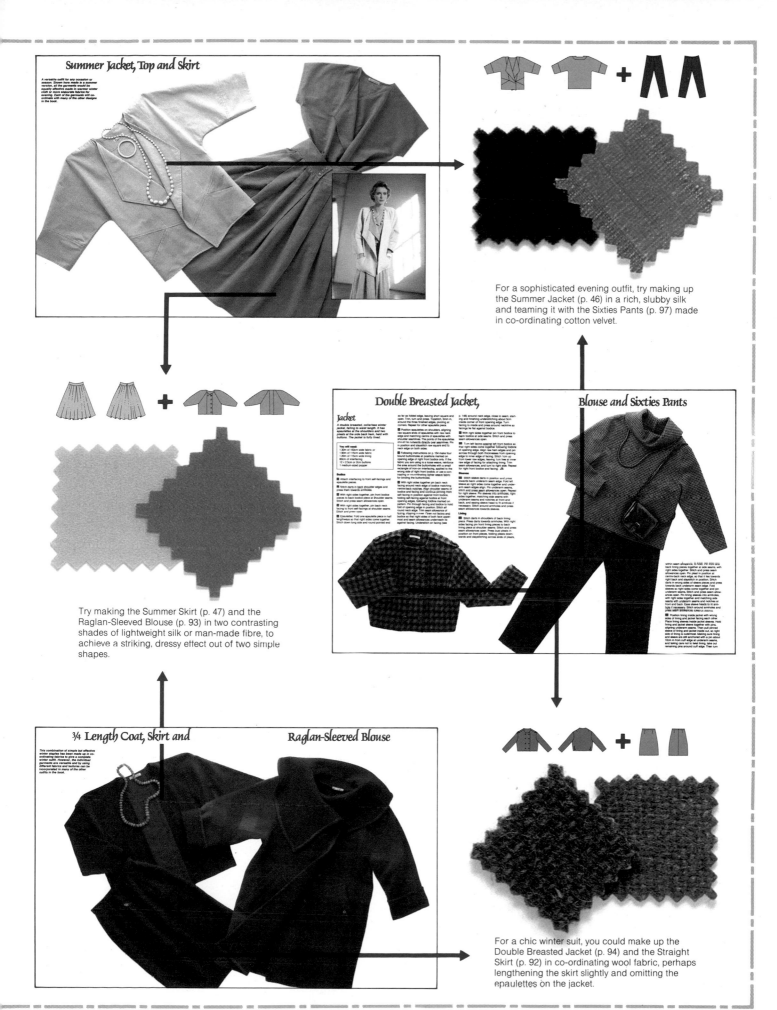

Summer Jacket, Top and Skirt

For a sophisticated evening outfit, try making up the Summer Jacket (p. 46) in a rich, slubby silk and teaming it with the Sixties Pants (p. 97) made in co-ordinating cotton velvet.

Try making the Summer Skirt (p. 47) and the Raglan-Sleeved Blouse (p. 93) in two contrasting shades of lightweight silk or man-made fibre, to achieve a striking, dressy effect out of two simple shapes.

Double Breasted Jacket, Blouse and Sixties Pants

Jacket

A double breasted, collarless winter jacket, falling to waist length. It has epaulettes at the shoulders and two pleats at the side back hem, held with buttons. The jacket is fully lined.

¾ Length Coat, Skirt and Raglan-Sleeved Blouse

For a chic winter suit, you could make up the Double Breasted Jacket (p. 94) and the Straight Skirt (p. 92) in co-ordinating wool fabric, perhaps lengthening the skirt slightly and omitting the epaulettes on the jacket.

Fabric suggestions – a plaid cotton shirt and plain canvas skirt give a more feminine effect.

Safari Jacket and Skirt

Jacket

A semi-fitting short-sleeved jacket with characteristic inverted pleat pockets and detailed pocket flaps. The wealth of top-stitching and lapelled collar lend it military style – team it with the safari skirt or shorts.

You will need:
1.50m of 150cm wide fabric *or*
1.90m of 115cm wide fabric
8 press-studs

Epaulettes

1 Place right sides of one pair of epaulette pieces together and stitch around both long sides and pointed end, allowing a 5mm seam allowance and leaving square ends open. Trim points, turn and press. Edgestitch close to seam edges then topstitch 5mm in from edgestitching. Repeat for other epaulette.

Pockets

2 *Pocket triangles:* Place right sides of one pair of triangle tab pieces together and stitch the two shorter seams of the triangle point, leaving the longest edge open. Trim point, turn and press. Edgestitch around the two seamed edges of the point and topstitch 5mm in from edgestitching. Repeat for other triangle tab.

3 *Pocket flaps:* Place right sides of one pair of pocket flap pieces together and insert a triangle between the two pieces, aligning notches and raw edges, so that the point faces inwards. Pin in position. Stitch around the flap, leaving a 5cm gap in the top seam through which to turn. Trim seam allowance of triangle and corners of flap, turn and press. Leaving top of flap unstitched, edgestitch around sides and lower edge of flap. Topstitch 5mm in from edgestitching. Repeat for other pocket flap.

4 *Pocket bags:* Set inverted pleat in pocket by folding pocket piece in half lengthways along centre foldline with right sides facing. Align notches to either side of centre foldline and stitch down from top edge as far as (a). Turn pocket to right side and align centre-front notch with stitching line, so the pleat lies evenly to either side of the stitching line. Press in pleat. Staystitch across top and bottom of pocket to hold pleat in place. Starting at the top of the pocket, edgestitch close to stitching line in centre of pleat around either side of the line, pivoting the needle at (a) and stitching through to the back of the pleat. Then topstitch 5mm out from edgestitching, forming a "V" at lower point (see fig. 1). Repeat for other pocket.

5 Turn over 1cm along top of one pocket to wrong side and stitch. Turn over 3cm to right side along foldline to form facing. Stitch down sides of fold. Turn, press and neaten all remaining raw seam allowances of pocket. On wrong side of pocket edgestitch along inner folded edge of facing, through to right side. Press in three remaining seam allowances to wrong side. Repeat for other pocket.

6 Pin a completed pocket in position on right bodice front. Tack and then edgestitch around

sides and bottom of pocket. Topstitch 5mm in from edgestitching.

7 Pin one pocket flap to right front, setting it into position 1cm above top of pocket so that centre of pocket triangle aligns with centre of pocket pleat. Stitch across top edge of flap to attach flap to jacket front, then topstitch 5mm in from edgestitching line. Repeat for left pocket and flap.

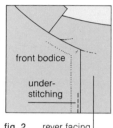

finished
topstitched
pocket
bag

fig. 1

Yoke

8 Placing right sides together, pin both jacket fronts to top yoke at shoulders. Stitch and press seam allowances up towards shoulderline. On right side, edgestitch on yoke close to seam through all seam allowances. Topstitch 5mm in from edgestitching. Pin right side of jacket back to right side of top yoke. Stitch and press seam allowances towards shoulder. Edgestitch close to seam on yoke through all seam allowances, and then topstitch 5mm in from edge-stitching.

Collar

9 Place right sides of collar pieces together and, leaving curved edge open, stitch around remaining three sides. Trim seams and corners, turn and press. Staystitch long raw curved edges together. Neaten inside edge of front facings. Placing right sides together pin shoulder of facing to shoulder of under yoke. Stitch and repeat for other front facing. Neaten seam allowances and press open.

10 Placing under side of collar to right side of bodice and aligning notches and all raw edges, pin collar in position and tack. Lay facing on top, right side downwards and aligning notches. Pin and tack facing to bodice, starting at centre-back of neck and working out to rever corners and down front bodice to hem. Repeat for other side, again working out from centre-back of neck. Stitch, trim corners and clip curves. Turn complete facing to right side.

Revers

11 Spread facing and bodice so that right sides of both face uppermost and seam allowances underneath lie against facing. Starting at a point about 6cm down from rever point on right side of front bodice, understitch on bodice through seam allowances, close to seam (see fig. 2 and p. 148). This will hold the underneath of the rever neatly in place when it is turned. Continue understitching to a point about 20cm down from rever point. Repeat for other side. Understitch around neck edge of yoke facing through seam allowances, starting understitching 4cm in from point where collar joins facing and continuing around neck edge of yoke to equivalent point 4cm in from opposite collar edge. Press all facings and collar. To edge-stitch rever it is necessary to stitch on upper surface of bodice from hem to start of rever,

and then transfer to upper surface of rever, so that the edgestitching is neat the whole way round. Starting at left front hem, edgestitch on right side of bodice, through all seam allowances and facing to a point level with halfway up the pocket. Break stitching here; draw threads to inside and tie off. Then turn jacket so rever facing is uppermost and continue edgestitching from the point where you broke off, up around the rever points, and around the collar edge, down the right side of the bodice, until you reach the point opposite where you broke the edgestitching on the left bodice. Again draw threads to inside and tie off. Turn to the right side of right bodice, and continue edgestitching down to hem. Using the same method of breaking stitching, topstitch 5mm in from edgestitching all the way round the bodice, revers and collar (see fig. 3).

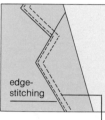

front bodice

under-
stitching

edge-
stitching

fig. 2   rever facing

fig. 3   topstitching

12 Turn jacket to inside and pin loose shoulder seam allowances of yoke facing to seam allowance of armhole openings, being careful not to pull the yoke too tight. Slipstitch yoke to armhole seam allowance. Press under seam allowance at lower edge of back yoke facing to wrong side. Adjusting pressed under seam allowance if necessary, pin in position over back yoke seam and slipstitch to top yoke seam allowance. With right sides together, pin both front bodice pieces to back bodice down side seams. Stitch, neaten seam allowances separately and press open.

Sleeves

13 With right sides facing, pin underarm seam of right sleeve and stitch. Neaten seam allowances and press open. Press under 5mm at hem of sleeve to wrong side, and then press under a further 3cm. Tack around fold through to right side of sleeve. On right side of sleeve, topstitch around sleeve, 3cm in from hem, catching inner edge of turnback in stitching. Topstitch again 5mm below this line of stitching. Repeat for left sleeve.

14 Pin epaulettes to shoulders, with points facing towards neck, aligning all raw edges and notches at armhole edge. Pin in sleeves, matching notches at front and back, easing any fullness around shoulder. Stitch and then trim 5mm from all seam allowances around armhole and neaten all raw edges together. Press seam allowances towards bodice. Press side seam allowances and underarm sleeve allowances flat at underarm point splitting seam allowance open to ease, and then edge-stitch around armhole seam on bodice through all seam allowances. Topstitch 5mm in from edgestitching. Repeat for other sleeve.

To finish

15 *Hem:* Turn under 5mm to wrong side around hem and stitch. Turn under a further

(see pattern charts on pp. 19, 20)

centimetre to wrong side and edgestitch along inner folded edge through to right side, all the way round the hem. Press thoroughly.

16 Attach four press-studs to jacket front where marked, one to each epaulette and pocket.

skirt

A close-fitting skirt with characteristic deep, inverted pleat pockets at either side. The skirt fastens with a front jeans style zip and studded waistband and also has inset front hip pockets with slight "rise" and tab detail at back waist. Shown here cut to just-above-the-knee, it can easily be lengthened and made in a heavier, winter fabric, with or without lower side pockets.

> **You will need:**
> 1.20m of 150cm wide fabric *or*
> 1.50m of 115cm wide fabric
> 75cm × 3cm of waistband stiffening
> 4 press-studs
> 2 hanging loops
> 20cm zip

1 Sew darts in back skirt piece, sewing them with right sides together and continuing stitching line of dart just beyond dart point. Press each dart towards side seam.

Hip pockets

2 With right sides facing, pin left pocket bag to left front of skirt around upper curved edge, matching notches. Stitch around curved edge, clip seam allowances and press towards pocket bag. Spread bag and skirt and understitch (see p. 148) on right side of pocket bag, close to original seamline through all seam allowances. Press pocket bag back against wrong side of skirt. On right side of skirt, edgestitch around curved seam edge and then topstitch 5mm in from edgestitching. Repeat for right front of skirt and pocket bag. **2**

3 With right sides together, pin left under pocket to left pocket bag, matching curves at inside edge. Stitch around curved inner seam and neaten seam allowances together. Press pocket and skirt section and position pocket against skirt, matching seam allowances at top and sides, allowing for the slight "rise" in the pocket for you to get your hand in. Staystitch across top and side of pocket to hold in position on skirt. Repeat for right pocket piece.

4 Placing right sides together pin left front skirt piece to back skirt piece at side seam. Stitch, neaten seam allowances separately and press open. Repeat for right front skirt piece.

Lower pockets

5 *Triangle tabs:* Place right sides of one pair of triangle tab pieces together and stitch the two shorter seams of the triangle point, leaving the longest edge open. Trim point, turn and press. Edgestitch around the two seamed edges of the point and then topstitch 5mm in from edgestitching. Repeat for other triangle tabs.

6 *Pocket flaps:* Place right sides of one pair of pocket flap pieces together and insert a triangle

between the two pieces, aligning notches and raw edges so that the point faces inwards. Pin in position. Stitch around the flap leaving a 5cm gap in the top edge through which to turn flaps. Trim seam allowance at edges of triangle and corners of flap, turn and press. Leaving top of flap unstitched, edgestitch around sides and lower edge of flap. Then topstitch 5mm in from edgestitching. Repeat for other pocket flap.

7 *Pocket bags:* Set inverted pleat in pocket by folding one pocket piece in half lengthways along centre foldline, with right sides together. Align notches at either side of centre foldline and stitch down from top edge as far as (**a**). Turn pocket to right side and align centre foldline with stitching line, so that the pleat lies evenly to either side. Press in pleat. Staystitch across top and bottom of pocket to hold pleat in place. Starting at the top edge of the pocket, edgestitch close to stitching line in centre of pleat around either side of the line, pivoting the needle at (**a**) and stitching through all thicknesses. Then topstitch 5mm out from edgestitching, forming a "V" in the stitching below (**a**) (see diagram on p. 11). Repeat for other lower pocket. **2**

8 Turn over 1cm along top of one pocket to wrong side and stitch. Turn over 3cm to right side along foldline, to form facing. Stitch down sides of fold. Turn, press and neaten all remaining raw seam allowances of pocket. On wrong side of pocket edgestitch along inner folded edge of facing, through to right side. Press in remaining three seam allowances to wrong side. Repeat for other pocket.

9 To attach pockets to skirt, lay skirt flat with right sides uppermost and pin pockets in position at points marked on pattern at either side of skirt. Edgestitch around the sides and bottom of pockets, stitching in a "V" at top edges to secure. Topstitch 5mm in from edgestitching around the three sides.

10 Pin pocket flaps to skirt, setting them in position 1cm above top of pockets so that centre of flap triangle aligns with centre of pocket pleat. Stitch across top edge of flap, stitching through unstitched gap, to attach flap to bodice. Then topstitch flap 5mm in from edgestitching. **2**

11 Turn skirt so that right sides of both front pieces come together along centre-front seam. Pin pieces together from (**b**), down and around curve of pleat as far as hem edge. Stitch seam. Neaten these seam allowances together, clipping across seam allowances at (**b**) to ease. On right side of skirt press pleat in position so that pleat seam points towards right side seam.

Inserting zip

12 *(Follow diagrams on p. 157 for displaced zip.)* With right side of fabric uppermost, place the zip face down on the left skirt front, so that the zip tape aligns with the opening edge of the front. Tack zip in position down this opening edge, following seamline, leaving other side of the zip free. Open zip for ease and stitch tacked side in position using zipper foot.

13 Press left front zip placket along foldline and neaten around lower curved edges. Place in position over stitched zip so that all raw edges lie along front opening edge and fold faces towards side seam. Tack in position along original stitching line and stitch through all thicknesses. Neaten all seam allowances together and turn so that placket and skirt front

lie flat, with seam allowances facing towards side seam. Edgestitch on skirt front down length of zip, close to original seam.

14 Neaten down and around long curved inside edge of right zip placket. With right sides together and aligning raw edges at front opening edge, tack this placket to right skirt front, allowing a 5mm seam allowance. Stitch down front opening edge. Press seam allowances towards side seam and turn placket to wrong side of skirt front. Following seamline at centre-front above pleat, press fold at front opening in position so that the seam between placket and skirt front lies slightly in from fold edge on inside.

15 Close zip and place skirt flat on table or ironing board so that skirt front faces upwards and zip also lies flat, facing upwards. Position free zip tape under right front, overlapping right front opening edge over left front opening edge so zip is completely concealed. The right front opening edge should join the centre-front seam neatly so that the entire opening, seam and pleat lie flat. Place a pin through all thicknesses at bottom of opening to hold all layers in position. Feeling through fabric, pin free zip tape to right placket and skirt front, taking care not to pin through to left placket underneath. Now open the zip and tack the free tape to the right placket *only,* in exactly the same position, but tacking so that your stitches do not come through to skirt front. Remove lower anchoring pin and stitch zip to right under placket only, close to zip teeth.

16 Tack single placket to right skirt front, 2cm from front opening edge, tacking from top of skirt round to (**b**). On right side of fabric, top-stitch through right skirt front and placket, using tacking line as your guide and topstitching from top edge down and around bottom curve of zip opening. Pull threads through at bottom and tie off. Make another line of top-stitching 5mm outside first line.

17 Turn to wrong side and with zip closed and plackets in position, stitch across lower ends of left and right plackets to hold both together.

18 *Belt loops:* Make loops for waistband by folding in 1cm to wrong side down each long side of one loop piece and pressing in position. Fold under 1cm at each short end and then fold strip in half again lengthways and press (see fig. 1). Edgestitch all around edge. Repeat for other five loops.

fig. 1

Waistband

19 Fold waistband in half lengthways along foldline, so that right sides come together. Stitch across short ends. Turn to right side and, with right sides facing, pin notched raw edge of waistband around top raw edge of skirt, matching notches and inserting one raw end of each belt loop at positions marked, so that they are sandwiched between waistband and skirt. Also sandwich in back triangle, aligning centre of triangle with first dart to the right of centre-back point, between belt loop and main skirt (see fig. 2). Stitch all around waist edge. Slip length of waistband stiffening inside waistband, positioning it behind seam allowances. Fold remain-

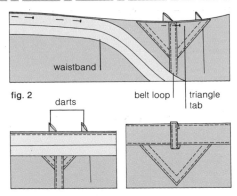

fig. 2

waistband

belt loop | triangle tab

darts

ing lower raw edge of waistband under to wrong side so that folded edge just covers original line of stitching, and tack in position. On right side of waistband, edgestitch around lower edge close to seam, catching in waistband underneath and inserting hanging loops. Continue edgestitching around front opening edges of band, round top and down other opening edge to point where you started. ⌐

To finish

20 *Hem:* Adjust hem length if necessary. Turn under 1cm to wrong side and stitch all round. Turn under a further 3cm to wrong side and press in position. Edgestitch on inside of skirt close to inner folded edge, through to right side. Turn skirt to right side and topstitch around hem, 5mm below line of edgestitching, to form a visible double row of stitching. ⌐

21 Attach studs to pocket triangles, back triangle and centre-front waistband.

Shorts

These loose-fitting shorts have double pleats into the waistband, side pockets and a jeans style zip fastening. Around the waist there are six belt loops and at each side seam, tabs and studs secure the roll-up hem. It would be possible to lengthen the legs to convert them into Bermuda shorts, or even longer pants.

> **You will need:**
> 1.00m of 150cm wide fabric *or*
> 1.20m of 115cm wide fabric
> 75cm × 3cm of waistband stiffening
> 7 press-studs
> 20cm zip

1 Folding material so that right sides come together, sew dart in each back piece, continuing line of stitching just beyond dart point. Press darts towards side seams.

Pockets

2 With right sides facing, pin left pocket bag to left front of shorts around upper curved edge, matching notches. Stitch around upper curved edge, clip seam allowances and press towards pocket bag. Spread bag and shorts front and understitch (see p. 148) on right side of pocket bag, close to original seamline, through all seam allowances. Press pocket bag back against wrong side of shorts front. On right side of shorts, edgestitch around curved seam edge and then topstitch 5mm in from edgestitching. Repeat for right pocket bag and right front of shorts. ⊐

3 With right sides together, pin left under pocket piece to left pocket bag, matching curves at inside edge. Stitch around curved inner seam and neaten seam allowances together. Press pocket and shorts section and position pocket against shorts, matching seam edges at waist and sides, allowing for the slight ''rise'' in the pocket for you to get your hand in. Staystitch across top and side of pocket to hold in position on shorts. Repeat for right pocket.

Inserting zip

4 Follow instructions on p. 157 for inserting a displaced zip; (c) on both front pieces is the point marking bottom of zip opening. When topstitching on right shorts front in step 8, first topstitch 2cm in from opening edge, starting at waist edge and stitching round in a curve to (c). Then topstitch again 5mm outside this line of stitching.

5 With right sides together, pin front pieces to both back pieces at side seams. Stitch down from waist edge as far as (a). At this point, clip across seam allowances as far as seamline. Turn seam so *wrong* sides come together and continue stitching seam down to hem. Neaten all seam allowances separately and press entire seam open on either side (see fig. 1).

6 Turn shorts inside out and pin right inside leg seams. Following same method as in step 5, stitch down to (b). Clip and turn seam to other side of fabric and stitch down to hem.

Neaten seam allowances separately, pressing open on either side. Repeat for remaining inside leg seam.

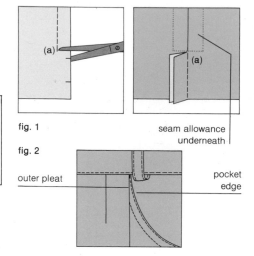

fig. 1

fig. 2

outer pleat | pocket edge

seam allowance underneath

7 Place right sides of back pieces together at centre-back seam. Aligning inside leg seams, pin entire seam together from (c) right round crotch point and up to top edge of centre-back. Stitch, continuing line of stitching at under crotch point round to back waist edge. Stitch entire seam again for strength. Clip curves and neaten seam allowances separately, pressing them open.

8 Pin pleat tucks in position at top front, pinning so that they face towards side seams. Overlap outer pleat on each side so that it aligns with top edge of pocket (see fig. 2).

9 Make belt loops by folding in 1cm to wrong side down each long side of one loop piece and pressing in position (see p. 12). Fold under 1cm at each short end and then fold strip in half again lengthways and press. Edgestitch all around edge. Repeat for remaining five loops.

Waistband

10 Fold waistband in half lengthways along foldline, so that right sides come together. Stitch across short ends. Turn to right side and with right sides facing, pin raw notched edge of waistband around raw waist edge of shorts, matching notches and inserting one raw end of each belt loop at each back dart, each side seam and just over each front pocket opening edge. The loops should be sandwiched between waistband and shorts. Stitch all around waist edge. Slip length of waistband stiffening inside waistband, positioning it behind seam allowances. Fold remaining lower raw edge of waistband under 1cm to wrong side and then fold band in half so that folded edge just covers original line of stitching. Tack in position. On right side of waistband, edgestitch around lower edge close to seam (catching in waistband underneath). Continue edgestitching around front opening edges of band, all around top and back down other opening edge to position where you started. ⊐

Side tabs

11 Place right sides of one pair of tab pieces together and stitch around both long sides and pointed end, allowing a 1cm seam allowance

and leaving square ends open. Trim points, turn and press. Fold in 1cm seam allowances at square ends to inside. Edgestitch close to seam around all edges and then topstitch 5mm in from edgestitching. Repeat for other tab. ⊐

To finish

12 *Hem:* Turn up 1cm to *right* side around hem edge and stitch. Turn up a further 4cm, press and edgestitch along inner folded edge through to wrong side. Repeat for hem of other leg. Roll up a further 4cm on each leg to right side and secure raw seam allowances inside fold at side seam with a few hand stitches.

13 Pin square end of one tab to inner folded edge of one leg at side seam so that point faces downwards. Slipstitch tab to side of shorts just inside folded edge, taking care not to catch turn up in stitching.

14 Repeat for other leg, and turn tabs up to right side of shorts so points face towards top edge of shorts. Attach press-studs at positions marked on pattern, placing one top stud on tab and three under studs on shorts side seam to allow for alternative positions of tabs. Hand stitch turn up of inside leg to inside leg seam to enclose all raw seam allowances.

15 Attach press-stud to centre-front point of waistband. ⊐

Vest

This simple vest top can be made in a variety of fabrics to co-ordinate with many of the other garments in the book. It is ideal for beginners or if you wish to make a garment quickly, and has machine-stitched bound neck and armholes.

> **You will need:**
> 1.00m of 150cm wide fabric *or*
> 1.00m of 115cm wide fabric

1 With right sides together, pin darts in place at side seams, where marked. Stitch darts, tapering stitching to a point just beyond bust point mark. Press darts downwards.

2 Pin right sides of back and front together at shoulder and side seams. Stitch, neaten seam allowances separately and press open.

3 At hem, turn in 5mm to wrong side and stitch all round hem. Turn in a further centimetre to wrong side and edgestitch close to inner folded edge, through to right side. ⊐

Binding armholes and neck opening

4 Pin armhole bias strip around armhole, placing right sides together. Beginning at underarm seam, stitch 5mm in from raw edge all the way round the armhole, trimming off and tucking under 5mm at end of strip to neaten when you arrive back at underarm seam. Press binding and seam allowances outwards, away from garment, and understitch on binding close to seam, through all seam allowances around armhole. Clip seam allowances and then turn in 5mm to wrong side along remaining raw

edge of binding and press. Pin or tack into position against wrong side of bodice and edgestitch around armhole close to inner folded edge of binding, through to right side. Repeat for other armhole. ⏛

5 Using the same method as for armhole above, bind neck opening. Press vest thoroughly.

Fabric suggestions – plain cotton for the vest, with a co-ordinating cotton poplin for the shorts transform the military theme into a more sporty look.

Safari Dress

This military-style dress has epaulettes, front tab opening, a back inverted pleat, flapped and triangled pockets with same pleat detail and a wealth of topstitching. Although it takes a while to make up, it is a dress which can be worn everyday for formal and informal occasions alike. Accessorize it with a leather belt threaded through the belt loops at the waist.

You will need:
2.30m of 150cm wide fabric or
3.10m of 115cm wide fabric
60cm of interfacing
11 press-studs or buttons

Epaulettes

1 Place right sides of one pair of epaulette pieces together and stitch around both long sides and pointed end, allowing a 5mm seam allowance and leaving square ends open. Trim points, turn and press. Edgestitch close to seam around stitched edges and then topstitch 5mm in from edgestitching. Repeat for other epaulette.

Pockets

2 *Pocket triangles:* Place right sides of one pair of triangle tab pieces together and stitch the two shorter seams of the triangle point, leaving the longest edge open. Trim point, turn and press. Edgestitch around the two seamed edges of the point and then topstitch 5mm in from edgestitching. Repeat for other three triangles.

3 *Pocket flaps:* Place right sides of one pair of pocket flap pieces together and insert a triangle in the middle of the two pieces, aligning all raw edges so that the point faces inwards. Pin in position. Stitch around the flap leaving a 5cm gap in the top edge unstitched through which to turn flaps. Trim seam allowance at edges of triangle and corners of flap, turn and press. Leaving top of flap unstitched, edgestitch around sides and lower edge of flap. Then topstitch 5mm in from edgestitching. Repeat for other two pocket flaps.

4 *Pocket bags:* Set inverted pleat in pocket by folding one pocket piece in half lengthways along centre foldline, with right sides together. Align notches at either side of centre foldline and stitch down from top edge as far as (**a**). Turn pocket to right side and align centre foldline with stitching line, so that the pleat lies evenly to either side. Press in pleat. Staystitch across top and bottom of pocket to hold pleat in place. Starting at the top edge of the pocket, edgestitch close to stitching line in centre of pleat around either side of the line, pivoting the needle at (**a**) and stitching through all thicknesses. Then topstitch 5mm out from edgestitching, forming a "V" in the stitching below (**a**) (see diagram on p. 11). Repeat for other two pockets.

5 Turn over 1cm along top of one pocket to wrong side and stitch. Turn over 3cm to right side along foldline, to form facing. Stitch down sides of fold. Turn, press and neaten all remaining raw seam allowances on pocket. On wrong side of pocket edgestitch along inner folded edge of facing. Press in remaining three seam allowances to wrong side. Repeat for other two pockets.

6 Pin completed *small* pocket to left dress front at pocket position marked on pattern. Tack in position and edgestitch around sides and bottom of pocket, starting and finishing stitching with a small triangle, to hold. Topstitch 5mm in from edgestitching. Set the two remaining larger pockets to one side. Pin smaller pocket flap to dress front, setting it into position 1cm above top of pocket so that centre of flap triangle aligns with centre of pocket pleat. Stitch across top edge of flap to attach flap to dress front then topstitch 5mm in from edge-stitching line.

7 *Front pleat:* On right dress front, at front pleat position marked, press 5cm in to wrong side down the length of pleat as far as hem edge. Pin right and left dress front pieces together along pleat seam and stitch. Neaten seam allowances together and press pleat towards right front of dress. Hold top of pleat in position with a line of staystitching just below diagonally cut edge, where tab will join.

Back split and inverted pleat

8 Turn 1cm to wrong side down each side of centre-back split and stitch. Neaten across bottom raw edge of centre-back inverted pleat. To position the pleat, fold dress back in half lengthways, with right sides together. Stitch from pleat point (**b**) at waist down to (**c**) above split, securing stitching at either end. With wrong side uppermost, spread pleat out evenly to either side of seam and pin in position. Edgestitch and then topstitch 5mm in all round pleat seam as in step 4, stitching a "V" at top and bottom of pleat seam. Position unstitched pleat in top edge of dress back, aligning notches. Staystitch across top of pleat. Turn neatened facings of split against wrong side of dress back and pin in position between bottom of pleat and edge of hem.

9 Pin remaining triangle to top edge of dress back so that all raw edges are together and point of triangle is aligned with centre of back pleat, pointing downwards. Staystitch in position. With right sides together pin back edge of top yoke to back of dress, and front edges of yoke to dress fronts. Stitch and press seam allowances upwards.

Front tab

10 With right sides facing, pin right front tab to right dress front, pinning down front opening edge, matching notches. Stitch down from neck to (**d**). Break stitching and slash seam allowances of dress and tab at corner almost to (**d**) (see fig. 1). Then pull over the lower raw edge of tab so it aligns with the top raw edge of pleat.

Continue stitching across top raw edge of pleat, starting at (**d**) and finishing at folded edge of pleat. Press seam allowances of tab and dress at front opening edge towards centre-front, and seam allowances along bottom of tab and top of pleat in, towards neck-line. Along remaining long raw edge of tab, press under 1cm to wrong side and tack in position. At top of tab, turn tab back on itself along foldline so that right sides come together. Stitch across top of tab, stitching 1.5cm down from top raw edge, starting at folded edge and finishing half way across width of tab. Turn tab so that wrong sides come together and set folded and tacked inner edge of tab over original line of stitching, so that all seam allowances are enclosed. Pin in position over original seam, leaving lower ends of tab pointing downwards. Slash across seam to (**e**) on left front of dress so that right tab lies flat.

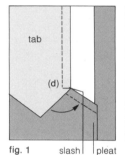
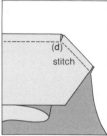

fig. 1   slash   pleat

11 Attach left tab to left dress front in the same way as right tab, but do not stitch around bottom of tab. Set fold in tab, and turn in 1cm seam allowance to wrong side down remaining raw edge and pin in position over original seam. Set left tab behind right tab, taking care not to tear slashed seam allowances, but making sure that both tabs lie flat at bottom of front opening.

Collar

12 Attach interfacing to under collar (see p. 153). With right sides facing pin top and under collar together and stitch around the three outer sides, leaving long curved inner edge open. Trim corners and seam allowances. Spread top and under collar and understitch on long stitched edge of under collar close to seamline, through under collar and seam allowances only, starting and finishing stitching 4cm inside collar points. Press collar, and edgestitch around the three finished sides and then topstitch 5mm in. Staystitch long curved raw edges of collar together. ⊐

13 Place under side of collar against right side of neck edge, matching centre-back and shoulderline seam notches, and aligning front edges with unstitched section of front tabs. Stitch all round neck edge, joining up to centre-front tabs where already stitched.

14 Pin right side of under yoke to neck opening, sandwiching collar between dress and under yoke. Stitch all around neck edge of yoke, following first line of stitching attaching collar. Trim seam allowances and clip curves, pressing seam allowances towards under yoke. Spread dress and under yoke and understitch on under yoke close to seam around neck edge, through seam allowances (see p. 148).

15 To finish under yoke press under 1.5cm along lower raw back edge and front shoulder edges to wrong side and tack. At centre-front of dress tuck raw front edges of under yoke under tab on each side and hold with a pin. Position under yoke on wrong side of dress at shoulder seams and back, placing folded edges directly over stitching lines. Tack in position and turn to right side. Edgestitch along lower edge of back yoke close to first stitching line through all thicknesses, catching in under yoke. Then topstitch 5mm in. Repeat edgestitching and topstitching along front yoke shoulder seams. Press.

16 To finish tabs, edgestitch on right side of inner seamed edge of left tab, close to first seamline, from top to bottom. Set right tab over left tab at bottom of front opening and hold with a pin. Edgestitch on right tab close to original seam down and around bottom of tab, catching in left tab along bottom of opening. Pivot needle and then stitch up outside folded edge of right tab for 3cm, stitching through left tab and all thicknesses. Break stitching, turn dress to wrong side and neaten seam allowances across bottom of tab together. Turn back to right side of dress and starting at the top, topstitch down inner folded edge of right tab, 5mm in from edgestitching, to a point 2cm above bottom of tab. Pull threads to inside and tie off. Position left tab behind right tab, so that both lie flat and continue line of topstitching through all thicknesses down to bottom of inner edge of tab, and across bottom to pleat edge. Pull threads to inside and tie off. ⊐

17 Finish side seams by placing right sides of dress front and back together and pin seams from armhole to hem. Stitch both seams, neaten seam allowances separately and press open.

Hip pockets

18 Arrange dress on ironing board so front is uppermost, and pin the two remaining pockets in position across side seams as marked on pattern. Follow step 6 for edgestitching and topstitching pockets and for attaching the two larger pocket flaps.

Sleeves

19 Fold left sleeve so right sides come together and align underarm seam edges, pinning in position. Stitch underarm seam, neaten seam allowances separately and press open. Turn under 5mm to wrong side around lower edge of sleeve and stitch. Turn under a further 3cm to

(see pattern charts on pp. 22, 23)

wrong side and press, holding in position with pins if necessary. Edgestitch around inner folded edge, stitching through to right side. Topstitch on right side of sleeve, 5mm below line of edgestitching, all around bottom of sleeve. Repeat for right sleeve.

20 Position an epaulette at each shoulder, aligning square raw edge between notches in shoulder edge, and with point of epaulette facing neck. Staystitch epaulettes to armhole edges. If necessary, ease top of sleeves (see p. 150 and p. 153) so that they fit armhole. Pin left sleeve into armhole opening, matching front and back notches, epaulette notches and underarm seams. Stitch, trim seam allowances to 1cm and neaten them together, clipping curves. Press seam allowances towards dress. Turn dress to right side and edgestitch all around armhole on dress, close to seamline. Topstitch again 5mm in from edgestitching all around armhole. Repeat for right sleeve. ◿

To finish

21 Turn back epaulettes so they lie flat along shoulder. Attach studs (or make buttonholes and sew on buttons) at stud positions marked (the epaulette should not pull the shoulder). Attach five studs down front tab at positions marked. Attach a stud to each of the three pocket triangles and centre-back triangle.

22 *Belt loops:* Try on dress with the belt you intend to wear and mark positions for four belt loops around waist, following positions marked on pattern, but checking for correct height. Also check length of hem at this point.

23 Make the four belt loops by folding in 1cm down each long side and then folding again in half lengthways, and tucking in 1cm at each end (see p. 12). Edgestitch all around the four edges of each loop. Attach each loop at positions marked on dress, stitching through belt loop and dress in a rectangle at each end of loop.

24 *Hem:* Having adjusted hem if necessary, turn under 1cm to wrong side, all around hem edge, and stitch. Turn under 3cm more and pin in position on wrong side. Edgestitch close to inner folded edge all around hem, pivoting needle 3cm in from folded edge of back split and turning stitching up and around split, stitching in a "V" at top of split. Continue stitching down other side of split, pivoting 3cm from hem edge and then stitch around hem catching in inner folded edge of hem. Topstitch 5mm below this line of edgestitching, following same course around split. Hand stitch corners of hem at lower edge of centre-back split (see figs. 3 and 4). ◿

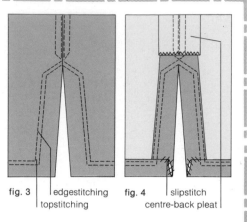

fig. 3 | edgestitching | topstitching

fig. 4 | slipstitch | centre-back pleat

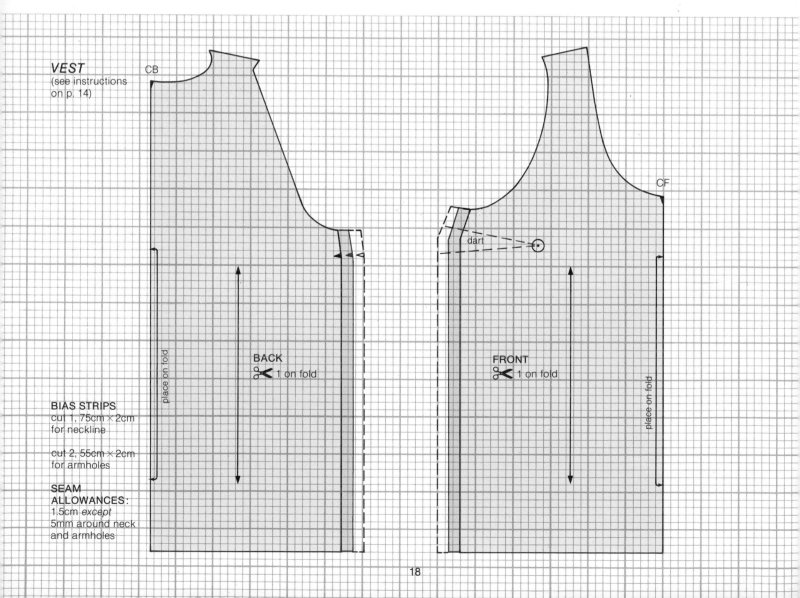

VEST
(see instructions on p. 14)

CB

CF

dart

place on fold

BACK
✂ 1 on fold

FRONT
✂ 1 on fold

place on fold

BIAS STRIPS
cut 1, 75cm × 2cm for neckline

cut 2, 55cm × 2cm for armholes

SEAM ALLOWANCES:
1.5cm *except* 5mm around neck and armholes

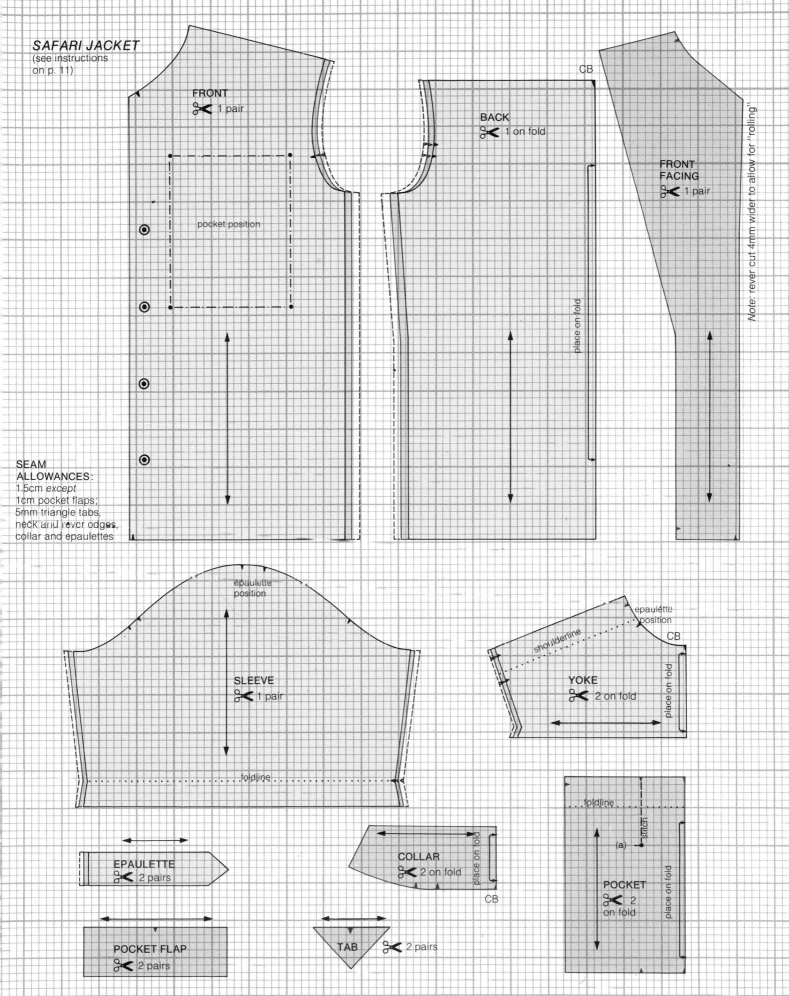

SAFARI JACKET
(see instructions on p. 11)

FRONT
✂ 1 pair

pocket position

SEAM ALLOWANCES:
1.5cm *except*
1cm pocket flaps;
5mm triangle tabs,
neck and rever edges,
collar and epaulettes

BACK
✂ 1 on fold

CB

place on fold

FRONT FACING
✂ 1 pair

Note: rever cut 4mm wider to allow for "rolling"

epaulette position

SLEEVE
✂ 1 pair

foldline

shoulderline

epaulette position

CB

YOKE
✂ 2 on fold

place on fold

EPAULETTE
✂ 2 pairs

COLLAR
✂ 2 on fold

place on fold

CB

foldline

stitch

(a)

POCKET
✂ 2 on fold

place on fold

POCKET FLAP
✂ 2 pairs

TAB ✂ 2 pairs

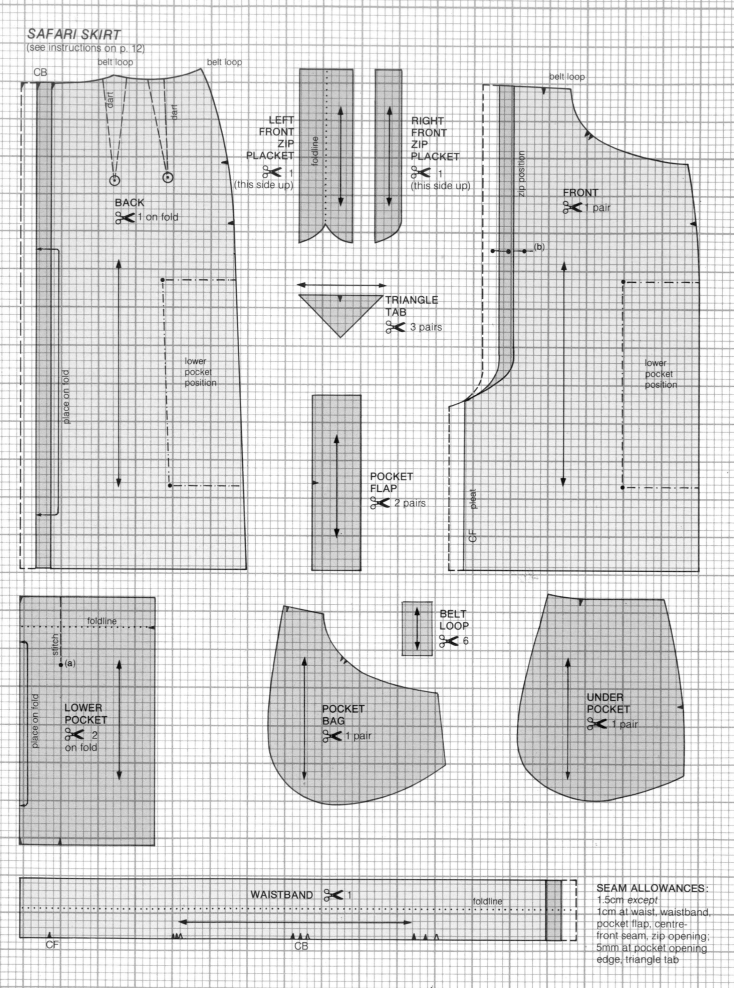

SAFARI SKIRT
(see instructions on p. 12)

CB

belt loop   belt loop   belt loop

dart   dart

LEFT FRONT ZIP PLACKET
✂ 1
(this side up)

RIGHT FRONT ZIP PLACKET
✂ 1
(this side up)

foldline

zip position

BACK
✂ 1 on fold

FRONT
✂ 1 pair

(b)

place on fold

lower pocket position

TRIANGLE TAB
✂ 3 pairs

lower pocket position

POCKET FLAP
✂ 2 pairs

CF pleat

foldline

stitch

(a)

place on fold

LOWER POCKET
✂ 2 on fold

POCKET BAG
✂ 1 pair

BELT LOOP
✂ 6

UNDER POCKET
✂ 1 pair

WAISTBAND ✂ 1

foldline

CF   CB

SEAM ALLOWANCES:
1.5cm *except*
1cm at waist, waistband, pocket flap, centre-front seam, zip opening; 5mm at pocket opening edge, triangle tab

20

SAFARI SHORTS
(see instructions on p. 14)

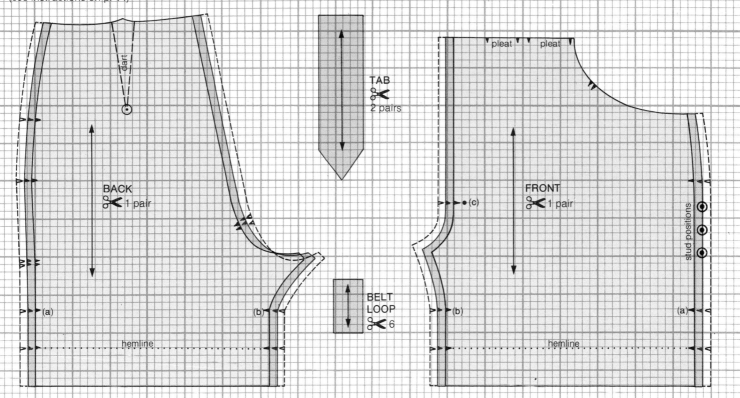

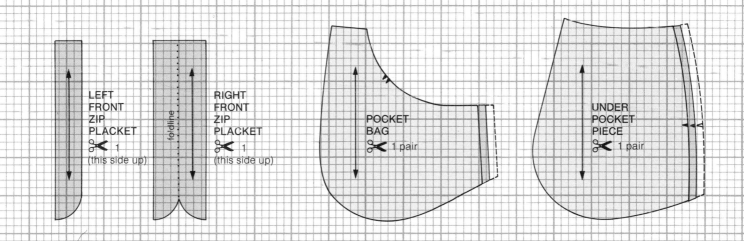

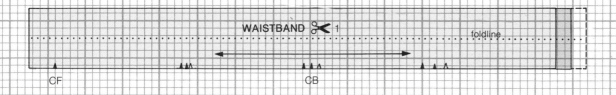

BACK ✂ 1 pair

dart

TAB ✂ 2 pairs

BELT LOOP ✂ 6

FRONT ✂ 1 pair

pleat pleat

stud positions

(a) (b) (c) (b) (a)

hemline

LEFT FRONT ZIP PLACKET ✂ 1 (this side up)

RIGHT FRONT ZIP PLACKET ✂ 1 (this side up)

foldline

POCKET BAG ✂ 1 pair

UNDER POCKET PIECE ✂ 1 pair

WAISTBAND ✂ 1

foldline

CF CB

SEAM ALLOWANCES:
1.5cm except
1cm at waist, waistband, tab, centre-front and back seam;
5mm at pocket opening edge

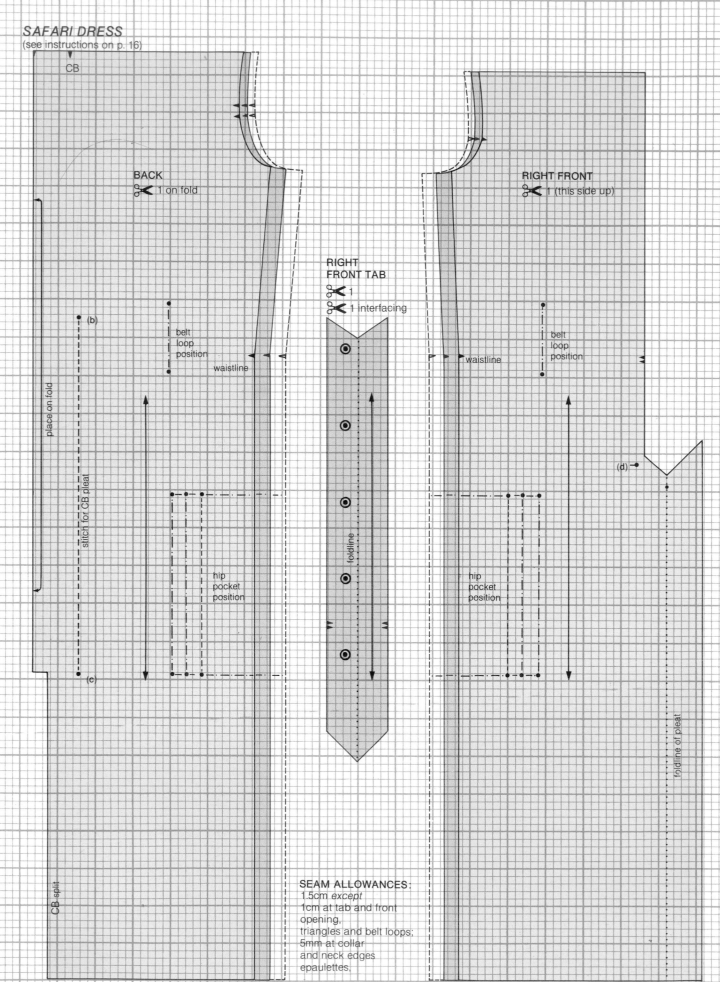

SAFARI DRESS
(see instructions on p. 16)

CB

BACK
✂ 1 on fold

RIGHT FRONT
✂ 1 (this side up)

RIGHT
FRONT TAB
✂ 1
✂ 1 interfacing

(b)

belt
loop
position

waistline

belt
loop
position

waistline

place on fold

stitch for CB pleat

(d)

hip
pocket
position

foldline

hip
pocket
position

(c)

foldline of pleat

CB split

SEAM ALLOWANCES:
1.5cm *except*
1cm at tab and front
opening,
triangles and belt loops;
5mm at collar
and neck edges
epaulettes,

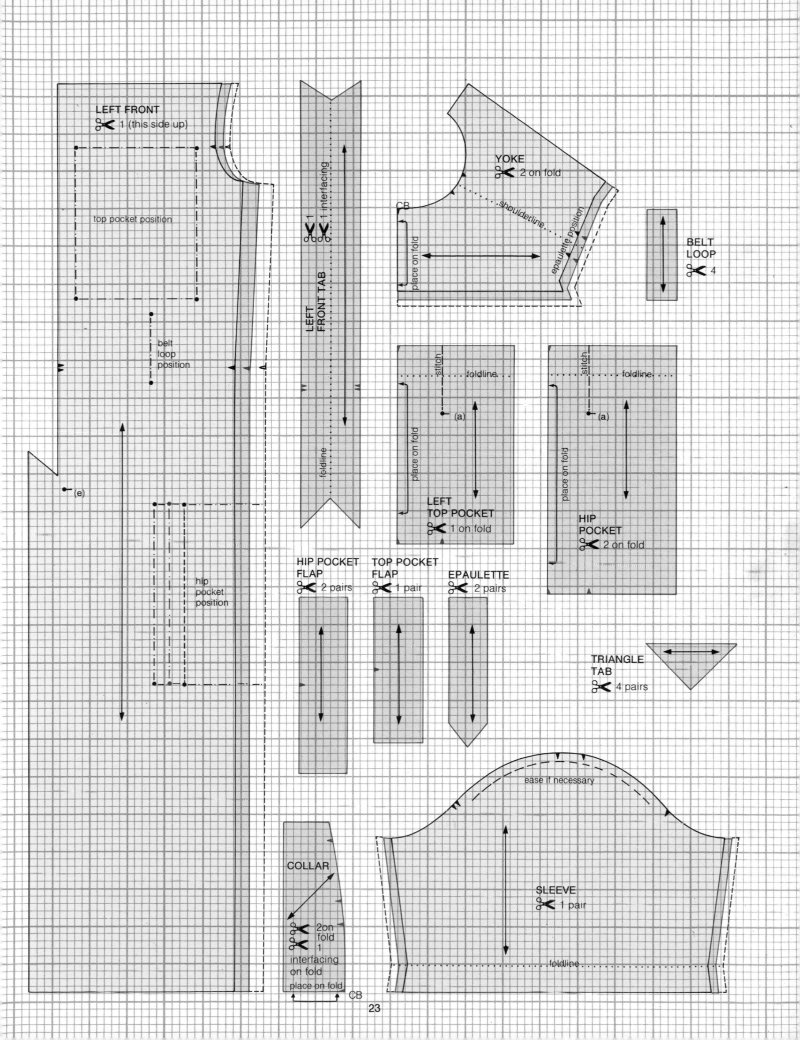

LEFT FRONT
✂ 1 (this side up)

top pocket position

belt loop position

(e)

hip pocket position

LEFT FRONT TAB
✂ 1 ✂ 1 interfacing

foldline

foldline

YOKE
✂ 2 on fold

CB

shoulderline

place on fold

epaulette position

BELT LOOP
✂ 4

stitch

foldline

place on fold

(a)

LEFT TOP POCKET
✂ 1 on fold

stitch

foldline

place on fold

(a)

HIP POCKET
✂ 2 on fold

HIP POCKET FLAP
✂ 2 pairs

TOP POCKET FLAP
✂ 1 pair

EPAULETTE
✂ 2 pairs

TRIANGLE TAB
✂ 4 pairs

COLLAR
✂ 2 on fold
✂ 1 interfacing on fold
place on fold

CB

SLEEVE
✂ 1 pair

ease if necessary

foldline

23

An easy-to-wear, low-waisted dress with gathered skirt and large cowl neckline. It has "V"-shaped pockets, back-buttoning and elbow length sleeves. Shown here in a short version, it would look equally good made in wool jersey or crepe with mid-calf length skirt, possibly with contrasting buttons and cowl for a stronger effect.

Fabric suggestions – experiment with different colourways for a stronger or contrast effect, or use a more ethnic print for a softer look.

24

Cowl-Neck Dress

You will need:
2.20m of 150cm wide fabric *or*
3.00m of 115cm wide fabric
7 buttons

Dress bodice

1 With right sides together, pin front bodice piece to both back bodice pieces at shoulder seams. Stitch, neaten seam allowances together, pressing them towards back and edgestitch close to seam on right side of back bodice pieces along shoulderline, through seam allowances.

2 At right back bodice opening edge, turn back 1cm to wrong side and stitch. Turn again down foldline marked on pattern, press and edgestitch along inner folded edge down whole length of back bodice, through to right side. Press and edgestitch again down outer folded edge of back bodice opening. Repeat for left back bodice.

Cowl

3 With right sides facing and matching notches, stitch a back cowl piece to each side seam of one front cowl piece. Repeat for remaining front and back cowl pieces. Press seam allowances open. With right sides facing, pin cowl pieces together, starting pinning at top of right centre-back opening, following notches for 3cm seam allowance down back opening (this makes a wide seam allowance for strengthening buttonholes) around outer curved edge of cowl, allowing a 5mm seam allowance, and then up left centre-back opening (allowing 3cm allowance) as far as neck edge of left back opening (see fig. 1). Stitch, clip curves and trim 3cm seam allowances at lower edge of curve only, below buttonhole points. Turn cowl and press.

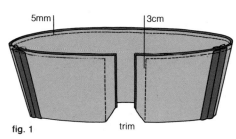

fig. 1   trim

4 With right sides facing, pin underneath cowl piece to right side of bodice at neckline, matching side seams and centre-front points and pinning underneath cowl piece so that its seam allowance around neck edge is 2mm wider than the bodice seam allowance (this is to allow for the "roll" of the upper side of the cowl). Stitch to neck edge, pivoting needle at shoulder seams. Clip seam allowances at shoulder seams and back opening, and press upwards away from dress.

5 Position upper cowl over underneath cowl, setting cowl "roll". Press under a 5mm seam allowance on inner raw edge of upper cowl to wrong side, clipping where necessary. Lay folded curved neck edge of upper cowl directly over the original stitching line around neck edge, and pin and tack in position. Edgestitch along this inner folded edge, through to right side of under cowl. Edgestitch upper cowl around outer edge, from neck edge of left back opening, down to corner of cowl, around outer curve and back up to neck edge of right back opening. ⏋

Sleeves

6 Pin lower edge of sleeve to sleeve facing, with right sides together. Stitch and press seam allowances open. Fold sleeve in half lengthwise and stitch underarm seam from edge of facing to underarm edge of sleeve. Neaten seam allowances separately on sleeve piece only and press open. Clip facing at "V" point where facing joins sleeve. Press under 1cm to wrong side at remaining raw edge of facing and press facing back to inside of sleeve. Pin in position on inside of sleeve and edgestitch close to inner folded edge of facing, through to right side. Turn sleeve to right side and edgestitch around lower cuff edge of sleeve. Repeat for other sleeve. ⏋

7 Placing right sides together, pin front bodice to back bodice at side seams. Stitch seams, neaten seam allowances separately and press open. Pin finished sleeves into armholes, matching underarm seams and notches at front and back. Stitch sleeve to bodice and neaten seam allowances together, splitting stitching on sleeve seam allowance at underarm point. Press seam allowances towards bodice. Turn dress to right side and edgestitch all around armhole on bodice, through seam allowances, close to seam. Press and repeat for other sleeve.

Skirt

8 With right sides facing, pin front and back skirt pieces together at side seams. Stitch, neaten seam allowances separately and press open. Stitch two lines of gathering stitches around top edge of skirt, just within seam allowance, breaking stitching at side seams for ease of gathering (see p. 148). Overlap back bodice opening edges by 3cm and hold with pins. Gather edge of skirt to fit lower edge of bodice, and, placing right sides together, pin gathered edge of skirt to bodice, matching side seams and centre-front and centre-back points. Stitch, neaten seam allowances together and press upwards, towards neck. Turn to right side and edgestitch on bodice, through seam allowances, close to seam. ⏋

Pockets

9 Neaten the two sides of the point of one pocket piece. Turn in 1cm to wrong side at top of pocket and stitch. Turn top of pocket back 3cm to right side along foldline and stitch down sides of fold to hold. Trim corners, turn and press. Edgestitch along inner folded edge, through to right side. Then edgestitch along top folded edge of pocket. Press remaining neatened seam allowances around pocket in to wrong side, tucking excess material at point of "V" to inside, and pin pocket in position against sides of skirt where marked. Edgestitch down two sides of pocket point, securing stitching at either side of top of pocket with a "V" to strengthen. Repeat for other pocket. ⏋

To finish

10 Adjust hem length if necessary. Turn in 5mm to wrong side around hem edge and stitch. Turn under a further centimetre and edgestitch close to inner folded edge, through to right side.

11 Make buttonholes on cowl and back bodice, and sew on buttons.

(see pattern charts on pp. 36, 37)

Sundress and Short-Sleeved Top

Sundress

A simple sundress with dropped waist, tie shoulders and a cowl neckline cut into a "V" at the front and back. The gathered skirt is made in two sections, one overlapping the other, allowing you to use contrasting fabrics. Wear it on its own or team it with the matching top.

You will need:
2.10m of 150cm wide main fabric
70cm of 150cm wide contrast fabric *or*
2.30m of 115cm wide main fabric
70cm of 115cm wide contrast fabric
(If you wish to make a self colour dress, use 2.80m of 150cm wide fabric *or* 3.00m of 115cm wide fabric.)

To attach cowl

1 Staystitch armhole edges of front and back bodice pieces. On front bodice turn in 5mm to wrong side at each armhole opening edge and stitch. Turn in a further centimetre and edge-stitch close to inner folded edge, through to right side. Repeat for back bodice, taking care not to stretch cross-grain fabric around armhole. ⏋

2 Placing right sides together, pin front bodice to back bodice at side seams. Stitch, neaten seam allowances separately and press open, slipstitching pressed back seam allowances to bodice at underarm points.

3 Turn in 5mm to wrong side along top edge of front cowl piece and stitch. Turn in a further centimetre and edgestitch close to inner folded edge, through to right side. Trim points at either end of cowl piece. Turn in and stitch same allowances around remainder of cowl ties as far as notch at (**a**) on front cowl. Repeat for back cowl, turning in top edge of back cowl and tie edges of cowl as far as (**b**).

4 With right sides together, pin lower neckline edge of front cowl to top edge of front bodice, clipping seam allowances around centre-front "V" to ease. Stitch, neaten seam allowances together, and press up towards neck edge. Repeat for dress back. Topstitch on front and back cowls, 1cm in from seams, through all seam allowances. ⏋

Wrapover skirt

5 Turn front wrap edge of main skirt piece in 5mm to wrong side and press. Turn in a further centimetre and edgestitch close to inner folded edge through to right side. Repeat for back wrap edge of main skirt piece.

6 Repeat step 5 for contrast skirt section.

7 Align main and contrast skirt sections matching notches on top edge so that they overlap at the front and the back and contrast skirt section lies underneath at front and back overlap. Pin and tack in position along top edge and staystitch along overlapping sections so that both skirt pieces are held together at front and back. Gather around the top of the skirt, breaking stitching at side seam positions on both sides for ease of gathering (see p. 148). Draw up the gathers so that skirt fits lower edge of bodice, matching notches at centre-front, centre-back and side seams. With right sides facing, pin skirt to bodice and stitch. Neaten seams together and press upwards. Turn dress to right side and topstitch 1cm above seam on bodice through all seam allowances. ⏋

To finish

8 *Hem:* Adjust length of hem on both skirt sections if necessary. Turn up 5mm to wrong side along hem edge of both sections and stitch. Turn up a further centimetre on both sections and edgestitch close to inner folded edge through to right side of fabric. ⏋

Top

A wide, boat-necked top with dropped shoulders and short sleeves, drawn up into gathers with adjustable ties. Make it in a matching fabric to wear underneath the sundress, or co-ordinate it with many of the other garments in this book.

You will need:
1.40m of 150cm wide fabric (in contrast colour if matching sundress) *or*
1.50m of 115cm wide fabric

Bodice

1 Placing right sides together, pin front piece to back piece at shoulders and side seams and stitch. Neaten seam allowances separately and press open.

2 Pin bias strip around neck edge, placing right sides together. Turn in raw short ends of binding at beginning and end of strip to neaten, and stitch 5mm in from raw edges all the way round the neck opening. Press binding and seam allowances outwards, away from garment, and understitch on binding through seam allowances, close to seam. Clip seam allowances. At remaining raw edge of binding turn

under 5mm to wrong side and stitch. Pin or tack binding in position against wrong side of bodice and edgestitch close to inner folded edge of binding, through to right side of top.

Sleeves

3 *Ties:* Take one straight-grain strip and turn in 1cm to wrong side along both long edges. Press and fold strip in half again, aligning folded edges to form a 1cm wide strip and tucking in one short end of the strip to neaten. Edgestitch around the two long edges and tucked in short end. Make the other three ties in the same way and press all four.

4 *Tie channels:* Turn in 5mm to wrong side around hem edges of both sleeves and stitch. Turn in a further centimetre and edgestitch close to inner folded edge. Place sleeve pieces flat, side by side and with right sides facing upwards. Fold channel pleat towards front along foldlines, aligning both (**a**) points and both (**b**) points (see fig. 1). Pin in position and stitch along edge of fold on right side from shoulder edge to hem. Press and turn sleeve pieces over to wrong side. Stitch other side of channel along edge of remaining fold. A double channel has thus been formed (see fig. 2).

5 Thread a tie through each channel so that both sleeves have two ties and secure the raw

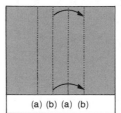
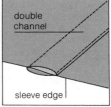

double channel

sleeve edge

fig. 1   fig. 2

7 With right sides together pin sleeves into armhole openings, matching notches and aligning channels so they lie in line with shoulder seams. Stitch, neaten seam allowances together and press towards neckline.

Turn garment to right side and topstitch on bodice 1cm in from seamline around armhole, through all seam allowances. Repeat for other sleeve.

To finish

8 *Hem:* Turn under 5mm to wrong side around hem edge and stitch. Turn under a further centimetre and edgestitch around inner folded edge, through to right side.

9 Press thoroughly. Draw up both pairs of sleeve ties, and tie in a bow or knot.

ends of the ties at shoulder edges of sleeves by stitching across ends of double channels and ties. Trim ends of ties at shoulder edge.

6 With right sides facing, pin underarm seam edges of one sleeve together and stitch. Neaten seam allowances separately and press open. Slipstitch seam allowances at hem to sleeve so they lie flat. Repeat for other sleeve.

(see pattern charts on pp. 37, 38, 39)

Tunic Top and Skirt

Top

This loose-fitting, kimono-style tunic top has tapered sleeves and a deep "V" back, fastening with overlapping button-hole band. The "tails" at the back can be brought to the front and tied at the waist.

You will need:
1.50m of 150cm wide fabric *or*
1.80m of 115cm wide fabric
4 small buttons

Bodice

1 Placing right sides together, stitch both back pieces of bodice to front piece at shoulder seams. Neaten seam allowances separately and press open.

2 Starting at centre-back "V" point, staystitch 3mm in from raw edge, all around neck opening edge to strengthen.

3 *Buttonhole band:* Fold buttonhole band in half along foldline so that right sides come together, and stitch across both short ends. Turn, press and topstitch 1cm in from edge, around the three closed sides. Place band against left back, aligning all raw edges between notches, and tack into position.

4 *Binding neck edge:* Join one straight-grain binding strip to one bias binding strip at one short end. Repeat for other straight-grain and bias strips. Press seams open. To attach binding, pin straight-grain section of one binding strip to left back opening edge, right sides together and sandwiching buttonhole band. Continue pinning bias section of binding around the neck edge as far as notch at centre-front "V". Starting at back hem edge, stitch 5mm in from raw edges around back and neck edges as far as point of centre-front "V". Repeat for other side of bodice. Cut off excess binding at centre-front "V", leaving 2cm extra on left front and 1cm extra on right front of binding strips. Press bindings and seam allowances outwards away from garment. Understitch on binding through seam allowances, close to original stitching line, all round back and neck edge on both sides. Press under 1cm to wrong side around remaining raw edge of bindings, and fold bindings flat against wrong side of dress.

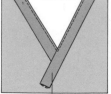
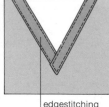

fig. 1 | tuck under | edgestitching

Fold left front binding around right front binding at centre-front "V" so that longer end of binding tucks under shorter end, to finish neatly (see fig. 1). Tack inner folded edge of binding to bodice and edgestitch around, stitching through to right side of bodice. ⊐

Sleeves

5 Placing right sides together and matching notches, pin sleeves to bodice around armhole edge. Stitch, leaving 1.5cm of seam unstitched at each underarm point for side seams. Neaten edges together leaving 1.5cm unneatened at either end. Press seam allowances towards bodice. Starting 4cm in from underarm point topstitch on bodice, stitching out from original seam in a half "V" shape to 1cm away from seam. Pivot needle and then continue top-stitching parallel to seamline, 1cm away from seam, until you reach corresponding point 4cm short of underarm point at other side. Pivot needle and angle stitching back to seamline.

6 With right sides of one sleeve facing, align underarm seam edges and stitch seam from underarm to cuff. Neaten seam allowances separately and press open. Turn under 5mm around cuff edge to wrong side and stitch. Turn under a further centimetre and edgestitch close to inner folded edge through to right side. Repeat for other sleeve and cuff. 🪧

7 Placing right sides together, pin front and back pieces together at side seams. Starting at underarm point, stitch seams down to 1.5cm above hem on front bodice. Neaten seam allowances separately and press open.

To finish

8 *Hem:* Turn in 5mm to wrong side around the two raw edges of the "tails" and stitch. Turn in 5mm around front hem and stitch. Turn in a further centimetre all round and edgestitch through to right side, close to inner folded edge in one continuous line, pivoting at point where back tails meet front (see fig. 2). 🪧

9 Make four buttonholes where marked and sew on buttons.

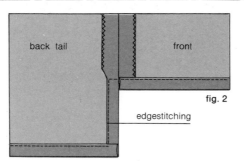

back tail   front

fig. 2

edgestitching

skirt

An unpressed pleated skirt with elasticated waist and deep hip-band. Make it up in soft, supple fabrics for summer, or lightweight jersey or wool for winter.

You will need:
1.70m of 150cm wide fabric *or*
1.70m of 115cm wide fabric
2 lengths of elastic, 51 (55, 59)cm × 5mm
2 hanging loops

Hip-band

1 With right sides facing, pin side seams of hip-band together and stitch. Neaten seam allowances separately and press open.

2 Turn over 1cm to wrong side at waist edge of hip-band and stitch. To make channels for elastic, turn over a further 3cm at top, along foldline marked on pattern. Edgestitch through to right side along inner folded edge, inserting hanging loops at sides and leaving a 2cm gap for inserting the elastic. Topstitch on right side of hip-band 2cm above line of edgestitching, again leaving another 2cm gap directly above the first. Then topstitch directly between the two lines of stitching. 🪧

Pleated skirt section

3 Placing right sides together, pin skirt front to skirt back at side seams. Stitch, neaten seam allowances separately and press open.

4 Turn the skirt so that right sides are outermost and pin each pleat in position, folding from left to right, matching pleat positions marked on the pattern so that (**a**) meets (**b**) and enclosing side seams in pleats (see p. 151). Staystitch around top of skirt within seam allowance to hold pleats in position. Placing right sides together, pin lower edge of hip-band to pleated edge of skirt, adjusting pleats at side seams if necessary so that hip-band and skirt fit exactly. Stitch, neaten seam allowances together and press upwards, towards waist. Turn skirt to right side and topstitch through hip-band, 1cm above seamline, stitching through all seam allowances. 🪧

To finish

5 Insert a piece of elastic through each channel and secure ends together. Topstitch insertion gaps to join original stitching lines on channel.

6 *Hem:* Adjust hem length if necessary. Turn under 5mm to wrong side around hem edge and stitch. Turn under a further centimetre and stitch close to inner folded edge, through to right side of skirt. 🪧

29

(see pattern charts on pp. 40, 41)

Sleeveless Top and Skirt

Skirt

This one-size, simple, front wrapover skirt has an elasticated waist, a fall-over frill around the top, and a split centre-back seam. Use a lightweight, reversible material to ensure that the frill gathers and falls correctly.

You will need:
2.10m of 150cm wide fabric *or*
2.10m of 115cm wide fabric
2 lengths of elastic, 51cm (55cm, 59cm)
  × 5mm
2 hanging loops

(*Note:* Since fabric is reversible, wrong and right sides mentioned in text merely refer to opposite sides of the fabric and not pattern of fabric.)

1 With *wrong* sides of skirt pieces together and matching notches, stitch centre-back seam from top edge to (**a**). Clip across seam allowance at (**a**), and turn skirt pieces so that *right* sides are facing and continue stitching down the centre-back seam as far as (**b**). Neaten seam allowances between (**a**) and (**b**) separately and press open.

2 Returning to the top section of centre-back seam, press seam allowances open between top edge of skirt and (**a**), turning in 5mm along each raw edge of seam to inside of seam. Edgestitch down folded edges of seam allowances through to right side, tucking in corners of clipped seam allowance at (**a**) and edgestitching in a "V" shape at this point (see fig. 1).

3 Neaten seam allowances around centre-back split in same way as step 2, folding in 5mm to inside of seam allowance down each side and edgestitching around inner folded edge, forming a "V" in edgestitching above (**b**) (see fig. 2). ⌐

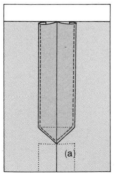
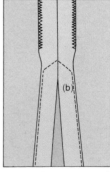

fig. 1   fig. 2

4 Turn in 5mm to wrong side down both front wrap edges and stitch. Turn in a further centimetre down both wrap edges and edgestitch close to inner folded edge, through to right side. ⌐

5 Now set front wraps in position by placing right front over left, matching notches along top edge. Pin through both pieces along channel line. Tack wrapover pieces together along channel line.

Elastic channels

6 Place right sides of the two channel pieces together. Stitch across both short ends to form a continuous band which will fit inside wrapped over skirt. Press 1cm to wrong side around both long raw edges of channel and stitch. Then pin channel in position against wrong side of skirt starting at (**a**) and following channel position marked on pattern. Edgestitch close to folded edge along top of channel, through to right side of skirt, leaving a 2cm gap in stitching for inserting elastic. Position hanging loops at side seam points and then edgestitch around lower folded edge leaving another 2cm gap for elastic at same point. Now stitch in a continuous straight line through the centre of the channel between the two rows of edgestitching to form a double channel through which to thread the two lengths of elastic (see fig. 3).

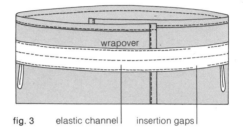
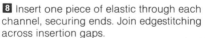

fig. 3   elastic channel   insertion gaps

To finish

7 To hem frill, turn over 5mm to right side and stitch around folded edge. Turn under a further centimetre and edgestitch along inner folded edge through all thicknesses. ⌐

8 Insert one piece of elastic through each channel, securing ends. Join edgestitching across insertion gaps.

9 *Hem:* Adjust length of hem if necessary, and then turn up 5mm to inside and stitch. Turn up a further centimetre and edgestitch close to inner folded edge through to right side of fabric around hem of both skirt pieces.

Top

A simple summer or evening top, with cut-away shoulders, a neat stand collar, left shoulder tab opening and right front pocket. All seams are decorated with top-stitching. Ideal worn with summer skirts, shorts or trousers, or teamed with a jacket. Use lightweight fabrics only.

You will need:
80cm of 150cm wide fabric *or*
1.30m of 115cm wide fabric
3 buttons
7cm of lightweight iron-on interfacing

1 Sew in bust darts on left and right front pieces of top, where marked on pattern, placing right sides together along dart, and tapering line of stitching just beyond marked point of dart (see p. 150). Press darts downwards.

Pocket

2 Turn over 1cm to wrong side along top edge of pocket piece and stitch. Then turn over 2.5cm along foldline to *right* side and stitch down fold at right hand side seam only to hold. Turn fold to right side and press in fold across top of pocket. Edgestitch along inner folded edge of pocket through to right side. Neaten around bottom and right hand side seam

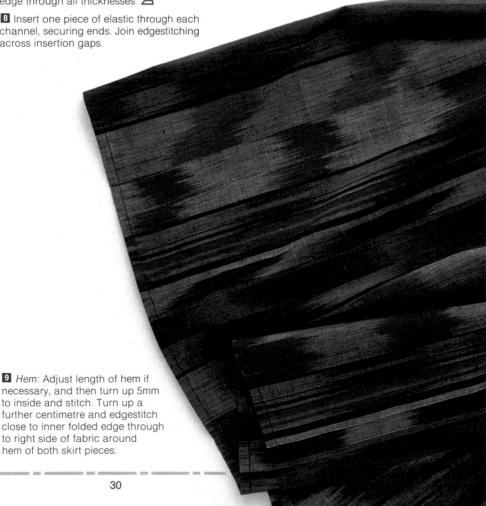

edges, and press in 1.5cm on both these edges to wrong side. Lay pocket flat on right front, with right sides uppermost and matching notches, and pin in position where marked. Staystitch inner raw edge of pocket to right front within seam allowances, to hold. Edgestitch around the two neatened edges and then topstitch 5mm in from edgestitching, through pocket and blouse front. ⌐

3 With right sides facing, pin right front of blouse to front centre panel, matching notches along seam edge and sandwiching the pocket in the seam. Stitch, neaten seam allowances together, pressing them towards centre. Edgestitch close to seamline on centre panel, down the seam. Then topstitch 5mm in from edgestitching. Pin left front piece to front centre panel, stitch, edgestitching and topstitching in the same way on centre panel. ⌐

4 Turn under 5mm to wrong side at each front armhole opening and stitch. Turn under a further centimetre, taking care not to stretch the fabric, and edgestitch along inner folded edges through to right side. On right side of top front, edgestitch each armhole opening around outside edges. Repeat for back armhole openings. ⌐

5 Place right sides of front and back pieces together and pin side seams. Stitch, neaten seam allowances separately and press open. Pin right shoulder seam together (with right sides of fabric still facing) and stitch. Neaten seam allowances separately and press open,

mitring at armhole edge and underarm seam, hand stitching mitred seam allowance back at underarm and shoulder points to neaten. Leave left shoulder seam unstitched.

Stand collar

6 Attach interfacing to wrong side of inner half of collar (see p. 153). With right sides facing pin notched edge of collar around neckline of bodice, aligning the notches at centre-front, centre-back and right shoulder seam. Clip across seam allowances to ease around neckline and turn collar along foldline to inside. Press under 1cm to wrong side at inner raw edge and stitch. Tack this folded edge to original neck seamline so that it just covers the stitching. Turn to right side and edgestitch on collar close to neck seam through all thicknesses, catching in folded edge of collar under-

neath. Edgestitch around upper folded edge of collar. Then topstitch on collar 5mm in from each line of edgestitching.

Shoulder fastening and tab

7 Attach interfacing to underneath half of front and back tabs. With right sides together and matching notches, pin front tab to left shoulder and collar edge. Fold tab in half so right sides come together, press in 1cm to wrong side along remaining long raw edge and stitch across both short ends. Turn to right side and tack this folded edge over original stitching line, so that the raw end of the collar is enclosed in the tab. Edgestitch all around edge of tab on right side, catching in underneath

folded edge of tab. Then topstitch 5mm in from edgestitching. Attach the back tab in exactly the same way, edgestitching and topstitching to finish off. ⌐

To finish

8 *Hem:* Around hem turn under 5mm to wrong side and stitch. Turn under a further centimetre and edgestitch close to inner folded edge through to right side. Turn to right side and edgestitch around lower edge of hem, parallel to first row of edgestitching.

9 *Buttonholes:* Make three buttonholes at positions marked on front tab, stitching buttonholes across the width of the tab. Attach buttons to back tab. ⌐

(see pattern charts on pp. 42, 43)

Pants

These pants are based on original karate pants and have an elasticated waist, and crotch and leg gussets, which give them a loose, but neat fit. Perfect as all-round casual pants for everyday and sports use, they are simple to make, and can be made in a multitude of medium-weight fabrics.

You will need:
1.10m of 150cm wide fabric or
2.10m of 115cm wide fabric
2 lengths of elastic 51cm (55cm, 59cm)
   ×5mm
2 hanging loops

1 Place right sides of the two pants pieces together at centre-front and centre-back seams, matching notches at front and back. Pin front seam and back seam as far as notch marking leg divide points (see fig. 1). Stitch and set aside.

fig. 1

2 With right sides together, pin one leg gusset piece to one unnotched side of crotch gusset piece (see fig. 2). Pin other leg gusset to opposite side of crotch gusset. Stitch both seams, neaten seam allowances separately and press open.

3 Open "legs" of pants out and with right sides together, pin front edge of entire crotch and leg gusset section to front pants pieces, matching front notches and ending at notch on leg 1.5cm from bottom of leg gusset section (see fig. 3). Stitch this seam, from notch on one pants piece to notch on opposite pants piece, breaking stitching at leg divide point. Repeat for back crotch and leg seams.

4 Pin front and back edges of remaining right inside leg seam together, and stitch from point

where leg section joins to hem of pants (see fig. 4). Repeat for remaining left inside leg seam.

5 Neaten all seam allowances separately and press open, pressing and hand stitching loose seam allowances at points where they overlap so that they lie flat.

To finish

6 *Hem:* At ankle, turn under 1cm to wrong side and stitch. Trim seam allowances, press

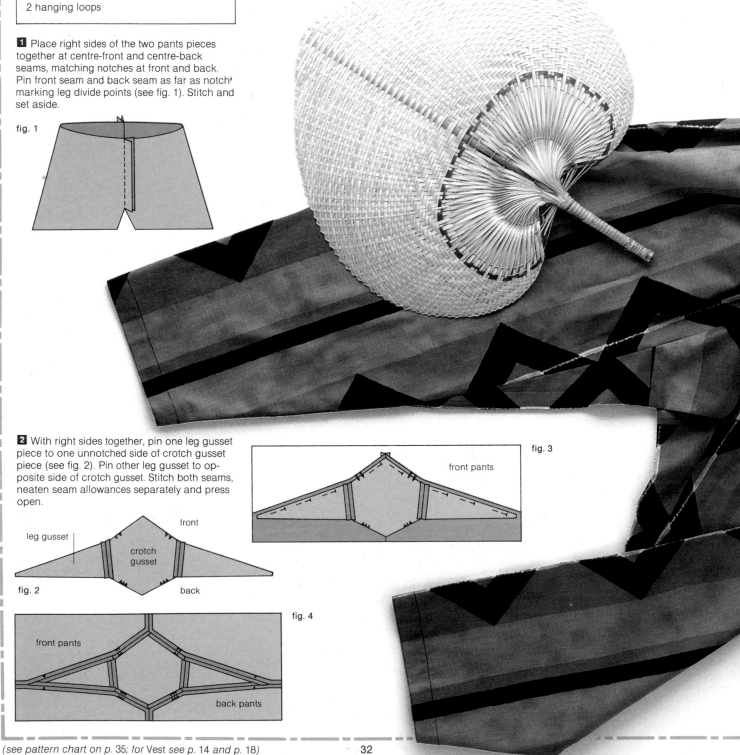

leg gusset
front
crotch gusset
back
fig. 2

front pants
fig. 3

front pants
back pants
fig. 4

(see pattern chart on p. 35; for Vest see p. 14 and p. 18)

under a further 2.5cm along hem foldline, and stitch close to inner folded edge of hem, through to right side. Edgestitch around lower edge of hem. Repeat for other ankle. ⌐

7 *Waist elastic channel:* Using the same method as for hemming ankles above, turn in the waist edge around waist foldline to make a channel for inserting elastic, leaving a 2cm gap in the inner folded edge and setting in hanging loops at either side under inner folded edge.

Topstitch around top edge and then again between the two rows of stitching, leaving another 2cm gap, so forming a double channel for elastic (see fig. 5). ⌐

fig. 5

insertion gaps

elastic channel

8 Thread a length of elastic through each channel, secure ends of elastic, and topstitch across both insertion gaps to make stitching lines continuous.

A simulated hand-print lends this outfit its ethnic, primitive flavour.

Kanga

A kanga is a length of fabric which can be wrapped and tied in various ways to form a wrap to wear on and around the beach. Wrap it around the waist for a simple skirt, tying it at the side hip, or tie it on one shoulder; even cross over the ends at the front and tie them at the back of the neck for a simple dress which can be worn belted or loose.

You will need:
2.50m of 150cm wide fabric *or*
2.50m of 115cm wide fabric

1 Take chosen width of fabric and turn in 5mm to the wrong side all around the four raw edges. Stitch.

2 Turn in a further centimetre all round and edgestitch through to right side, close to inner folded edge. ⌐

Bikini

This strapless bikini has a ruched top which is boned at the side seams for support, and ties at the back. The pants are cut very brief and fasten on both hips with ties. The bikini is self-lined.

You will need:
90cm of 150cm wide fabric *or*
90cm of 115cm wide fabric
1.20m lingerie elastic, 5mm wide
2 pieces nylon "boning" 5cm long

(*Note:* It is difficult to make this bikini if your machine does not have a zigzag stitch.)

Pants

1 With right sides facing place front and back pants pieces together, aligning them at crotch seam. Pin seam and stitch across. Press seam allowance open. Repeat for front and back lining pieces. ⌐

2 Lay pants over lining so that wrong sides are together, all raw edges match and both pieces lie flat. Pin together around raw edges and then zigzag neaten these edges so that pants and lining are joined to form one double piece. ⌐

3 With lining side uppermost, lay elastic against top of pants front. Pulling elastic tight, pin it 5mm in from top edge of pants front, leaving a few centimetres of extra elastic at either end. Still pulling it tight stitch the elastic to the top of the pants with a wide zigzag stitch. As you stitch the elastic to the bikini, the material will gather up (see fig. 1 overleaf). Repeat for top edge of pants back.

4 Using extra few centimetres of elastic at either end to pull fabric and elastic taut, turn over 5mm to wrong side along elasticated top front edge, and pin in position. Pull tight and zigzag stitch on right side through all thicknesses. Repeat for top back edge.

Bikini and Kanga

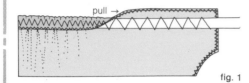

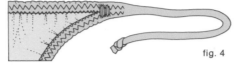

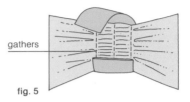

fig. 1

fig. 4

gathers

fig. 5

5 Use same method as in steps 3 and 4 to elasticate and finish off both leg openings.

6 *Side ties:* Fold one bias tie strip in half lengthways. Lay a length of silk thread or fine string along the inside of the fold – the string should be longer than the strip. Tie a substantial knot at one end of the length of thread and position it just beyond the end of the strip. Stitch across this end, stitching through folded fabric and thread just below knot, using small stitches to hold thread and knot in place. Stitch to within about 2mm of raw edges then turn and stitch down long raw edge (see fig. 2), tapering stitching inwards to 5mm from raw edges, 3cm down from top edge. Continue stitching remainder of strip allowing 5mm seam allowance. Gently pull unknotted end of thread, so that stitched end is pulled through channel (you will probably need to ease it through with your fingers) and strip is turned to right side (see fig. 3). Cut across stitched short end of strip about 2mm inside seam to get rid of knot and any bulk, leaving a raw end. Pull string out of strip and press flat. Repeat for remaining three ties.

fig. 2

2mm | 5mm

fig. 3

7 Turn in raw ends at wider end of tie and position on inside of one corner of pants, overlapping tie and corner 1.5cm. Secure firmly by zigzag stitching through tie and pants corner (see fig. 4). Attach remaining three ties to other three corners of pants. Tie knots in unfinished ends of ties to finish them off, trimming any excess tie close to knot.

Top

8 Sew in darts at positions marked and press towards side seams.

9 Place right sides of lining and top together, matching seam edges. Pin around edges and then stitch all round, leaving a 5cm gap in stitching along lower centre-front edge, through which to turn. Trim corners, turn and press. Slipstitch opening together. Mark top and bottom centre-front points and side seam points with pins, so that you can identify them.

10 Make three lines of gather-stitching, 5mm apart, across centre-front, from top to bottom. Gather up each line so that it measures 4cm. Tie off gathering threads, secure with a few stitches and cut off loose thread ends. Fold 8cm × 10cm rectangle in half lengthways, so that right sides come together, and stitch down long seam edge and across one short end. Trim corners and turn to right side. Press. Wrap strip around gathered centre-front point, tucking raw end under finished end of strip on inside (see fig. 5). Slipstitch finished edge over raw edge of strip to neaten and then slipstitch either side of strip to back of bikini top to hold.

11 Gather down side seams with two lines of gather stitching at each side seam point, pulling them up so that they measure 6cm.

12 Make two short strips out of the 4cm × 8cm lengths, using same method as in step 6, but allowing 5mm seam allowance for entire long seam. Turn strips and tuck in 1cm at one end of each strip, slipstitching across opening. Turn in 1cm to inside at remaining raw end and press each strip. Position one strip at each side seam point, and edgestitch around both long edges and stitched short end of strip, through to bikini top. Leave strip open at top. Remove gathering stitches, and then insert a piece of "boning" into each strip and slipstitch across ends of strips to close. ⏚

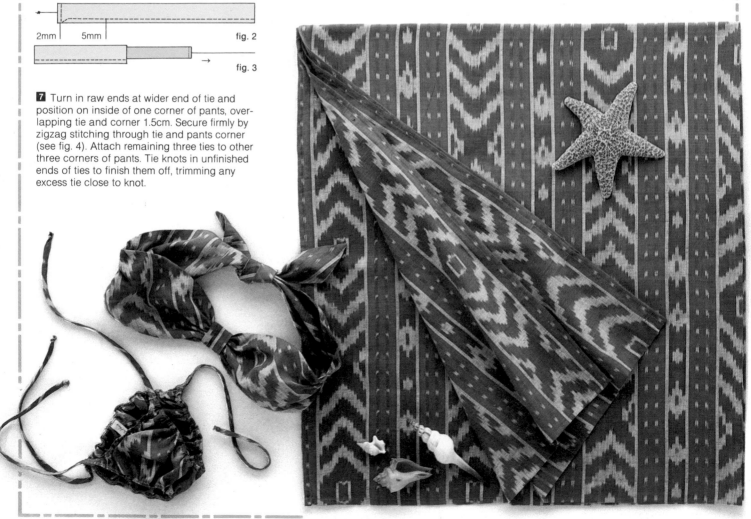

(see pattern charts on p. 43)

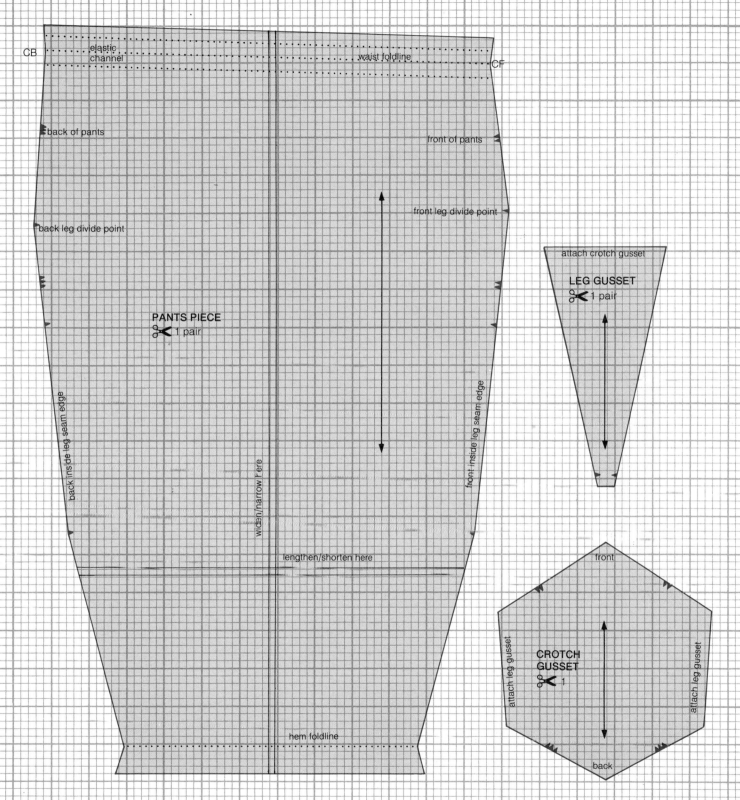

PANTS
(see instructions on p. 32)

CB

elastic
channel

waist foldline

CF

back of pants

front of pants

front leg divide point

back leg divide point

attach crotch gusset

LEG GUSSET
✂ 1 pair

PANTS PIECE
✂ 1 pair

back inside leg seam edge

widen/narrow here

front inside leg seam edge

lengthen/shorten here

front

attach leg gusset

CROTCH
GUSSET
✂ 1

attach leg gusset

hem foldline

back

SEAM ALLOWANCES:
1.5cm throughout

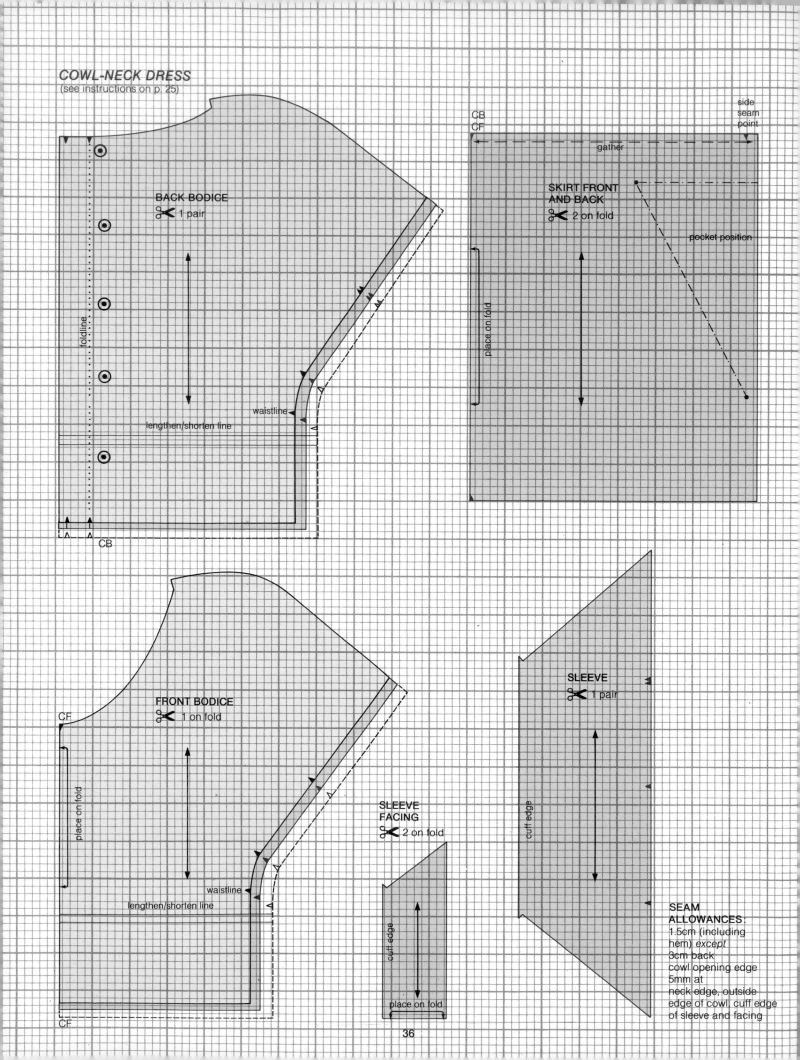

COWL-NECK DRESS
(see instructions on p. 25)

BACK BODICE
✂ 1 pair

foldline

lengthen/shorten line

waistline

CB

SKIRT FRONT AND BACK
✂ 2 on fold

CB
CF

side seam point

gather

place on fold

pocket position

FRONT BODICE
✂ 1 on fold

CF

place on fold

lengthen/shorten line

waistline

CF

SLEEVE FACING
✂ 2 on fold

cuff edge

place on fold

SLEEVE
✂ 1 pair

cuff edge

SEAM ALLOWANCES:
1.5cm (including hem) *except* 3cm back cowl opening edge 5mm at neck edge, outside edge of cowl, cuff edge of sleeve and facing

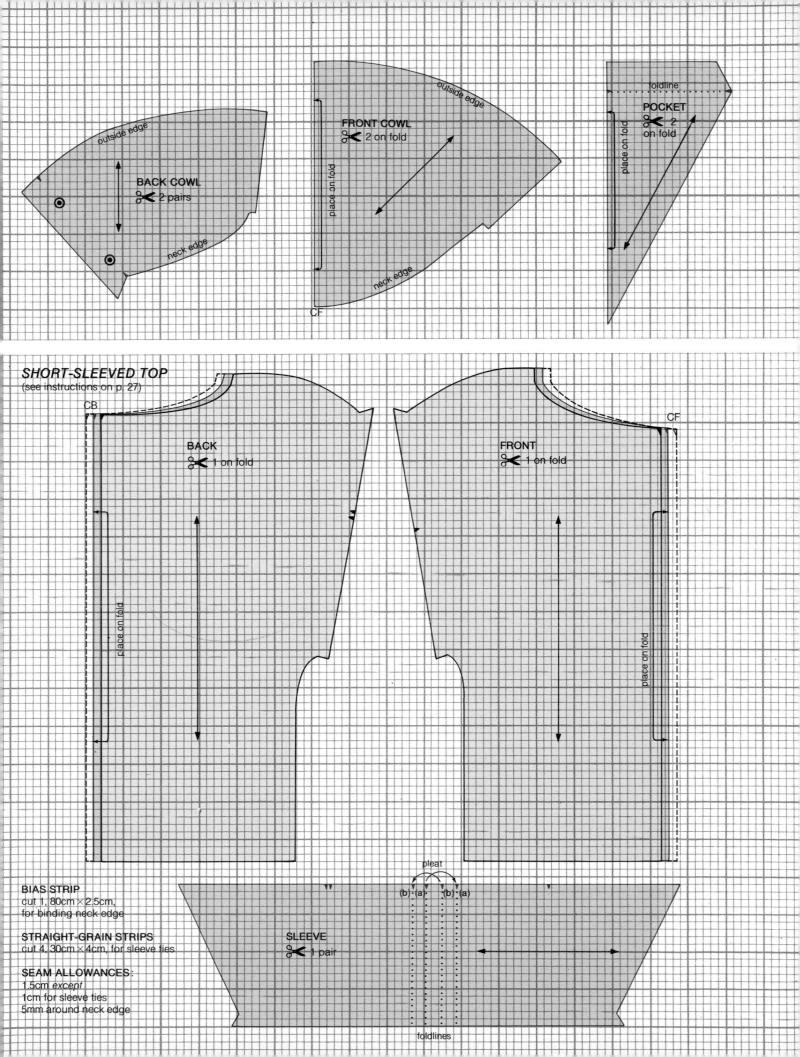

outside edge

BACK COWL
✂ 2 pairs

neck edge

FRONT COWL
✂ 2 on fold

outside edge

place on fold

neck edge

CF

foldline

POCKET
✂ 2
on fold

place on fold

SHORT-SLEEVED TOP
(see instructions on p. 27)

CB

BACK
✂ 1 on fold

place on fold

CF

FRONT
✂ 1 on fold

place on fold

pleat

(b) (a) (b) (a)

BIAS STRIP
cut 1, 80cm × 2.5cm,
for binding neck edge

STRAIGHT-GRAIN STRIPS
cut 4, 30cm × 4cm, for sleeve ties

SEAM ALLOWANCES:
1.5cm *except*
1cm for sleeve ties
5mm around neck edge

SLEEVE
✂ 1 pair

foldlines

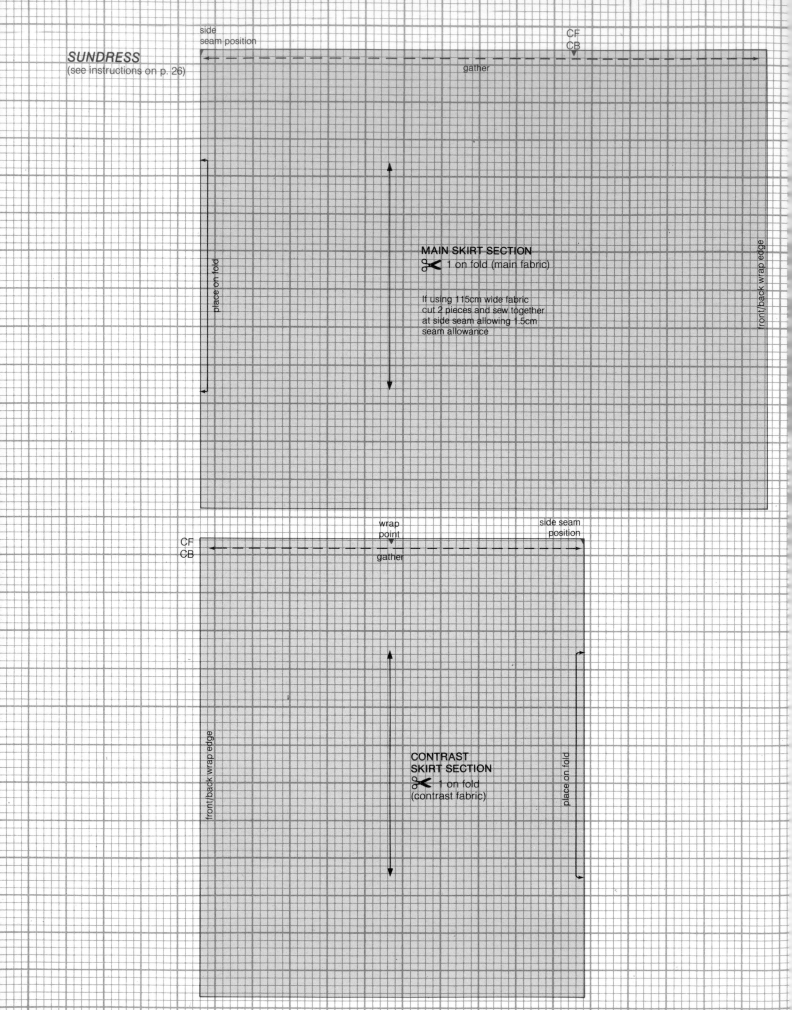

SUNDRESS
(see instructions on p. 26)

side seam position

CF
CB

gather

place on fold

MAIN SKIRT SECTION
✂ 1 on fold (main fabric)

If using 115cm wide fabric
cut 2 pieces and sew together
at side seam allowing 1.5cm
seam allowance

front/back wrap edge

wrap point

side seam position

CF
CB

gather

front/back wrap edge

place on fold

CONTRAST SKIRT SECTION
✂ 1 on fold
(contrast fabric)

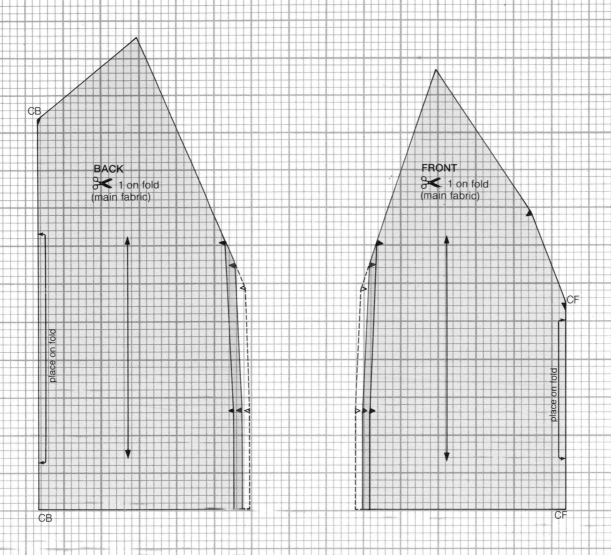

BACK
✂ 1 on fold
(main fabric)

place on fold

CB

CB

FRONT
✂ 1 on fold
(main fabric)

place on fold

CF

CF

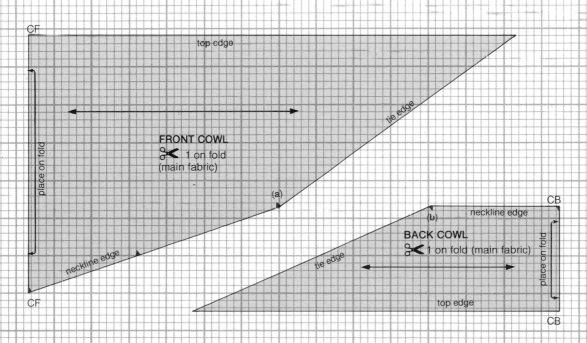

CF

top edge

FRONT COWL
✂ 1 on fold
(main fabric)

place on fold

tie edge

(a)

neckline edge

CF

(b)

neckline edge

CB

BACK COWL
✂ 1 on fold (main fabric)

tie edge

place on fold

top edge

CB

SEAM ALLOWANCES:
1.5cm throughout

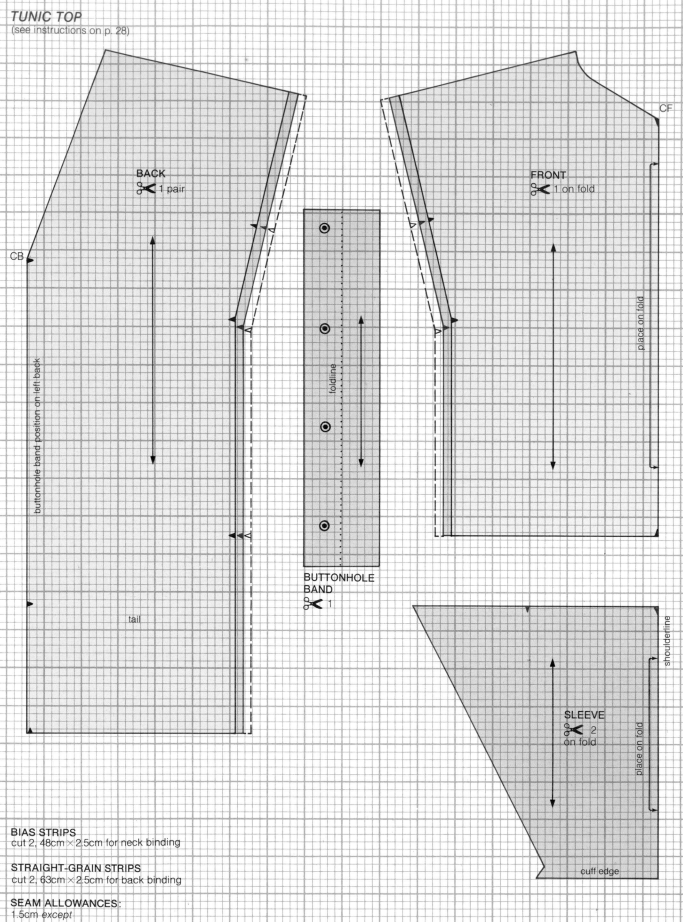

TUNIC TOP
(see instructions on p. 28)

BACK
✂ 1 pair

CB

buttonhole band position on left back

tail

FRONT
✂ 1 on fold

CF

place on fold

BUTTONHOLE
BAND
✂ 1

foldline

SLEEVE
✂ 2
on fold

shoulderline

place on fold

cuff edge

BIAS STRIPS
cut 2, 48cm × 2.5cm for neck binding

STRAIGHT-GRAIN STRIPS
cut 2, 63cm × 2.5cm for back binding

SEAM ALLOWANCES:
1.5cm *except*
1cm at top and bottom of buttonhole band
5mm at neck opening and centre-back edge of back and buttonhole band

SKIRT

(see instructions on p. 29)

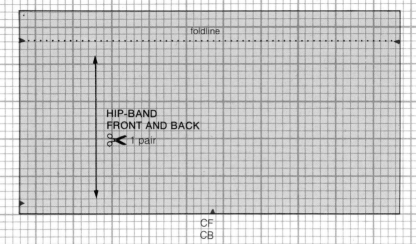

foldline

HIP-BAND
FRONT AND BACK
✂ 1 pair

CF
CB

CB
CF continue marking around
remainder of top finishing
on (a) at side seam

b a b a b a b a b a b a b a b a b a b a b a

SKIRT FRONT
AND BACK
✂ 2 on fold

place on fold

SEAM ALLOWANCES:
1.5cm throughout

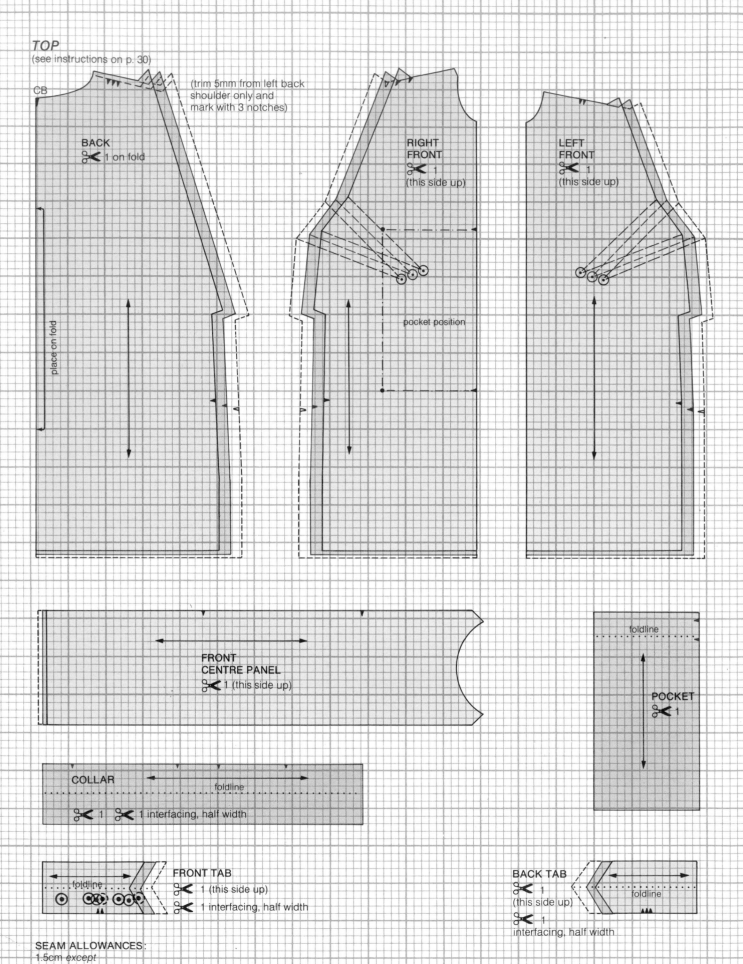

TOP
(see instructions on p. 30)

CB

(trim 5mm from left back
shoulder only and
mark with 3 notches)

BACK
✂ 1 on fold

place on fold

RIGHT
FRONT
✂ 1
(this side up)

pocket position

LEFT
FRONT
✂ 1
(this side up)

FRONT
CENTRE PANEL
✂ 1 (this side up)

foldline

POCKET
✂ 1

COLLAR
foldline
✂ 1   ✂ 1 interfacing, half width

foldline
FRONT TAB
✂ 1 (this side up)
✂ 1 interfacing, half width

BACK TAB
✂ 1
(this side up)
foldline
✂ 1
interfacing, half width

SEAM ALLOWANCES:
1.5cm *except*
1cm at left shoulder opening and tabs, collar and neck edge

SARONG SKIRT
(see instructions on p. 30)

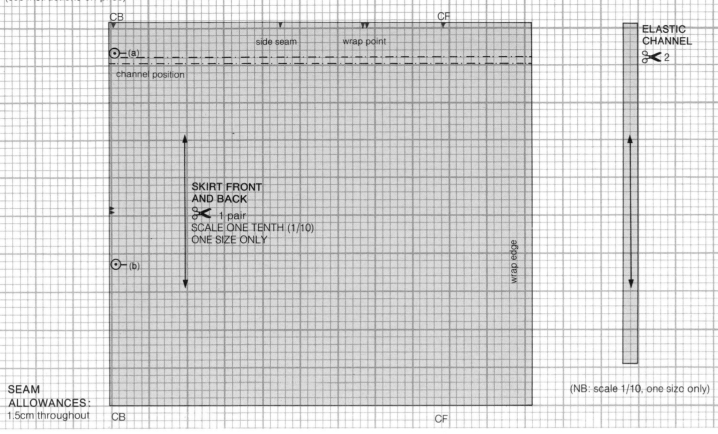

CB

CF

side seam   wrap point

⊙—(a)

channel position

ELASTIC
CHANNEL
✂2

SKIRT FRONT
AND BACK
✂ 1 pair
SCALE ONE TENTH (1/10)
ONE SIZE ONLY

⊙—(b)

wrap edge

SEAM
ALLOWANCES:
1.5cm throughout

CB

CF

(NB: scale 1/10, one size only)

BIKINI
(see instructions on p. 33)

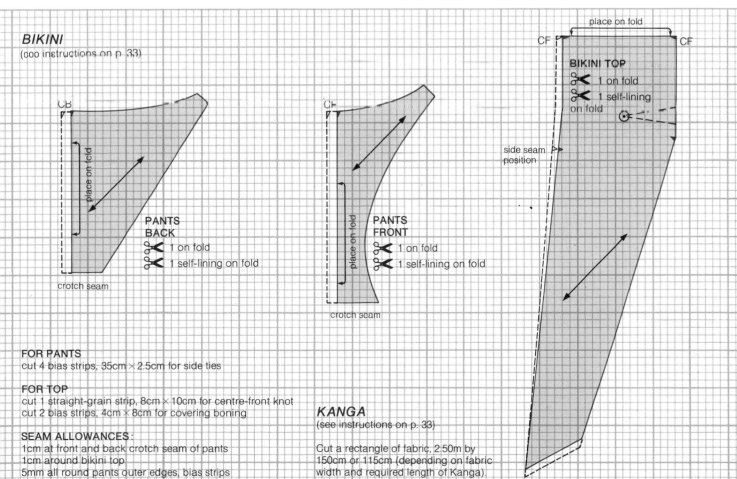

place on fold

CF   CF

BIKINI TOP
✂ 1 on fold
✂ 1 self-lining
on fold

CB

CF

place on fold

place on fold

side seam
position

PANTS
BACK
✂ 1 on fold
✂ 1 self-lining on fold

PANTS
FRONT
✂ 1 on fold
✂ 1 self-lining on fold

crotch seam

crotch seam

FOR PANTS
cut 4 bias strips, 35cm × 2.5cm for side ties

FOR TOP
cut 1 straight-grain strip, 8cm × 10cm for centre-front knot
cut 2 bias strips, 4cm × 8cm for covering boning

SEAM ALLOWANCES:
1cm at front and back crotch seam of pants
1cm around bikini top
5mm all round pants outer edges, bias strips

KANGA
(see instructions on p. 33)

Cut a rectangle of fabric, 2.50m by
150cm or 115cm (depending on fabric
width and required length of Kanga).

Summer Jacket, Top and Skirt

A versatile outfit for any occasion or season. Shown here made in a summer version, all the garments would be equally effective made in warmer winter cloth or more elaborate fabrics for evening. Each of the garments will co-ordinate with many of the other designs in the book.

Fabric suggestions - *different colourways in the same fabrics strengthen the overall effect.*

44

(see pattern charts on pp. 52, 53, 54, 55, 57)

Jacket

An unlined, loose-fitting, casual jacket with assymetrical front opening. Bodice and sleeves are cut in one piece with wide emphasized shoulders. Made here in heavy-weight cotton, it can also be made in a wool cloth for winter, or velvet for evening. Experiment with contrasting fabrics for cuffs and pockets, such as leather for winter or silks for evenings.

You will need:
2.30m of 150cm wide fabric *or*
3.10m of 115cm wide fabric
(includes self-lining for pockets)
1.00m of interfacing
50cm of lining (if using heavy-weight fabric)

(*Note:* If using wool or loose-weave fabric bind seam allowances with bias tape in matching or contrasting colour.)

1 If necessary, apply interfacing to wrong sides of pockets, cuffs and front and neck facings (see p. 153).

2 Staystitch upper front bodice pieces around the two rever edges to strengthen where fabric is cut on the cross.

Pockets

3 Pin pocket lining to pocket bag along opening edge, with right sides facing and matching notches. Stitch, allowing 1cm seam allowance. Press both seam allowances towards lining. Turn to right side, and understitch on lining close to seam, through lining and seam allowances, to hold. Turn lining so wrong sides come together, setting fold along top edge of pocket. Press and topstitch finished edge, stitching on pocket 1cm in from pocket edge. Repeat for other pocket.

4 Set left lined pocket bag flat against left lower front bodice piece, with right sides of pocket and bodice uppermost and aligning hem and side seam edges. Staystitch around the raw edges to hold the two pieces together. Repeat for right pocket (see fig. 1). ⏎

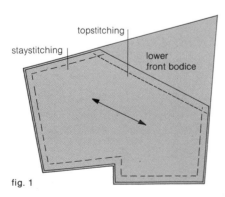

fig. 1

Bodice

5 Pin left lower front bodice, with attached pocket bag, to left upper front bodice along lower seam edge, right sides together and matching notches. Stitch, neaten seam allowances together, pressing them upwards, towards upper bodice. Topstitch on right side of upper front bodice, 1cm away from seam-

line, through bodice and seam allowances. Repeat for right front.

6 With right sides facing, pin front and back bodice pieces together at shoulder seams. Stitch, neaten seam allowances separately and press open.

7 Pin left and right front facings to back neck facing at shoulder seam edges, right sides of fabric together, to form one continuous facing strip. Stitch and press seam allowances open. Neaten all round inner raw edge of complete facing. Pin unfinished edge of jacket facing to jacket around neck edge and front opening edges, down and around hem edges of facing. Stitch facing to jacket, allowing 1cm seam allowance and stitching from beginning of left front facing hemline, up and round to right front facing hemline, so that facing is totally attached. Stitch again within seam allowance down revers, 2mm in from seamline, to strengthen. Trim corners, clip curves and press seam allowances around neck towards facing. Open out back neck facing from back of jacket and understitch on back neck facing, close to seamline through facing and seam allowances only, from shoulder seam to shoulder seam. Turn facing to inside of jacket and press carefully all around jacket opening, so facing lies flat against jacket.

8 With right sides together, pin jacket fronts to jacket back at the side and underarm seams. Stitch, neaten seam allowances separately, clipping them at underarm curves, then stitch again around curve, within seam allowance, to strengthen. Press seam allowances open.

Cuffs

9 With right sides together pin underarm seam of one upper cuff piece together and stitch. Repeat for other upper cuff and both under cuff (or lining) pieces. Press seam allowances open and with right sides together and matching underarm seams, pin upper cuff to under cuff. Stitch 1cm in from raw edge all round lower edge of cuff. Spread upper and under cuff so right sides are uppermost and seam allowances underneath lie against under cuff. Understitch on under cuff just inside seamline. Press under cuff against upper cuff, wrong sides together. Topstitch cuff around wrist edge 1cm in from edge. Staystitch through cuff and facing around upper raw edge to hold (see fig. 2). Repeat for other cuff.

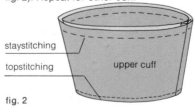

staystitching
topstitching
upper cuff

fig. 2

10 Pin staystitched edge of left cuff to left armhole opening, right sides together, and aligning underarm seams and matching notches. Stitch, neaten all seam allowances together and press them back towards wrist, tacking in position to hold if necessary. Topstitch on upper edge of cuff, 1cm in from seam-line, all round, through all thicknesses. Repeat for other cuff. ⏎

To finish

11 *Hem:* Neaten round raw edge of hem between inner edges of facing. Turn under 4cm to wrong side and tack in position against jacket.

12 Turn jacket to right side and, starting at right side seam, topstitch 1cm in from bottom edge of hem round to left front opening edge; pivot needle and continue topstitching up, around rever points and neck edge, down right front opening edge and along remaining unstitched hem, until you meet your starting point. ⏎

13 Slipstitch upper neatened edge of hem to jacket back, taking care that your stitches are invisible on the right side and catching hem to facing at right and left front. Tack inner raw edges of facing against jacket, around front opening and neck. Stitch on facing 1cm in from neatened edge of facing through to right side of jacket, starting at left front where lower bodice meets upper front bodice, so forming a line of topstitching on jacket all around facing.

Top

A very quick and easy-to-make, loose-fitting top, with assymetrical, overlapping front fastening, held in place by an angled line of stitching. Shown here made in a lightweight cotton, it can also be made in almost any fabric you choose to co-ordinate with many of the garments in the book. Wear it tucked in or belted at the waist.

You will need:
1.40m of 150cm wide fabric *or*
1.40m of 115cm wide fabric

1 Placing right sides together, pin front bodice pieces to back bodice piece at shoulder seams. Stitch, trim seam allowances to 1cm, neaten together and press towards back.

2 Pin both side seams together, with right sides facing. Stitch, trim seam allowances also to 1cm, neaten together and press towards back.

3 Topstitch 5mm in from seamline along back bodice at shoulders, through seam allowances. Repeat for side seams, topstitching on back bodice.

4 Turn in 5mm to wrong side down left front opening edge and stitch. Turn under a further centimetre and edgestitch close to inner folded edge, through to right side. Repeat for right front opening edge.

5 With right sides facing, pin bias strip around neck opening edge (see p. 145 for instructions about joining bias strips), starting at top left front opening edge of top and folding in raw short end at beginning of binding to neaten. Stitch 5mm in from edge all around neck opening, taking care not to stretch the fabric cut on the cross. Trim other end of binding and turn in raw short end to neaten. Clip seam allowances at curves and press binding and seam allowances away from top. Understitch all around on binding through seam allowances, close to seamline.

6 Press in 5mm to wrong side around remaining raw edge of binding and turn inner folded edge of binding against wrong side of neck edge. Pin in position and edgestitch close to inner folded edge of binding, through to right side. ⏎

7 Repeat steps 5. and 6. for armhole openings and bias strips.

To finish

8 At hem, turn under 5mm to wrong side and stitch all round. Turn under a further centimetre and edgestitch all round close to inner folded edge, through to right side.

9 Place top on a flat surface or ironing board and press flat, wrapping right front opening over left front, and matching wrap points at (**a**) and (**b**) as marked on pattern. Pin and tack the two overlapping pieces together from (**a**) on right front opening edge, diagonally across to (**b**), as marked on pattern. Stitch the two front wraps together along this line, stitching on upper side of right front wrap through to under side of left front wrap. Draw threads at each end of line of stitching through to wrong side, and tie off. ▱

Skirt

This unpressed pleated skirt has a shaped, fitted hip-band, front press-stud opening and set-in side pockets. Equally good for summer and winter alike, it can be made in almost any light- to medium-weight fabric.

> **You will need:**
> 2.10m of 150cm wide fabric
> 40cm of interfacing
> 3 press-studs (*or buttons*)
> 2 hanging loops
> 1 small popper

(*Note:* For winter fabric, such as wool or corduroy, make the set-in pockets in lining fabric to reduce bulk.)

Front opening

1 With right sides together, pin long edge of front opening strip to front opening of skirt, aligning raw edges and pulling split in front of skirt straight as you pin (see fig. 1). Stitch strip to skirt 5mm in from raw edges from waist edge down to (**a**). Pivot needle at (**a**) and clip across seam allowance to ease, then stitch up other side of front opening taking care not to pucker skirt at (**a**). Trim away excess strip.

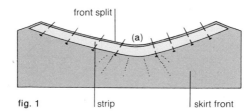

fig. 1 | strip | skirt front

front split

(a)

2 Turn in 5mm along remaining raw edge of strip to wrong side and fold strip over against wrong side of skirt front, so that this folded edge just overlaps the original stitching line (see fig. 2). Pin and tack in position. Turn to right side and edgestitch on strip close to seam through all thicknesses of fabric, pulling the fabric so that the strip is straight at (**a**) and catching inner folded edge of binding strip in stitching. ▱

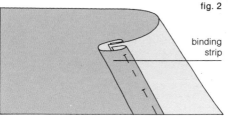

fig. 2

binding strip

3 Pin front pleats of skirt into position, matching notches marked on pattern and leaving front opening free. The front opening should fall at the back of the pleat, slightly to the right of the centre-front notch (see fig. 3). Staystitch across the top edge of the pleats to hold, again leaving front opening free. ▱

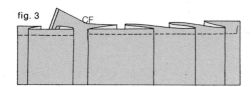

fig. 3   CF

4 With right sides facing, pin left angled pocket bag to left pocket opening edge of skirt front. Stitch, neaten seam allowances together and press towards pocket bag. On right side of pocket bag, understitch along seam through seam allowances (see p. 148). Turn pocket piece back against wrong side of skirt and topstitch 5mm in from opening edge on right side of skirt, unpicking nearest pleat where necessary. Repeat for right pocket.

5 Pin left full pocket bag to left angled pocket bag, placing right sides together and matching notches in curved inner edge of pocket. Stitch around inner curved edge from top of skirt to side seam. Trim seam allowances and neaten together. Repeat for right pocket. Place right side of skirt front downwards on table, arranging pocket bags so they lie flat against skirt front. Pin into position along top edge and side seam edge, attaching pocket to skirt front. Staystitch across top and down side seams to hold.

6 Follow same method as in step 3 to pin pleats in back skirt piece, but omit the front opening details. Staystitch across top edge of pleats to hold. ▱

7 With right sides facing and matching notches at side seams, pin front and back skirt pieces together. Stitch right side seam, stitching from top edge of full pocket piece, continuing down to hem. Neaten side seam allowances together and press towards back of skirt. Topstitch on skirt back, 5mm in from seamline, down the entire length of the seam. Repeat for left side seam.

Hip-band

8 Attach interfacings to underneath piece of back hip-band and left and right underneath pieces of front hip-band (see p. 153). Pin front and back top hip-band pieces together at side seams, matching notches and placing right sides together. Stitch and press seam allowances open. Pin front and back interfaced underneath pieces together at side seams. Stitch and press seam allowances open. Place right sides of under hip-band and top hip-band together, pinning around top and both front opening edges. Allowing 1.5cm seam allowances at left and right front opening edges and a 5mm seam allowance at top edge of hip-band, stitch around hip-band leaving lower edge free. Clip seam allowance along top edge and press towards under hip-band. Open out stitched hip-band so that right sides of both top and underneath hip-band face upwards and understitch (see p. 148) on under hip-band through all seam allowances, close to first line of stitching, starting and finishing understitching 4cm in from front opening edges. Turn hip-band to right side. ▱

9 *To attach hip-band:* Place right side of top hip-band against right side of skirt, aligning lower raw edge of hip-band with top raw edge of skirt. Start pinning at left front opening, folding back front opening strip to wrong side (see fig. 4), matching side seams of skirt and band, and aligning centre-back "V" of band with centre-back pleat. Stitch all round, clipping seam allowances at centre-back "V" point to ease. Trim seam allowances at side seams and press entire seam allowance of band and skirt upwards, away from skirt. Neaten all around raw edge of under hip-band and pin in position behind top hip-band, laying it flat, with neatened seam allowance of under hip-band pointing downwards (this is not a turned-in edge). Tack in position, setting skirt loops at either side. Turn to right side and stitch all around top edge of skirt, immediately below hip-band and directly on top of first line of stitching, catching under hip-band in topstitching. Then topstitch on hip-band, 5mm in from edge and starting at bottom of left front opening edge. Stitch up left front opening, around top edge, down right front opening, and along lower edge of hip-band, 5mm in from seamline and pivoting at centre-back "V", finishing at starting point. ▱

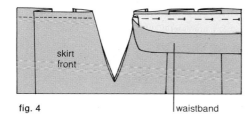

skirt front

fig. 4 | waistband

To finish

10 *Hem:* Adjust hem length if necessary. Turn under 5mm along hem edge to wrong side and stitch all round. Turn under a further centimetre and edgestitch close to inner folded edge through to right side, all around hem. ▱

11 Attach three studs on hip-band at positions marked on pattern (or make buttonholes and sew on buttons). Attach an extra small popper to the bottom of the hip-band opening, below the line of studs, to hold the skirt opening together.

Summer Dress

This loose, dropped waist summer dress has short sleeves pleated into a cuff, a "V" back and topstitching detail. It fastens at the back with an overlapping buttonhole band and can be worn wrapped on the hip with a sash or loose, perhaps shortened to above-knee length.

You will need:
2.50m of 150cm wide fabric *or*
3.20m of 115cm wide fabric
4 small buttons

Bodice

1 Placing right sides together, pin back bodice pieces to front bodice piece at shoulder seams and side seams, and stitch. Neaten seam allowances separately and press open.

2 *Buttonhole band:* Fold buttonhole band in half along foldline so that right sides come together. Stitch across top edge allowing 1cm seam allowance. Turn and press. Staystitch the two long raw edges of band together to hold. Pin band to left back opening edge where marked, aligning raw edges. Stitch through band and bodice 5mm in from raw edges.

3 *Facings:* With right sides together, stitch back facings to front neck facing at shoulder seams. Press seams open.

4 Placing right sides together, pin facing to bodice, starting at centre-front "V" and working outwards, matching shoulder seams and notches and enclosing buttonhole band on left back bodice (see fig. 1). Tack in position. Then stitch all round, 5mm in from raw edge, taking care not to stretch fabric where it is cut on the cross.

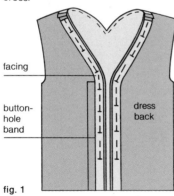

facing

button-hole band

dress back

fig. 1

5 Clip seam allowances at centre-front "V" point and curves. Press facing and seam allowances away from bodice. Understitch close to seam on right side of facing, through seam allowances, all the way round facing, but breaking stitching at centre-front "V" point to allow "V" to lie flat.

6 On remaining long raw edge of facing, turn in 5mm to wrong side and stitch close to fold-line all the way round, clipping edge of facing at bend in centre-back opening. Turn facing against wrong side of bodice, pressing carefully into position. Pin or tack in place on bodice. Edgestitch through to right side of bodice along inner, stitched edge of facing, all the way around neck and back opening. This

will form a line of stitching 3cm in from the edge on the right side of the bodice. Take care not to pull and pucker the fabric where it is cut on the cross. ⌐

Sleeves

7 Fold left sleeve so right sides are facing and pin underarm seam. Stitch, neaten seam allowances separately and press open. Repeat for right sleeve. Pin the four pleats in position to fit edge of one sleeve, matching notches and folding the pleats forwards as marked on pattern. Staystitch across bottom of pleats to hold and repeat for other sleeve. With right sides facing, align seam edges at short ends of one cuff piece, and stitch together to form a continuous band. Press seam allowances open. Pin cuff to hem of sleeve, right sides together and matching underarm seam with cuff seam. Stitch all round, 1cm from edge. Turn cuff to right side, press cuff and seam allowances away from sleeve and understitch on cuff, through seam allowances close to seam. Turn cuff to inside and press 1cm to wrong side along remaining raw edge of cuff. Pin this folded edge over the original seamline, slightly overlapping the seam, and tack in position. Turn sleeve back to right side and carefully stitch through original seamline on sleeve so that stitching is barely visible, catching inner folded edge of cuff in stitching on the wrong side (see fig. 2). Press cuff and topstitch on cuff close to seam. Repeat for other cuff and sleeve.

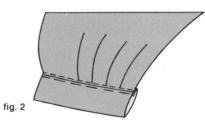

fig. 2

8 Ease one sleeve to fit armhole by gather stitching around the top of the sleeve, starting line of stitching about 8cm up from underarm seam and finishing at the same point on the other side of the sleeve. Draw up stitching so sleeve fits armhole and notches on sleeve and bodice align. Pin in position with right sides facing and stitch. Neaten seam allowances together and press towards neckline. Edge-stitch on right side of bodice through pressed seam allowances, close to armhole seamline. Repeat for other sleeve.

Skirt

9 With right sides of skirt facing, pin side seams of front and back pieces together and stitch. Neaten seam allowances separately and press open. Pin pleats in position, working on the right side of the fabric and folding top edge of skirt piece so that each (**a**) point meets the next (**b**) point and the pleated edge of the skirt fits the lower edge of the bodice (adjust pleat depth at side seams for sizes 10 and 12) (see p. 151). Staystitch around top edge of skirt to hold pleats in position. Placing right sides together, pin lower edge of bodice to pleated edge of skirt and stitch all round. Neaten seam allowances together and press upwards towards neckline. Turn dress to right side and

edgestitch on bodice close to seam around hipline, through all seam allowances. ⌐

To finish

10 *Hem:* Adjust hem length if necessary. Then turn under 5mm to wrong side around hem edge and stitch all round. Turn under a further centimetre and stitch close to inner folded edge, through to right side. ⌐

11 Make four buttonholes on band at positions marked on pattern and sew buttons on to right back bodice.

Fabric suggestions – a uniform stripe would give the dress a more slender line, whilst a floral print would give a bolder effect.

(see pattern charts on pp. 56, 57)

Wrapover Dress and Tie Belt

A loose and simple collarless, sleeve-less dress with contrasting revers and wide wrapover front opening. It is tied with a shaped hip tie belt also made in contrasting fabric.

5 Set lower front opening edges in the same way, but this time understitch through the *facing* and seam allowances, and not through dress fronts. Clip across seam allowances at waistline and then understitch on facing, close to the seam, from a point 6cm below waistline, to 5cm above hem edge. Repeat for other front facing. Then understitch back neck facing in the same way, stitching through neck facing and seam allowances, and not through dress back, from shoulder point to shoulder point.

6 Neaten inner raw edges of facings by turning in 5mm to wrong side and stitching all round edge. ⊿

You will need:
2.70m of 150cm wide main fabric
1.40m of 150cm wide contrast fabric *or*
2.80m of 115cm wide main fabric
1.40m of 115cm wide contrast fabric

1 With right sides together, stitch dress front pieces to dress back piece at shoulders. Neaten seam allowances separately and press open.

Facings

2 Placing right sides together, pin left front facing to left front, matching notches. Starting at the hem, stitch up front and around point of rever, 5mm in from raw edges, stopping at notch 5cm in from shoulder seam edge. Take care not to stretch fabric where cut on the cross. Repeat for right front and facing.

3 With right sides together, stitch back neck facing to front facings at shoulders. Neaten seam allowances separately and press open. Pin neck facing to neck edge, right sides together. Stitch around neck edge to join

stitching of front facings at notches so that entire facing is attached. ⊿

4 To ensure that revers turn and sit properly, understitch on dress front close to seam, through seam allowances but not through the front facings underneath (see p. 148). Start understitching at a point 6cm up from the waistline, and stitch almost to point of rever. Break stitching here, and then continue understitching around neck edge as far as notch 5cm from shoulder seam. Repeat for other side, trim rever points and clip seam allowances around curve of neck.

Pockets

7 With right sides together, pin one pocket piece to the dress back, matching notches at side seams. Stitch down side seam, 1.3cm from raw edges. Repeat for other side of back and both front pieces, again matching notches, so that all four pocket pieces are attached. Press pocket pieces away from dress.

8 Placing right sides together, pin side seams of dress, starting at the armhole, down to notch point at top of pocket. Then pin out and around pocket pieces to form "ears" facing outwards from side seams. Continue pinning down from bottom of pocket to hem (see fig. 1). Stitch this seam, pivoting needle at top and bottom of pocket. Clip across seam allowances

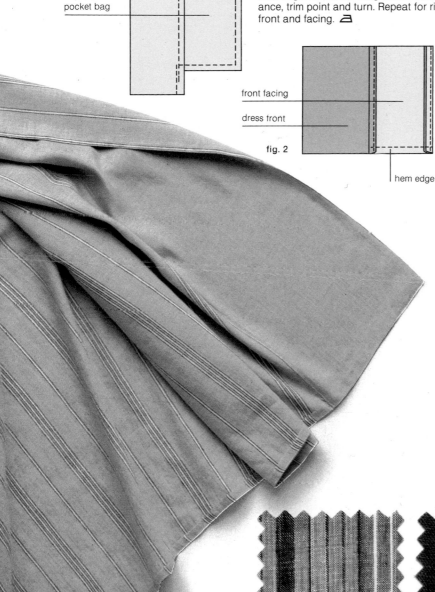

fig. 1

dress front

pocket bag

front facing

dress front

fig. 2

hem edge

at top and bottom of pocket and press seam allowances of dress and pockets outwards away from dress. Following side seam, stitch up from point where bottom of pocket joins side seam, as far as (a), stitching through front and back dress pieces only. Stitch again for strength. Repeat for other side seam and pocket. Neaten side seam allowances separately and press open. Neaten pocket seam allowances together. Turn dress inside out and turn the complete pockets flat against the front of dress. Pin or tack in position against fronts of dress, and press. Following seamline of pocket bag, stitch through pockets and dress fronts, so that pockets are fastened against dress fronts and stitching is visible on right side of dress fronts. ⊒

9 Adjust hem length if necessary. Then, with dress lying flat, turn left front so that right sides of front and facing come together (see fig. 2). Making sure that facing does not pull dress out of shape, pin through facing and dress along hem edge. Stitch, allowing 1.5cm seam allowance, trim point and turn. Repeat for right dress front and facing. ⊒

10 Turn up 5mm to wrong side around remaining hem edge and stitch. Turn under a further centimetre and tack into position along inner folded edge, beginning and ending line of tacking just inside rever facing at each end of hem. Pin inner stitched edges of facings in position on inside of dress fronts and back, again making sure they lie flat and do not pull dress out of shape. With inside of dress facing uppermost, edgestitch along tacking line all the way round from left front hem, up and around back neck and down to right front hem. Pivot needle 1cm above hem edge and stitch around inner folded and stitched edge of hem round to point where you started. ⊒

11 Edgestitch on left front of dress close to front opening edge, down from waist point, around hem edge and up to right front waist point. Break stitching here, pull threads to inside and tie off. Turn dress so that right side of facing is uppermost. Continue edgestitching up around right rever, neck edge and down left rever, ending edgestitching at starting point. Pull threads to inside and tie off. ⊒

12 Stitch around underarm curve at armhole, along seamline, to strengthen. Trim seam allowance to 5mm around underarm curve only and neaten. With right sides facing pin one armhole bias strip to armhole all around opening, trimming off any excess and tucking in short ends of binding at start and finish to neaten. Stitch, and press binding and seam allowances away from dress. Understitch on binding close to seam through binding and seam allowances, all the way round armhole (see p. 148). Press 5mm to wrong side along remaining raw edge of binding, pin in position against wrong side of dress and tack binding to dress along this inner folded edge. Edgestitch along inner folded edge of binding through to right side. On right side, edgestitch around outer edge of armhole opening. Repeat for other armhole.

Belt

13 Place right sides of main fabric belt pieces together and pin centre-back seam. Stitch and press seam allowances open. Repeat for contrast fabric pieces. Place right sides of joined main fabric pieces and contrast fabric pieces together, matching outer raw edges. Pin together and then stitch all round, leaving a 10cm gap at top centre-back edge through which to turn. Trim corners, turn belt to right side (see p. 153) and press. Slipstitch across opening. Edgestitch all around belt on main fabric side.

Fabric suggestions – *an ethnic print will give a gentler, less formal impression while a deep colour will accentuate the line and allow even stronger contrast effects.*

(see pattern charts on pp. 58, 59)

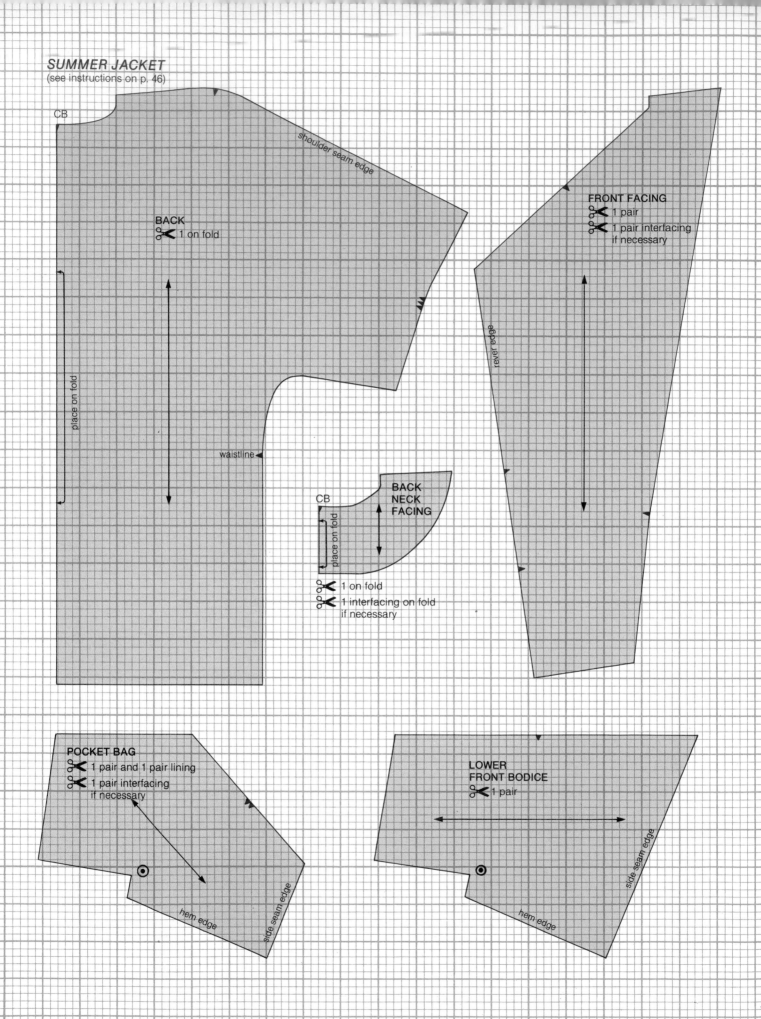

SUMMER JACKET
(see instructions on p. 46)

CB

shoulder seam edge

BACK
✂ 1 on fold

place on fold

waistline ◄

FRONT FACING
✂ 1 pair
✂ 1 pair interfacing
if necessary

rever edge

BACK
NECK
FACING

CB

place on fold

✂ 1 on fold
✂ 1 interfacing on fold
if necessary

POCKET BAG
✂ 1 pair and 1 pair lining
✂ 1 pair interfacing
if necessary

hem edge

side seam edge

LOWER
FRONT BODICE
✂ 1 pair

side seam edge

hem edge

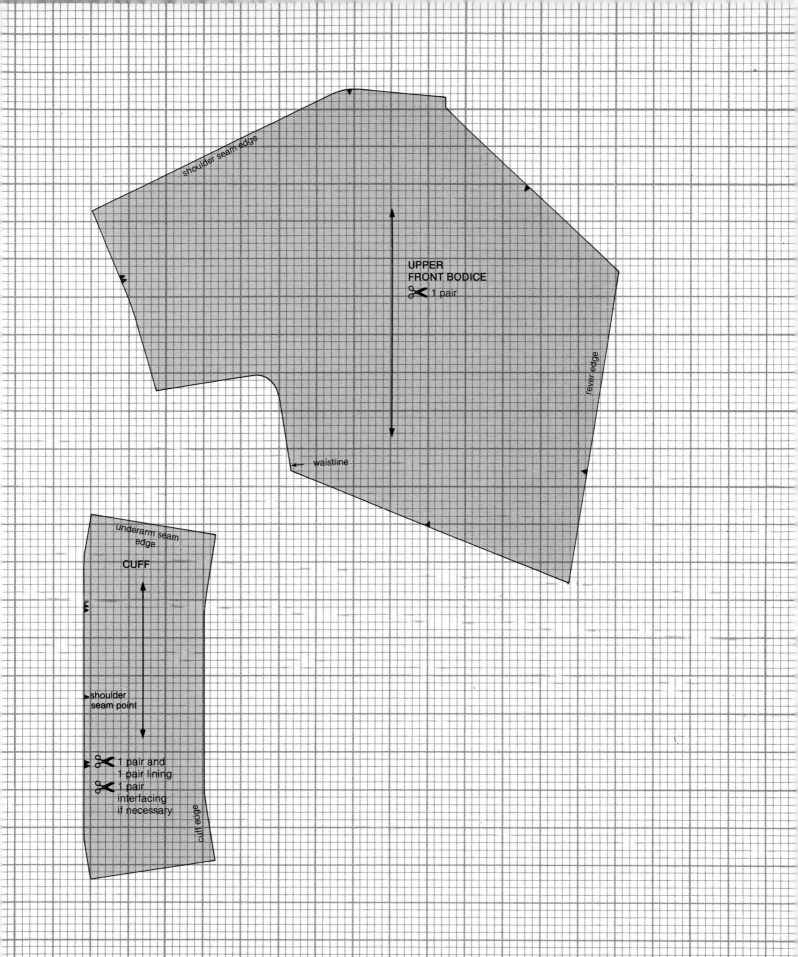

shoulder seam edge

UPPER
FRONT BODICE
✂ 1 pair

rever edge

waistline

underarm seam
edge

CUFF

shoulder
seam point

✂ 1 pair and
1 pair lining
✂ 1 pair
interfacing
if necessary

cuff edge

SEAM ALLOWANCES:
1.5cm *except*
1cm at revers, front facing, back neck facing, wrist edge of cuff, pocket opening edge

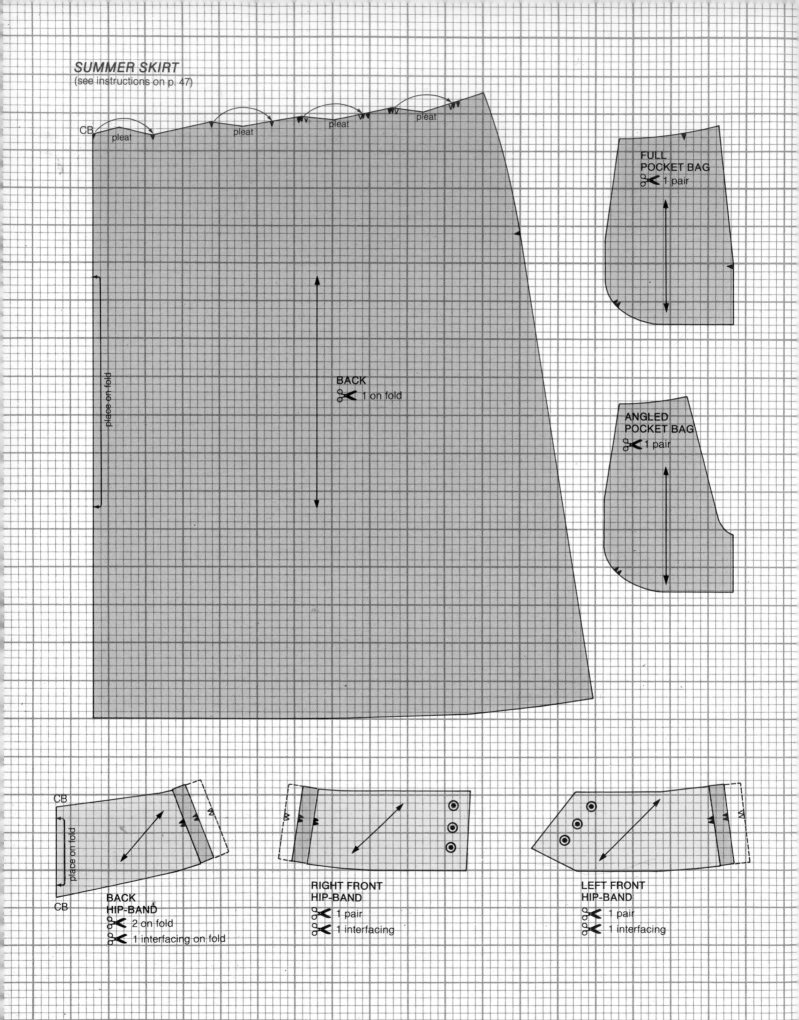

SUMMER SKIRT
(see instructions on p. 47)

CB

pleat   pleat   pleat   pleat   pleat

place on fold

BACK
✂ 1 on fold

FULL
POCKET BAG
✂ 1 pair

ANGLED
POCKET BAG
✂ 1 pair

CB

place on fold

CB

BACK
HIP-BAND
✂ 2 on fold
✂ 1 interfacing on fold

RIGHT FRONT
HIP-BAND
✂ 1 pair
✂ 1 interfacing

LEFT FRONT
HIP-BAND
✂ 1 pair
✂ 1 interfacing

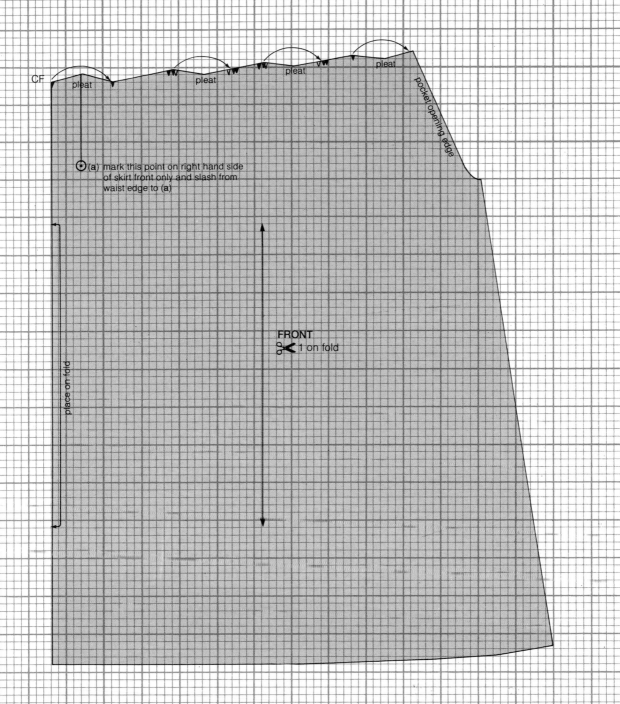

CF

pleat pleat pleat pleat

pocket opening edge

⊙(a) mark this point on right hand side
of skirt front only and slash from
waist edge to (a)

place on fold

FRONT
✂ 1 on fold

FRONT
OPENING STRIP

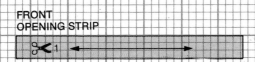

✂ 1

SEAM ALLOWANCES:
1.5cm *except*
5mm at pocket opening, front skirt slash opening, front opening strip, waist edge of hip-band

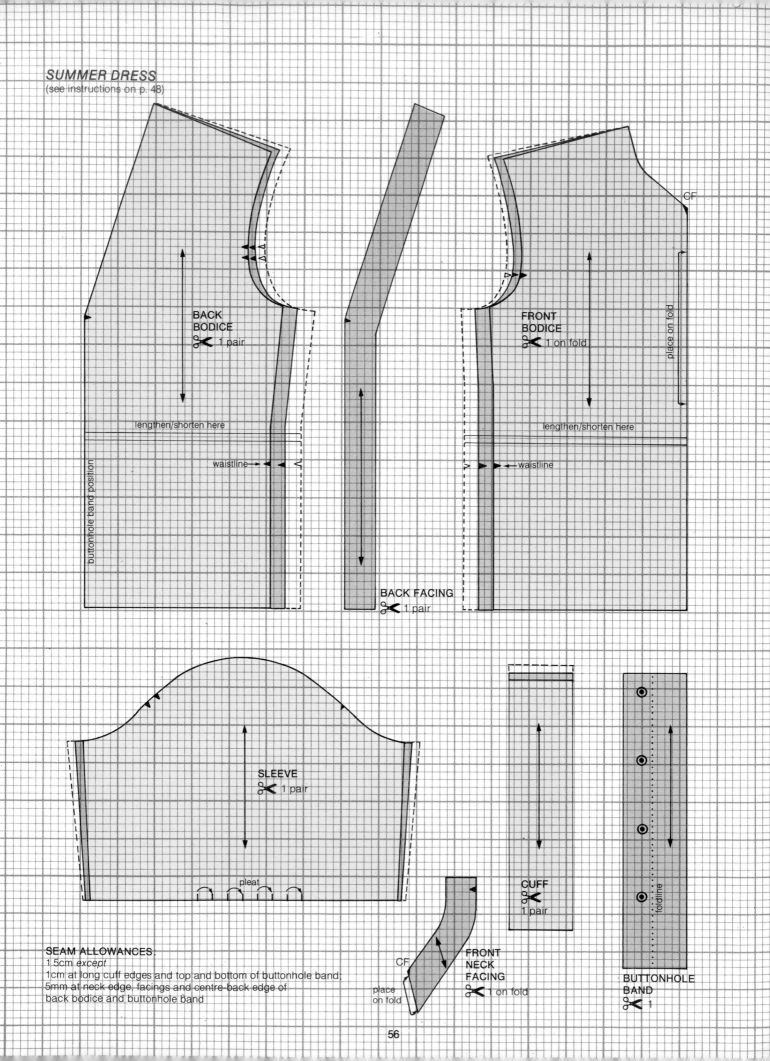

SUMMER DRESS
(see instructions on p. 48)

BACK
BODICE
✂ 1 pair

buttonhole band position

lengthen/shorten here

waistline

BACK FACING
✂ 1 pair

FRONT
BODICE
✂ 1 on fold

CF

place on fold

lengthen/shorten here

waistline

SLEEVE
✂ 1 pair

pleat

CUFF
✂ 1 pair

BUTTONHOLE
BAND
✂ 1

foldline

FRONT
NECK
FACING
✂ 1 on fold

CF

place
on fold

SEAM ALLOWANCES:
1.5cm except
1cm at long cuff edges and top and bottom of buttonhole band
5mm at neck edge, facings and centre-back edge of
back bodice and buttonhole band

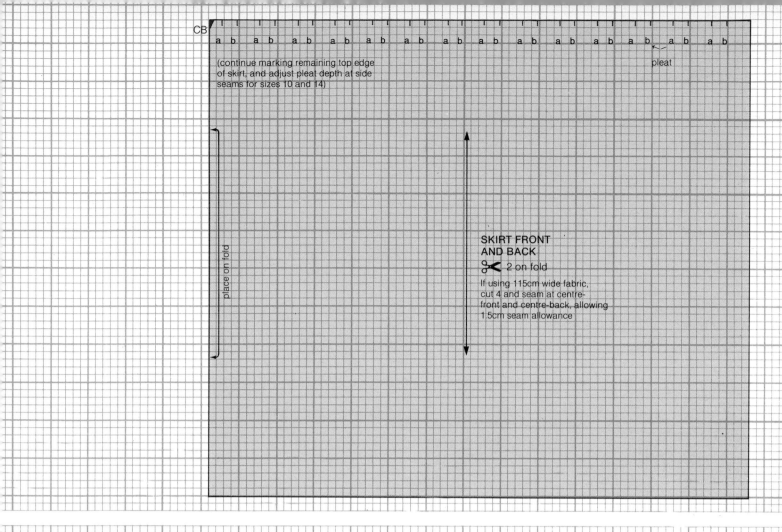

CB

a b a b a b a b a b a b a b a b a b a b a b a b a b a b a b a b a b a b

pleat

(continue marking remaining top edge
of skirt, and adjust pleat depth at side
seams for sizes 10 and 14)

place on fold

**SKIRT FRONT
AND BACK**

✂ 2 on fold

If using 115cm wide fabric,
cut 4 and seam at centre-
front and centre-back, allowing
1.5cm seam allowance

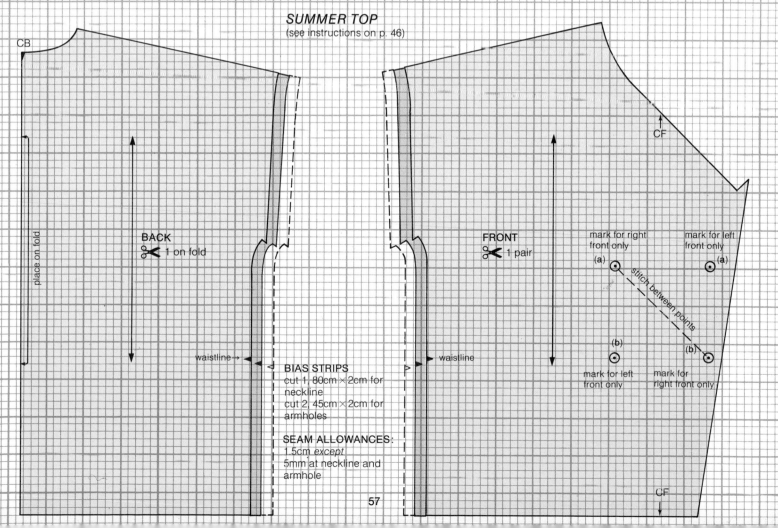

SUMMER TOP
(see instructions on p. 46)

CB

place on fold

BACK

✂ 1 on fold

waistline →

BIAS STRIPS
cut 1, 80cm × 2cm for
neckline
cut 2, 45cm × 2cm for
armholes

SEAM ALLOWANCES:
1.5cm *except*
5mm at neckline and
armhole

CF

FRONT

✂ 1 pair

← waistline

mark for right
front only

(a)

stitch between points

mark for left
front only

(a)

(b)

mark for left
front only

(b)

mark for
right front only

CF

57

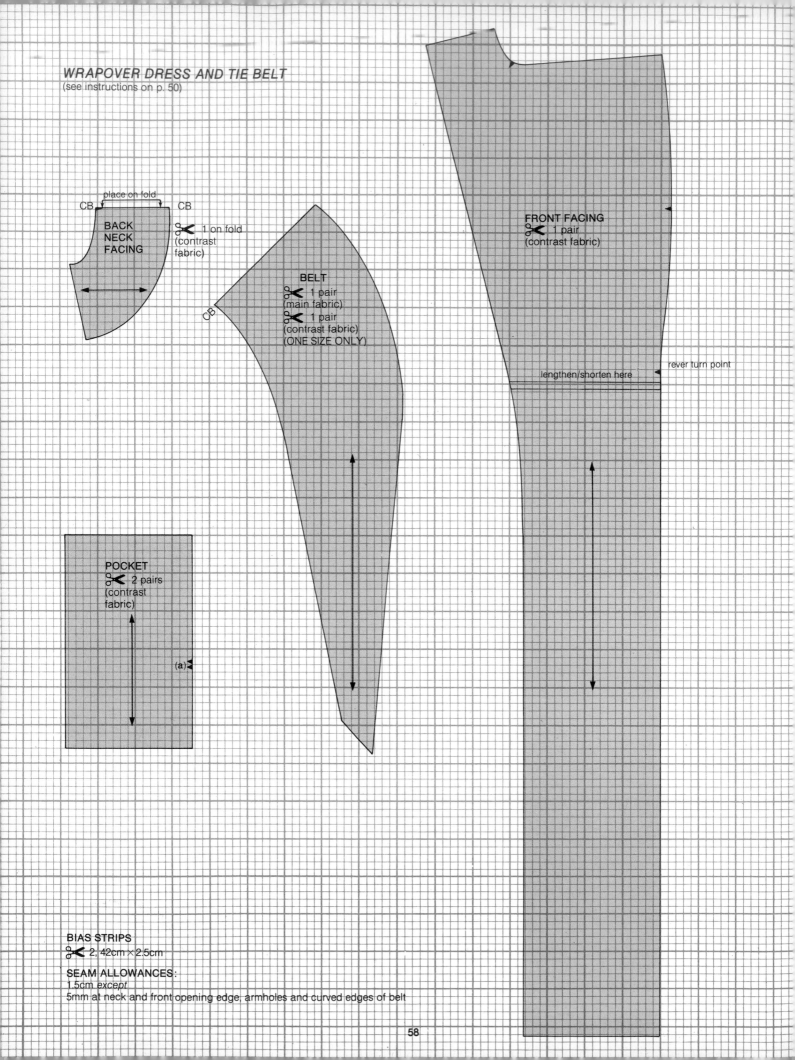

WRAPOVER DRESS AND TIE BELT
(see instructions on p. 50)

place on fold

CB   CB

BACK NECK FACING

✂ 1 on fold
(contrast fabric)

CB

BELT
✂ 1 pair
(main fabric)
✂ 1 pair
(contrast fabric)
(ONE SIZE ONLY)

FRONT FACING
✂ 1 pair
(contrast fabric)

lengthen/shorten here

rever turn point

POCKET
✂ 2 pairs
(contrast fabric)

(a)

BIAS STRIPS
✂ 2, 42cm × 2.5cm

SEAM ALLOWANCES:
1.5cm *except*
5mm at neck and front opening edge, armholes and curved edges of belt

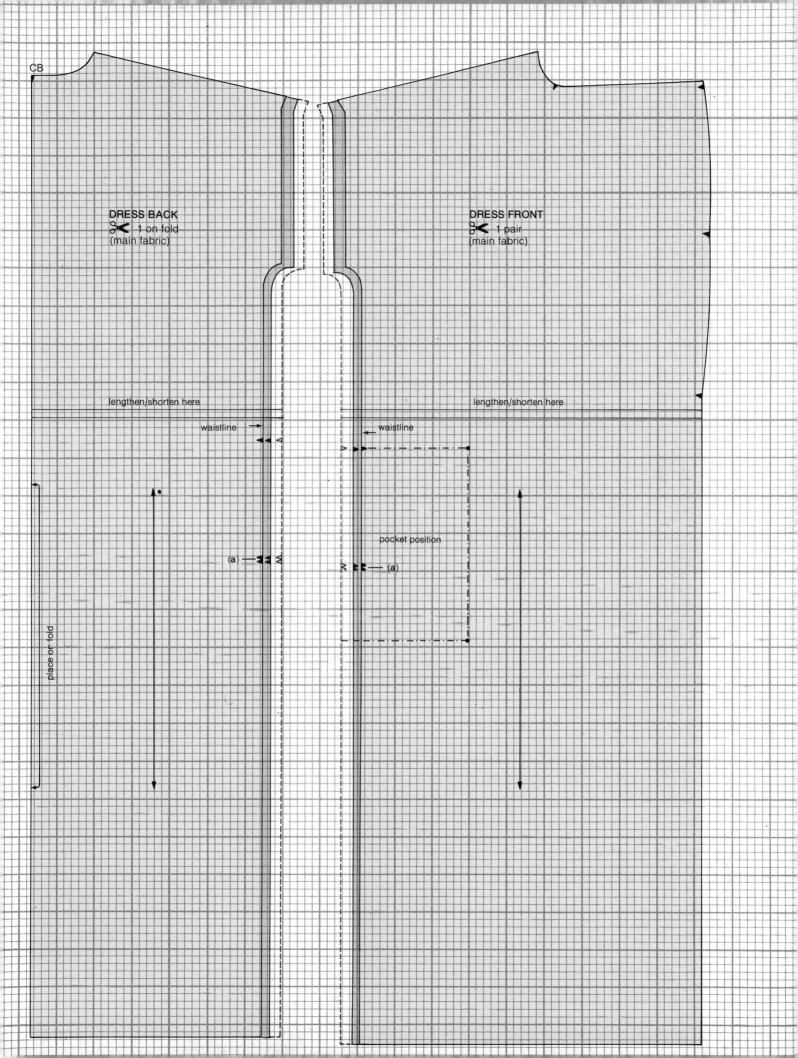

CB

DRESS BACK
✂ 1 on fold
(main fabric)

DRESS FRONT
✂ 1 pair
(main fabric)

lengthen/shorten here

lengthen/shorten here

waistline

waistline

pocket position

(a)

(a)

place or fold

Denim Jacket and Pants

Jacket

A generously-cut casual jacket, with assymetrical front fastening, deep side pockets and long sleeves. The front opening plackets fasten with press-studs, the cuffs and side seams are held with tabs and studs, and there is a triangle tab detail in the centre-back yoke. The front, back, sleeves and pockets are all made up of panels which make use of different grains in the fabric. Time and care are needed to achieve the finer details which make this a rewarding couture-style garment.

2 Placing right sides together, pin top back yoke to both top front yoke pieces at shoulder seams. Stitch along shoulder seams and press seam allowances towards back. Edgestitch on back yoke close to shoulder seams through all seam allowances. Repeat for under yoke pieces, but press seam allowances open and omit edgestitching.

fig. 1

understitching

under collar

top collar

You will need:
2.50m of 150cm wide fabric *or*
3.20m of 115cm wide fabric
90cm of interfacing
15 press-studs

1 Attach interfacing to wrong sides of relevant jacket pieces, i.e. to left and right under placket pieces, all pocket pieces, under yoke pieces, under collar piece, four tab pieces and one centre-back triangle tab piece (see p. 153 for interfacing instructions).

Collar

3 With right sides together pin top collar piece to under collar piece, leaving long curved edge of collar open. Stitch around three pinned sides. Trim corners and turn collar to right side. Spread top collar and under collar so that both face upwards and seam allowances underneath lie against under collar. Understitch on under collar (see p. 148) close to long seam, through all seam allowances, starting and finishing stitching about 3cm away from collar points, to hold under collar in position (see fig. 1). Staystitch along curved raw edges of collar to hold. Edgestitch on top collar, through to under collar, around the three finished edges.

Pockets

4 Matching notches and with right sides facing, pin side pocket panel to main pocket piece. Stitch, neaten seam allowances together and press them out towards side seam edges. Edgestitch on pocket panel, down seamline, through seam allowances. Neaten top edge of pocket and turn back facing along foldline marked on pattern, so that right sides come together. Stitch facing down along shorter side of pocket only (see fig. 2). Turn to right side. Neaten seam allowance on this side of the pocket only. Stitch across top of pocket on right side, 4cm in from folded top edge, catching the facing underneath in the stitching. Edgestitch along folded edge of pocket top. Turn in seam allowance (1.5cm) along shorter

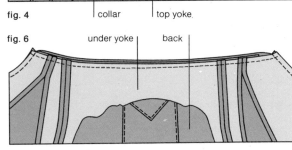

fig. 2

side of pocket and tack in place. Repeat for other pocket.

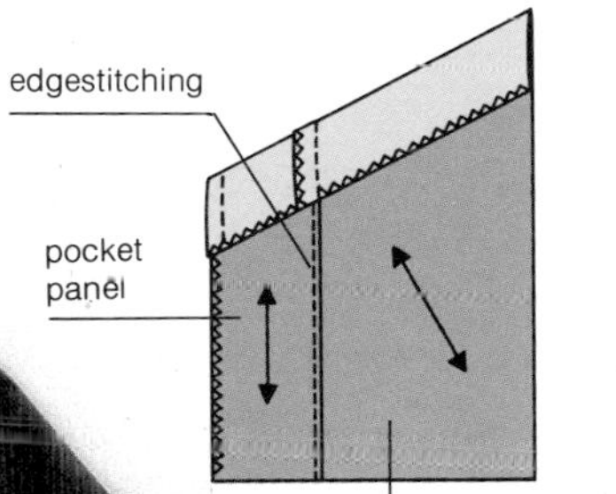

Plackets

5 Place right top placket against right under placket, with right sides facing. Starting at the neck edge, stitch down front opening edge of placket (allowing 1cm seam allowance) and around hem, finishing 1.5cm from inner raw edge. Trim corner at hem. Turn in seam allowance down long raw inner edge of under placket to wrong side. Press and tack along folded edge to hold. Repeat for left placket.

6 Pin long side of finished right pocket against right front panel matching notches and hemlines. Stitch and press. Repeat for left pocket. Pin long raw edge of top right placket to right front opening edge, with right sides together, sandwiching pocket and matching notches. Stitch and press seam allowances towards centre-front. Edgestitch close to seam on right side of right top placket, from neck to hem, taking care not to catch under placket in edgestitching (see fig. 3). Repeat for left placket.

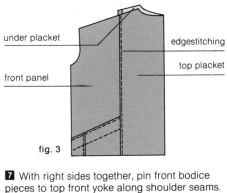

fig. 3

7 With right sides together, pin front bodice pieces to top front yoke along shoulder seams. Stitch and press seam allowances up, towards yoke.

8 Pin both back panels to centre-back panel, matching notches and with right sides together. Stitch, neaten seam allowances together and press towards centre-back. On right side of material, edgestitch on either side of centre-back panel close to seams, through all seam allowances.

Centre-back triangle tab

9 Pin right sides of triangle tab together and stitch the two shorter sides down to point, leaving notched edges open. Trim seam allow-

ances and turn to right side. Edgestitch around the two finished sides. Set tab in position against centre-back panel, aligning raw edges and notches. Staystitch tab in place. Place right side of top back yoke against finished back bodice, matching centre-back notches, and pin in position. Stitch and press seam allowances towards neckline.

Finishing yoke and collar

10 Pin and tack underneath side of finished collar to right side of top yoke, matching centre-back and shoulder seam notches. The collar should align with the opening edge of the left placket and centre-front notch of right placket (see fig. 4). Pin raw edge of left front under yoke to shoulder edge of left front under placket, placing right sides together. Stitch, press seam allowances upwards and repeat for right front under yoke and placket (see fig. 5). Keeping right sides together, pin under plackets and under yokes to top plackets and top yokes around neck edge, sandwiching collar. Stitch through all thicknesses, following line of staystitching on under collar and continuing stitching line through to front opening edges of left and right plackets (see fig. 6). Trim corners, clip curves and layer seam bulk. Turn so that right sides are uppermost. With seam allowances at neck edge lying against under yoke, understitch along neck edge of under yoke the length of the collar, through all seam allowances (see p. 148).

11 With inside of jacket uppermost, press under seam allowances at front shoulders of right under yoke and pin in position directly over original seamlines. Tack, turn jacket to right side and edgestitch close to seam on top yoke, from collar edge to armhole opening, stitching through all thicknesses, catching under yoke in stitching. Repeat for left front shoulder edge of under yoke. Repeat for back edge of under yoke, laying the jacket flat on the

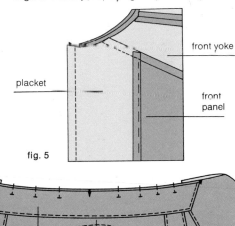

fig. 5

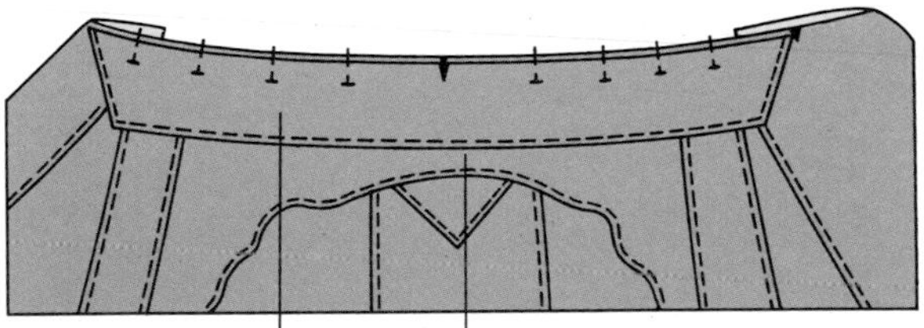

fig. 4

fig. 6

(see pattern charts on pp. 70, 71, 72)

ironing board whilst you pin under yoke in position for ease, and adjusting pressed in seam allowances if necessary. Hand stitch any sections of under yoke which may not have been caught in the topstitching, to yoke seam.

Sleeves

12 With right sides together, pin front and back sleeve pieces to either side of sleeve panel. Stitch, neaten seam allowances together and press towards sleeve panel. Turn to right side and edgestitch down each side of sleeve panel, close to seams, through seam allowances. With right sides facing, stitch underarm seam of sleeve. Neaten seam allowances separately and press open. Repeat for other sleeve.

13 *Cuff:* To finish cuff, place right sides of cuff facings together and stitch across short ends. Pin raw edge of cuff facing around cuff edge of sleeve, with right sides together and aligning underarm seams and stitch. Open out sleeve and facing so that right sides of sleeve and facing both face uppermost, and seam allowances lie against facing. Understitch on facing close to seam, through seam allowances. Turn under 1cm to wrong side at inner raw edge of facing and stitch all around. Pin and tack facing in position against inside of sleeve. Edgestitch around inner folded edge of facing through to right side of sleeve. Edgestitch again around bottom edge of cuff on right side of sleeve. Repeat for other cuff. ⊒

14 Placing right sides together, pin jacket fronts to back at side seams, taking care not to include pockets in side seams. Stitch, neaten seam allowances together and press towards back. On right side, edgestitch close to seam on back panel, from underarm point to hem. Repeat for other side seam.

15 Pin finished right sleeve into right armhole opening, matching front and back notches and underarm seams and with right sides together. Stitch, neaten seam allowances together and press back allowances towards neck of jacket, clipping seam allowances at underarm point to ease. Turn to right side and edgestitch on bodice close to armhole seam, all around armhole. Repeat for left sleeve.

16 Lay jacket flat with front uppermost. Position pockets flat against jacket, aligning raw hem edges and pinning tacked back edge of pocket in position against back of jacket. Edgestitch close to back edge of pocket, from hem to top of pocket, ending in a small stitched "V" for strength. Staystitch across raw hem edge of pocket through to jacket, stitching 1cm from raw edge. Repeat for other pocket. ⊒

17 Turn under 1cm around raw hem edge to wrong side and stitch all round. Trim side seam allowances within hem. Turn under a further 2.5cm and pin and tack in position against jacket, between inner placket edges. Edgestitch hem, close to inner folded edge, through to right side. (If you are making this jacket in denim or another very thick fabric, you may have to just neaten the hem edge firstly, rather than turning it under, to avoid bulk.)

To finish

18 Turn jacket so that *inside* faces outermost and fronts are uppermost. Position edge of tacked seam allowance of right under placket over original placket stitching line. Pin and tack in position from neck edge to hem edge. Then slipstitch this inner folded edge to the jacket

front, directly over original seamline, taking care that your stitches do not show on the right side. Repeat for left placket and under placket.

19 Edgestitch all round jacket on right side, starting at point where edge of right inner placket joins front edge of yoke, underneath collar. Stitch across top of right placket, down front edge of right placket, round hem to left opening edge, up left placket and then across to point underneath collar corresponding with starting point. ⊒

20 *Tabs:* Place right sides of one pair of tab pieces together and stitch around long edges and point, leaving square end open. Turn to right side and press, turning in seam allowance at raw edges of square end. Edgestitch all round tab, closing opening at square end. Repeat for remaining three tabs. Pin tabs to back of jacket and sleeves where marked, aligning them with bottom of hem and cuff. Stitch in place, stitching in a narrow rectangle (5mm wide) through all thicknesses across square end; all tab points should face backwards.

21 *Applying studs:* Attach studs at positions marked on front plackets. The sides and cuffs of the jacket have two alternative fastening positions so you will need to apply one top stud to the tab, and two under studs to each side and cuff, following positions on pattern. Attach stud to triangle tab.

Pants

These semi-fitting pants have a high waist with belt tabs around waistline, back darts and short split at the centre-back waist. On each outside leg there is a deep thigh pocket and the legs are drawn in at the ankles with tabs. The trousers fasten with an extended centre-front zip, and the tabs are held with snap fasteners. Gather in the waist with a chunky belt.

> **You will need:**
> 1.60m of 150cm wide fabric *or*
> 2.10m of 115cm wide fabric
> 10cm of interfacing
> 26cm zip   6 press-studs

1 If necessary attach interfacing to the tabs (see p. 153). Place right sides of one pair of tab pieces together and, leaving a 4cm gap at square end through which to turn tab, stitch around remaining sides. Trim corners, turn tab to right side and press, turning in seam allowance at square end. Repeat for remaining five tabs. ⊒

2 Stitch darts in each back pants piece. Press darts flat towards side seams.

3 Following instructions on p. 157 for inserting a displaced zip, sew in zip in front opening edge, topstitching down at an angle towards opening edge at bottom of zip.

4 Place back pants pieces against joined front pieces, so that right sides are facing. Pin together at side seams, matching notches and stitch. Trim seam allowances, neaten together and press towards back. Edgestitch down seam

on right side of both back pants pieces, close to side seams, through seam allowances.

Pockets

5 Neaten across top edge of each pocket. Turn over 3cm along foldline at top of pocket to right side. Stitch down sides of facing to hold. Neaten around remaining raw edges. Turn to right side and press. Topstitch 1cm in from neatened raw edge of facing, stitching through both thicknesses and then edgestitch along top edge of pocket. Press in 1.5cm seam allowance around three remaining neatened edges to wrong side. Repeat for other pocket.

6 Pin a pocket in position at each side seam where marked, so that pocket tops slope downwards towards back. Edgestitch around the three neatened lower sides of pockets, starting and finishing stitching in a "V" at top edge to secure. ⊒

Waist facing

7 Neaten unnotched long sides of both waist facings. With right sides together, pin right waist facing to waist edge of right pants aligning raw edges at centre-back and waist edge. Stitch right round from bottom of centre-back split, up around waist edge to centre-front zip point, stitching through zip placket (see fig. 1). At centre-front zip point, trim any excess facing along angled edge, leaving a 1cm seam allowance. Press in this seam allowance to wrong side. Trim and clip seam allowance around waist edge and press facing against wrong side of pants, folding along seam. Pin or tack inner neatened edge of facing flat against pants. Stitch through all thicknesses, 1cm in from inner neatened edge, from point at base of back split all the way around facing as far as angled edge of facing at front. Pivot needle here and continue edgestitching along diagonal folded edge up to top edge of centre-front (see fig. 2). Pivot needle again here and then edgestitch along top edge of waist, round to top of centre-back split. Pivot needle and then stitch down edge to meet the point where you started. Repeat for left trousers front, taking care to break stitching where it meets zip teeth. Clip across seam allowances at bottom of centre-back split. ⊒

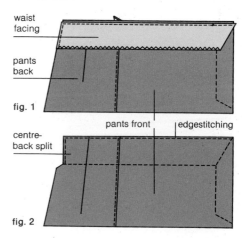

fig. 1

fig. 2

waist facing

pants back

centre-back split

pants front   edgestitching

8 Pin tabs in position around waist where marked, so that tab points face downwards. Stitch to trousers by stitching a small rectangle through all thicknesses at each square end, leaving pointed end of tab free for attaching stud.

9 Place right sides of front and back left leg pieces together at inside leg seam and pin seam. Stitch, neaten seam allowances separately and press open. Repeat for right inside leg seam. Pin remaining unstitched section of crotch seam together, and stitch as far as centre-back split. Stitch seam again at crotch point to strengthen. Neaten seam allowances separately and press open.

To finish

10 *Hem:* Allowing 4cm turn up, adjust length of legs if necessary. Neaten raw hem edge on both legs and turn under 4cm to wrong side. Pin in position. Stitch all round, stitching 1cm in from inner neatened edge through to right side. Repeat for other leg. Edgestitch around lower hem edge of each leg. Attach tabs at outer sides of legs where marked, using same method as for waist tabs, so that points of tabs face backwards. The square end should be positioned about 4cm in front of side seam.

11 At centre-back split topstitch a triangle shape 3cm wide at base of split to strengthen, catching all seam allowances in topstitching (see fig. 3).

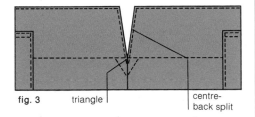

fig. 3   triangle | centre-
                              | back split

12 Apply press-studs to tabs around waist and at ankles and to corresponding positions on pants, at positions marked on pattern.

Work shirt

A loose-fitting shirt top with assymetrical front opening, fastening with press-studs. The wide-cut, three-quarter length sleeves are held at the cuff with a simple pleat and wrap stud fastening. The front plackets and breast pocket are cut on a different grain for contrast effect here.

You will need:
1.70m of 150cm wide fabric *or*
2.10m of 115cm wide fabric
7 press-studs

1 With right sides facing, pin back piece to one (top) yoke piece, matching notches. Stitch and press seam allowances towards neck. Put aside under yoke.

2 Pin shirt front pieces to top yoke at front shoulders with right sides together. Stitch and press seam allowances towards neck.

Pocket

3 Neaten right hand side and bottom raw seam edges of pocket piece. Fold under 5mm at top of pocket to wrong side and stitch. Fold back 2.5cm along foldline marked on pattern to right side to form self-facing and stitch fold down at right hand side only, to hold. Trim, turn and press fold in position along top of pocket. Edgestitch along inner folded edge of pocket facing, through to right side. Edgestitch along top of pocket. Press in seam allowance around both neatened edges of pocket and pin pocket in position on right front where marked. Edgestitch down right hand side of pocket and along bottom, through shirt front, stitching a "V" for strength at top right edge of pocket. Staystitch up left side of pocket through pocket and shirt front, just inside seam allowance, to hold.

Plackets

4 Placing right sides together, pin right front placket to right front, enclosing raw edge of pocket and matching notches. Allowing a 1cm seam allowance, stitch placket to bodice and press seam allowances towards centre-front. Press in 1cm to wrong side along remaining long raw edge of placket and tack this edge. Repeat for narrower left placket.

Collar

5 If necessary attach interfacing to top collar (see p. 153). Place right sides of collar pieces together and stitch around three sides, leaving long curved edges of collar open. Trim corners, turn collar to right side and spread under collar and top collar so that right sides, of both face upwards and seam allowances lie against under collar. Understitch on under collar

through seam allowances, close to seam (see p. 148), starting and finishing line of understitching about 3cm inside collar points. Press collar carefully and staystitch along curved raw edge of collar, through top and under collar, to hold.

6 Matching centre-back and remaining notches, pin collar to neck edge, placing right sides of under collar and top yoke together, and aligning collar edges with centre-front notches of plackets. Tack in position. Turn back plackets along centre foldline, so that right sides come together and ends of collar are sandwiched between plackets. Pin in position and then stitch from opening edge of placket to inner edge of placket, on each side (see fig. 1). Press

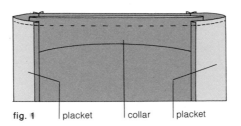

fig. 1 | placket | collar | placket

seam allowances at shoulder and back edges of under yoke piece to wrong side. With right side of under yoke against top collar, pin neck edge of under yoke to neck edge of shirt, sandwiching collar between yokes. Stitch around neck edge, through all thicknesses. Trim and

Fabric suggestions – keep the same batik theme, but experiment with brighter colours, for a jazzier, more casual look.

layer seam allowances, and clip to ease. Understitch on under yoke around neck edge close to seam, catching all seam allowances underneath in understitching. Turn shirt to right side.

7 Lay shirt flat on table or ironing board. Set under yoke in position against top yoke, tucking front raw edges of under yoke under the folded inner placket edges to neaten (see fig. 2). Pin pressed shoulder edges of under yoke directly over original top yoke shoulder seams. Tack or slipstitch under yoke to top yoke at shoulder seams. Repeat for back under yoke, making sure that it lies flat against top yoke and re-adjusting pressed seam allowance where necessary. Turn shirt to right side and edgestitch on shoulder edges of top yoke close to seamlines, through all thicknesses and catching in shoulder edges of under yoke. Edgestitch lower edge of back yoke in same way.

Sleeves

8 With right sides together, pin right sleeve to armhole, matching notches at front and back. Stitch from underarm point to opposite underarm point. Neaten seam allowances together, leaving 1.5cm free at either side for underarm seam. Press seam allowances towards collar.

Turn shirt inside out and align underarm seam edges of sleeve. Pin underarm seam and stitch from underarm point to edge of cuff. Place right sides of front and back bodice together at side seams and stitch from underarm point down to hem. Neaten all seam allowances separately and press open. Repeat for left sleeve and side seam.

9 *Cuff:* Turn in 5mm to wrong side at right cuff edge and stitch. Turn in a further 2.5cm to wrong side to form cuff facing and pin in position against sleeve. Edgestitch close to inner folded edge of facing through to right side, all the way round cuff. Then edgestitch around bottom edge of cuff. Repeat for left sleeve and cuff. ⊒

To finish

10 *Hem:* Turn right placket inside out, so that right sides come together. Align hem edges of placket and stitch across through both layers allowing 1.5cm seam allowance. Repeat for left placket. Turn in 5mm to wrong side around remaining hem of shirt and stitch all round, from just inside inner left placket edge to just inside inner right placket. Turn in a further centimetre to wrong side, pin in position and edgestitch along inner folded edge, from placket to placket, through to right side.

11 Turn right placket to right side and position inner tacked edge of placket directly over original seam. Pin in position and tack. With right side of shirt uppermost, edgestitch down inner edge of placket close to seam, from neck to hem, catching underneath edge of placket in stitching. Repeat for left placket.

12 Edgestitch on bodice around right armhole, stitching close to seam, through seam allowances, beginning and ending at underarm point. Repeat for left armhole. Beginning at bottom of right placket where placket joins bodice and with inside of shirt uppermost, edgestitch from this point across to opening edge. Pivot at corner and then continue edgestitching up right placket opening edge; pivot again at top corner of placket, then stitch around edge of collar and down left placket edge, finishing at corresponding point where left placket joins bodice. ⊒

13 Fold right cuff edge at pleat marked on pattern, so that both top stud positions come together (see fig. 3). Apply top studs (or make buttonholes) through both thicknesses, 1.5cm in from cuff edge. Apply bottom stud at position marked. Repeat for left cuff. Apply remaining five studs to front opening edge where marked.

tuck

placket

fig. 2

under yoke

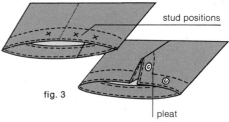

stud positions

fig. 3

pleat

(see pattern charts on p. 73)

Jacket

A tough, unlined jacket made in heavy
denim. Four zipped front pockets, patches
of rubberized (contrast) fabric, a large
collar and emphasized raglan sleeves
contribute to the sporty look of the jacket.
The denim is reversible and the reverse
side has been used for contrast effect on
facings, cuffs and collar. The jacket
fastens with an open-ended zip and
drawstring waist.

You will need:
2.60m of 150cm wide main fabric
40cm of 150cm wide contrast fabric *or*
3.50m of 115cm wide main fabric
30cm of 115cm wide contrast fabric
4 × 18cm zips
65cm open-ended zip
2m of drawstring
20cm Velcro
4 strips of iron-on interfacing,
    22cm × 4cm

Leisure Jacket and Full Skirt

Pockets

1 Mark positions for the four pocket zips on both front bodice pieces with tailor's chalk. Attach strips of iron-on interfacing to wrong side of jacket, placing them over zip position lines. Cut along one zip opening line, snipping a "V" shape 5mm deep at both ends of each line. Turn back the 5mm flaps so formed to wrong side around each slit, pressing them in position against wrong side of front bodice (see fig. 1). With right side of jacket front uppermost, position one zip behind one opening so that turned in edges lie evenly around teeth. Pin and tack zip to front bodice (see fig. 2), then stitch all round zip on bodice close to folded edges, pivoting needle at each corner. Repeat for the three remaining zips.

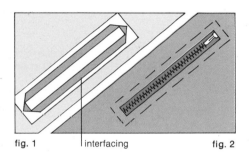

fig. 1   interfacing   fig. 2

2 Neaten around all raw edges of the four pocket pieces. Pin right side of one upper pocket piece to wrong side of each front bodice piece at positions marked (see fig 3). Tack upper pocket pieces to bodice fronts, tacking around curved edges only and leaving straight edges near shoulder seam free. Stitch pocket to bodice, using contrasting cotton if you wish, and stitching 1cm in from neatened raw edges, through to right side of bodice. Pin right sides of lower pocket pieces to wrong side of front bodice at positions marked. Tack in position around curved and straight sides, and then stitch all round, 1cm in from neatened edge of pocket, through to right side, again using contrasting cotton if you wish. Tie off all thread ends on wrong side.

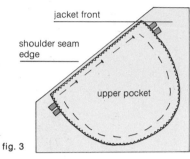

jacket front

shoulder seam edge

upper pocket

fig. 3

3 With right sides together, pin front bodice pieces to back bodice piece at side seams. Stitch, neaten seam allowances separately and press open.

Sleeves

4 *Shoulder pads:* Turn in 5mm to wrong side along straight bottom edges of front and back shoulder pad pieces and tack fold in position. Pin and tack left front shoulder piece, right side uppermost, to right side of left front sleeve piece. Edgestitch along lower edge of shoulder pad, close to folded edge, through sleeve. Repeat for remaining front sleeve and both back sleeves and shoulder pad pieces. Stay-stitch remaining raw edges of shoulder pads to sleeve pieces, within seam allowance. With right sides together, pin left front sleeve piece to left back sleeve piece along shoulder seam, matching notches and making sure lower edges of shoulder pads align. Stitch, neaten seam allowances separately and press open. Repeat for right sleeve.

5 *Elbow pads:* Press in 5mm to wrong side around raw edges of elbow pads, clipping seam allowances around curves for ease, if necessary. Tack folded edges in position. With right side of joined left sleeve piece uppermost, pin one pad in position, as marked on pattern. Tack and then edgestitch all round turned in edge of pad, through pad and sleeve. Fold sleeve so right sides come together and underarm seam edges align. Pin underarm seam and then stitch. Neaten seam allowances separately and press open. Repeat for right sleeve.

6 *Cuffs:* With right sides together, pin left front cuff facing to left back cuff facing at underarm and shoulder seams and stitch. Press seam allowances open. Repeat for right cuff facings. With sleeve still inside out, pin right side of finished left cuff facing inside left sleeve, aligning raw cuff edges and matching seamlines. Stitch all round cuff edge. Trim seam allowances and turn sleeve to right side. Fold cuff facing back against inside of sleeve, so wrong sides come together and press cuff edge, allowing facing to overlap sleeve edge slightly (see fig. 4). Topstitch 5mm in from fold at edge, all around cuff. Repeat for right sleeve.

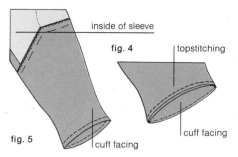

inside of sleeve

fig. 4   topstitching

fig. 5   cuff facing   cuff facing

7 Turn sleeve back to wrong side and neaten around inner raw edges of cuff facings. Position each facing against inside of sleeve, matching underarm seams of cuffs and sleeves. Pin and tack neatened edge of facing to sleeve as marked on pattern (see fig. 5). Stitch 1.5cm in from neatened edge, stopping and starting stitching at either side of elbow pad. Slipstitch unstitched section of facing to sleeve under elbow pad. Repeat for other sleeve. ⧗

8 With right sides together pin front bodice pieces to back bodice piece at side seams. Stitch, neaten seam allowances separately and press open. Pin left sleeve in position in left armhole opening, matching underarm seamlines and notches at front and back, and enclosing unstitched pocket edge. Stitch all round, neaten seam allowances together and press towards sleeve. Turn jacket to right side and topstitch on sleeve 5mm in from seam, all around armhole. Repeat for right sleeve.

9 *Waist tab:* Attach Velcro to right side of underneath waist tab piece. Then place right sides of tab pieces together and stitch all round curve of tab. Trim and clip seam allowances, turn tab to right side and edgestitch all around outer curved edge. Pin into position at waist where marked on right front edge so that right sides are together and straight raw edge of tab aligns with right front opening edge. Stitch tab to right front.

10 *Inserting open-ended zip:* Pin left side of open-ended zip to left front, so that right side of zip lies against right side of left front. Tack in position so that edge of zip tape and raw edge of left front align. Place left front facing over zip, right side of fabric facing downwards, aligning raw edges of facing and bodice, and sandwiching zip. Tack in position, over original line of tacking. Using zipper foot and a strong needle, stitch through zip tape, facing and bodice from neck to hem. Open out left facing and left front bodice so that seam allowances and zip tape lie against front bodice. Understitch down left front bodice close to edge of zip, through all seam allowances.

11 With right sides together and aligning raw front opening edges, pin right front facing to right front bodice. Stitch, open out facing and front so that seam allowances lie against facing and edgestitch on facing close to seamline, through all seam allowances. Pin right hand side of zip to right front facing, right side of zip against right side of fabric, following zip position marked on pattern, and matching top and bottom of right zip piece to left zip piece already attached. Tack in position. Stitch zip to facing, using zipper foot, leaving right front free. Neaten inner raw edges of both left and right front facings. ⧗

(see pattern charts on pp. 69, 74, 75)

12 *Collar:* Pin right sides of both collar pieces together. Stitch the two short ends and larger, outside curved edge, allowing 1cm seam allowance for short ends and 5mm seam allowance for curved edge. Leave inner curved edges open. Trim corners, clip curves and turn collar to right side and press. Staystitch along inner raw edges of collar, to hold both layers together. ⧈

13 With right sides together, stitch neck facing to front facings at shoulder seams and press seam allowances open. Pin collar around neck, laying right side of under collar against right side of neck edge and matching notches at centre-front, centre-back and side seams. Stitch collar to bodice, stitching through upper collar and lower collar and bodice. Lay right side of joined front and neck facing over top collar, aligning centre-back notch and shoulder seams. Pin in position and stitch all round from opening edge of left facing to opening edge of right facing, sandwiching collar. Then open out facing and bodice, so that right sides of both face uppermost and seam allowances lie against facing. Understitch on facing close to seam (see p. 148), catching in seam allowances and starting and finishing understitching about 5cm inside front opening edges. Neaten remaining inner raw edge of neck facing. Trim and clip seam allowances around neck edge. Turn facing so that it lies against inside of jacket and press in position.

14 *Hem:* Turn facings inside out at hem edge so that right sides of facings lie against right side of jacket. Stitch across from opening edge to inner neatened edge of facing, through facing and jacket, 3cm up from raw hem edge, following hemline. Repeat for other front facing. Trim facings and turn back to right side. Neaten remaining raw edge of hem and turn up 3cm to wrong side of jacket all around hem following hemline. Pin in position. With right side of jacket uppermost, set facings flat behind jacket fronts. Pin and tack right front facing to right front down zip position, pinning and tacking through zip tape, to secure. Topstitch on right side of jacket over tacking line, from neck edge as far as first line of topstitching around upper pocket. Stop topstitching here; pull threads through to inside and tie off. Begin topstitching again at bottom edge of top pocket, tying threads inside as you start, and stitch to top of lower pocket. Stop, pull threads through and start again at bottom of lower pocket, continuing down towards hem. Stop stitching 5mm above hemline. Pull threads through at this point and tie off on wrong side. Turn jacket to inside and starting at topstitching line down right front, 2.5cm above hem edge, stitch around hem as far as left front opening edge. Then topstitch around the three sides of the collar, starting at left front neck edge of top collar and stitching 5mm in from edge, round to right front neck edge. Break stitching here, turn to right side of right front bodice and continue topstitching 5mm in, down right front opening edge to point 5mm above hem edge. Pivot needle here and continue stitching across bottom of hem, 5mm in, to join line of topstitching down inner facing edge. Stop here, pull threads through to wrong side and tie off.

15 Zip up jacket and pin underneath piece of Velcro for waist tab in position on left front, aligning it with upper piece of Velcro on tab. Pin in position and stitch all round edge of Velcro through left front.

16 *Neck tab:* Pin Velcro to right side of underneath tab piece across outer opening edge. Stitch in position on tab piece. Then place tab pieces so right sides come together and stitch all round edges, but leaving a gap in top edge through which to turn tab. Turn, and slipstitch across gap. Press tab and then edgestitch all round on right side of tab. Pin to right front bodice just inside shoulder seam and 3.5cm down from neck edge. Stitch to jacket, stitching a narrow rectangle at right short end through all thicknesses. Position underneath piece of Velcro on left bodice front by zipping up jacket and aligning with neck tab. Pin in position and stitch to left bodice.

17 *Drawstring waist:* Neaten both long edges of channel and then pin in position against inside of jacket at channel position marked on pattern. Turn in short ends of channel where it meets inner facing edges, slightly overlapping facing edges. Stitch all along top and bottom neatened edges of channel, stitching 1cm in from neatened edge, through to right side. Leave turned in short ends unstitched for inserting drawstring. Using a bodkin or safety pin, thread drawstring through channel and tie knots in each end of string. ⧈

skirt

A calf-length skirt with wide, unstitched pleats into the waistband and side inset pockets. Shown here in denim it can be made in almost any fabric, for day or evening wear. If the fabric you choose is lightweight, omit the lining fabric for pockets and make the entire pocket in self-fabric.

You will need:
1.90m of 150cm wide fabric *or*
2.40m of 115cm wide fabric
30cm of 115cm wide lining (for pockets)
70cm × 2.5cm of waistband stiffening
20cm zip
2 hanging loops
1 hook and eye *or* button

---

1 Following marks on pattern, pin pleats in position on skirt front, starting at centre-front point and working out to each side, aligning notches. Staystitch across top of pleats, within seam allowances to hold. ⧈

2 With right sides together pin both skirt back pieces together at centre-back seam. Stitch from notch marking bottom of zip opening to hem edge. Neaten seam allowances separately and press open. Set pleats in position in skirt back in same way as skirt front, aligning folds to either side of centre-back seam 1.5cm in from raw seam edges to leave seam allowance for zip free. Staystitch across top of pleats to point 3cm in from opening edge. ⧈

3 Tack remaining unstitched section of centre-back seam together following seamline. Press seam open and position zip behind seam. Pin and tack zip in position down each side (see p. 156). Hand or machine stitch zip to skirt.

4 Neaten side seam edges of front and back skirt pieces.

Pockets

5 Neaten around curved edges of the four pocket bag pieces. With right sides facing, pin straight edges of each self fabric pocket bag to skirt back at side seams, following positions marked. Stitch 2mm inside seam allowance. Press pockets and seam allowances away from skirt. Stitch pocket lining pieces to front of skirt in the same way.

6 Place front skirt piece over back skirt piece, so right sides are facing. Align side seams and curved outer edges of pockets on either side and pin the two pieces together from waist edge, around pocket pieces, and down remaining side seam to hem. Stitch seams, pivoting needle at top and bottom of pockets, stitching around pocket bags to hem. Stitch from (**a**) on side seam to bottom of pocket, meeting stitching of lower section of side seam below pocket and stitching through front and back skirt pieces only. Repeat for other side of skirt. Clip across seam allowance of back skirt at top and bottom of pocket curve. Turn skirt to right side, pin and tack bag in position against wrong side of skirt front, so that pocket bags lie flat. Turn skirt to wrong side again and stitch around curved seamline of pocket, through pocket and skirt front. Press side seam allowances above and below pocket open and seam allowances down straight edge of pocket towards pocket.

Waistband

7 Gather top edge of skirt at side seams where marked. Fold waistband in half lengthways so right sides come together. Stitch across both short ends. Turn to right side and pin long raw edge of top side of waistband around waist edge of skirt, right sides of fabric together, matching centre-front, side seam and centre-back notches and overlapping waistband at centre-back point of right skirt back. Stitch waistband to skirt and press seam allowances upwards. Neaten remaining long raw edge of waistband. Insert stiffening inside waistband. Pin and tack neatened inner edge of waistband over original line of stitching, so that all seam allowances are covered and neatened seam edge overlaps original seam by 1cm. Turn in seam allowance on lower edges of overlapping section of waistband at right centre-back and slipstitch across both layers from edge of waistband to centre-back of skirt. Topstitch on right side of skirt, just below waistband and directly over original seam, starting at centre-back of right skirt back and stitching around waist edge, catching underneath part of waistband in topstitching and inserting hanging loops at side seams. Pivot needle at centre-back edge of left back of skirt and then edgestitch up short end of waistband, around top edge, down remaining short edge and around extended right edge of waistband to starting point.

To finish

8 *Hem:* Adjust hem length if necessary allowing 1.5cm for hem turn up. Neaten around raw edge of hem. Turn up 1.5cm to wrong side and pin in position. On inside of skirt, stitch all round hem, close to inner neatened edge, through to right side. ⧈

9 Sew hook and eye at centre-back opening (or make buttonhole and sew on button).

FULL SKIRT
(see instructions on p. 68)

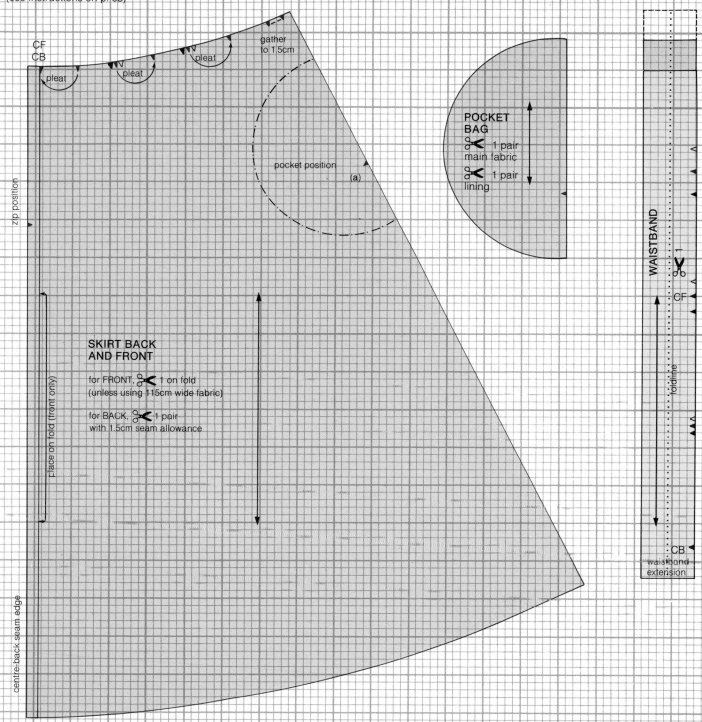

CF
CB

pleat
pleat
pleat
pleat

gather
to 1.5cm

zip position

pocket position

(a)

POCKET
BAG
✂ 1 pair
main fabric
✂ 1 pair
lining

WAISTBAND

CF

foldline

CB
waistband
extension

SKIRT BACK
AND FRONT

for FRONT, ✂ 1 on fold
(unless using 115cm wide fabric)

for BACK, ✂ 1 pair
with 1.5cm seam allowance

place on fold (front only)

centre-back seam edge

Note: If using 115cm wide fabric, cut skirt
front as for skirt back allowing for centre-
front seam. Stitch both front pieces together
and continue as for 150cm wide fabric

SEAM ALLOWANCES:
1.5cm *except*
1cm waist edge of skirt and waistband

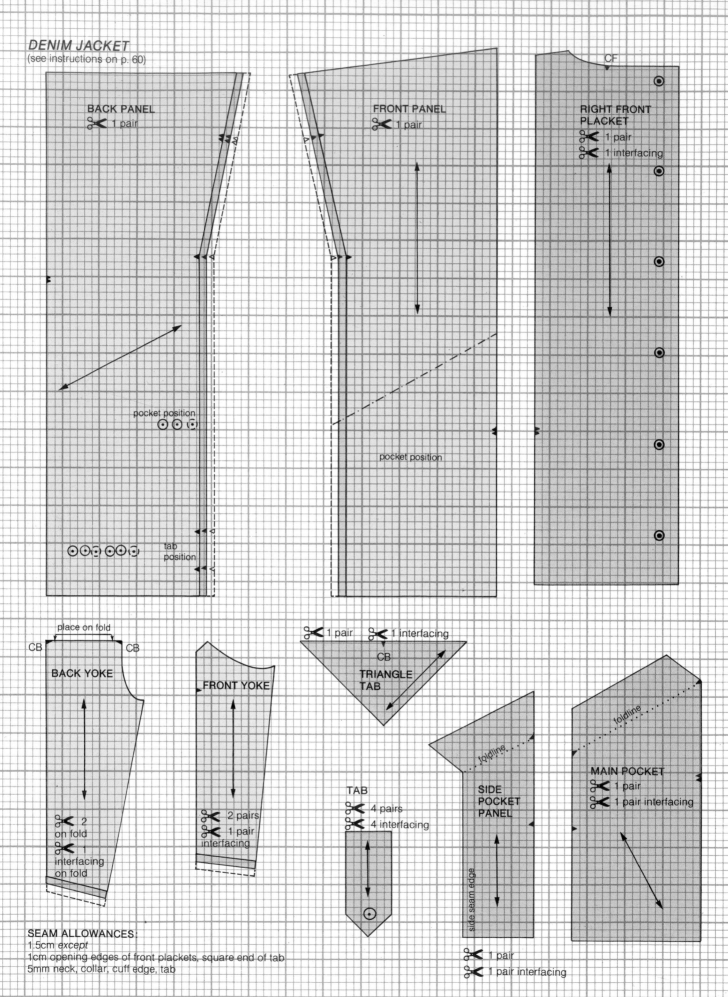

DENIM JACKET
(see instructions on p. 60)

BACK PANEL
✂ 1 pair

FRONT PANEL
✂ 1 pair

RIGHT FRONT PLACKET
✂ 1 pair
✂ 1 interfacing

CF

pocket position

pocket position

tab position

place on fold

CB   CB

BACK YOKE

FRONT YOKE

✂ 1 pair   ✂ 1 interfacing

CB

TRIANGLE TAB

✂ 2 on fold
✂ 1 interfacing on fold

✂ 2 pairs
✂ 1 pair interfacing

TAB
✂ 4 pairs
✂ 4 interfacing

foldline

foldline

SIDE POCKET PANEL

MAIN POCKET
✂ 1 pair
✂ 1 pair interfacing

side seam edge

SEAM ALLOWANCES:
1.5cm *except*
1cm opening edges of front plackets, square end of tab
5mm neck, collar, cuff edge, tab

✂ 1 pair
✂ 1 pair interfacing

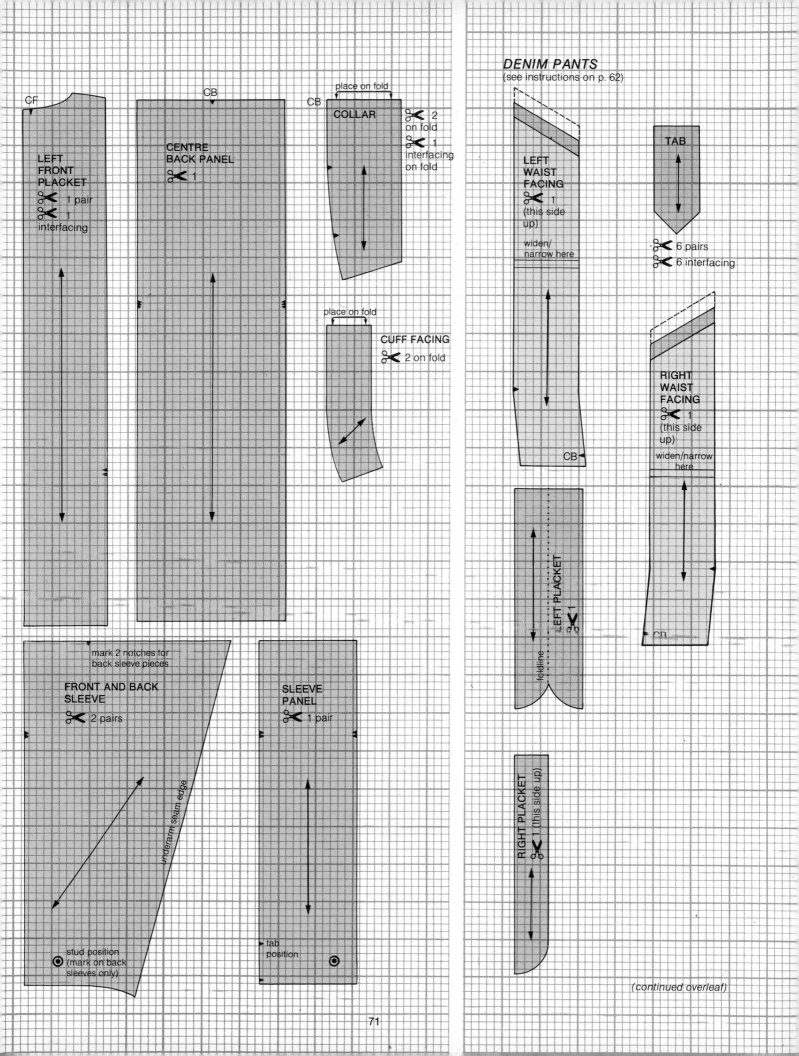

CF

LEFT
FRONT
PLACKET
✂ 1 pair
✂ 1
interfacing

CB

CENTRE
BACK PANEL
✂ 1

CB

place on fold

COLLAR

✂ 2
on fold
✂ 1
interfacing
on fold

place on fold

CUFF FACING
✂ 2 on fold

mark 2 notches for
back sleeve pieces

FRONT AND BACK
SLEEVE
✂ 2 pairs

underarm seam edge

stud position
⊙ (mark on back
sleeves only)

SLEEVE
PANEL
✂ 1 pair

→ tab
position

⊙

DENIM PANTS
(see instructions on p. 62)

LEFT
WAIST
FACING
✂ 1
(this side
up)

widen/
narrow here

CB

TAB

✂ 6 pairs
✂ 6 interfacing

RIGHT
WAIST
FACING
✂ 1
(this side
up)

widen/narrow
here

CB

LEFT PLACKET
✂ 1

foldline

RIGHT PLACKET
✂ 1 (this side up)

(continued overleaf)

DENIM PANTS CONTINUED
(see instructions on p. 62)

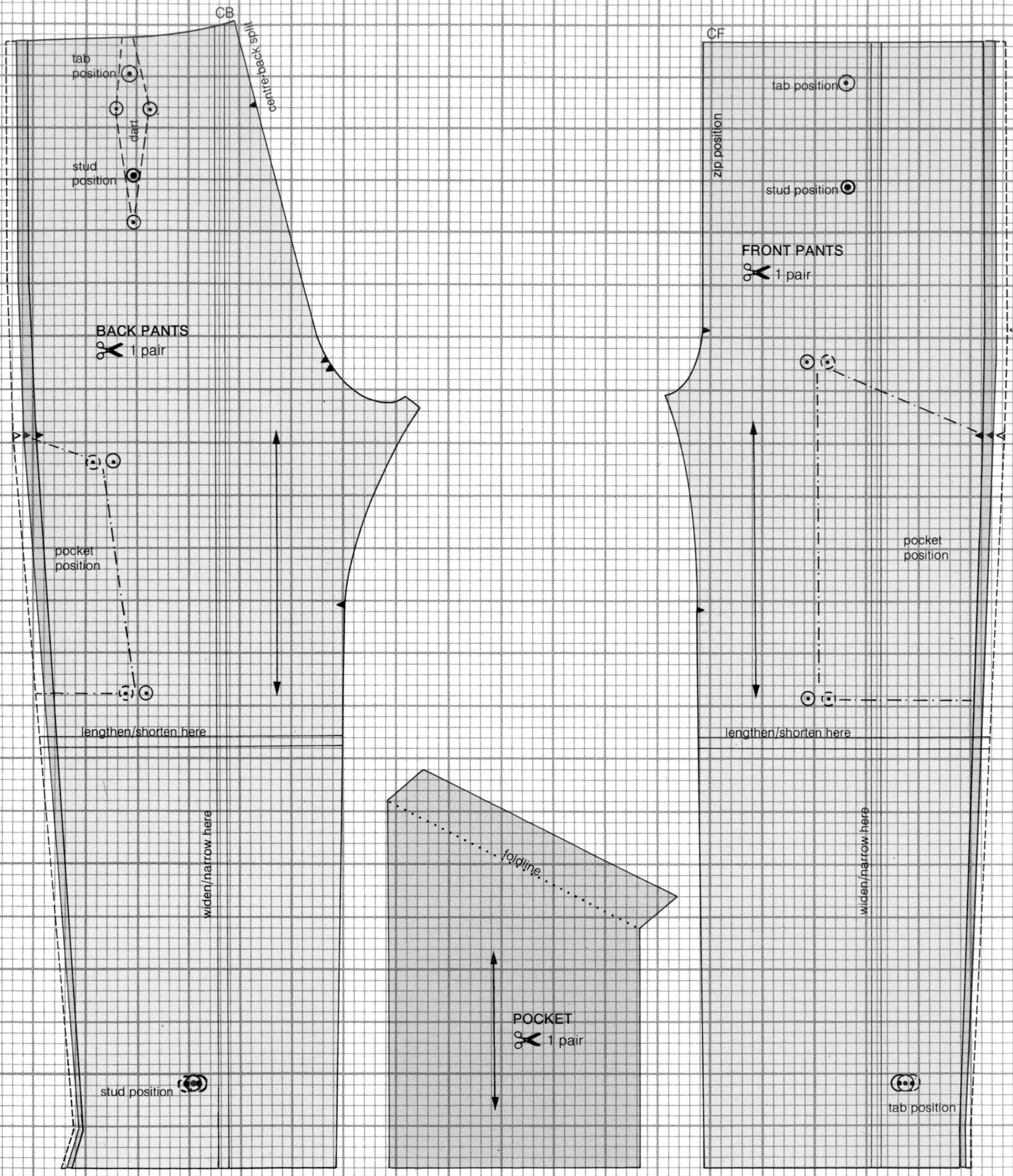

CB

centre back split

tab position

dart

stud position

BACK PANTS
✂ 1 pair

pocket position

lengthen/shorten here

widen/narrow here

stud position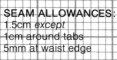

CF

zip position

tab position

stud position

FRONT PANTS
✂ 1 pair

pocket position

lengthen/shorten here

widen/narrow here

tab position

foldline

POCKET
✂ 1 pair

SEAM ALLOWANCES:
1.5cm *except*
1cm around tabs
5mm at waist edge

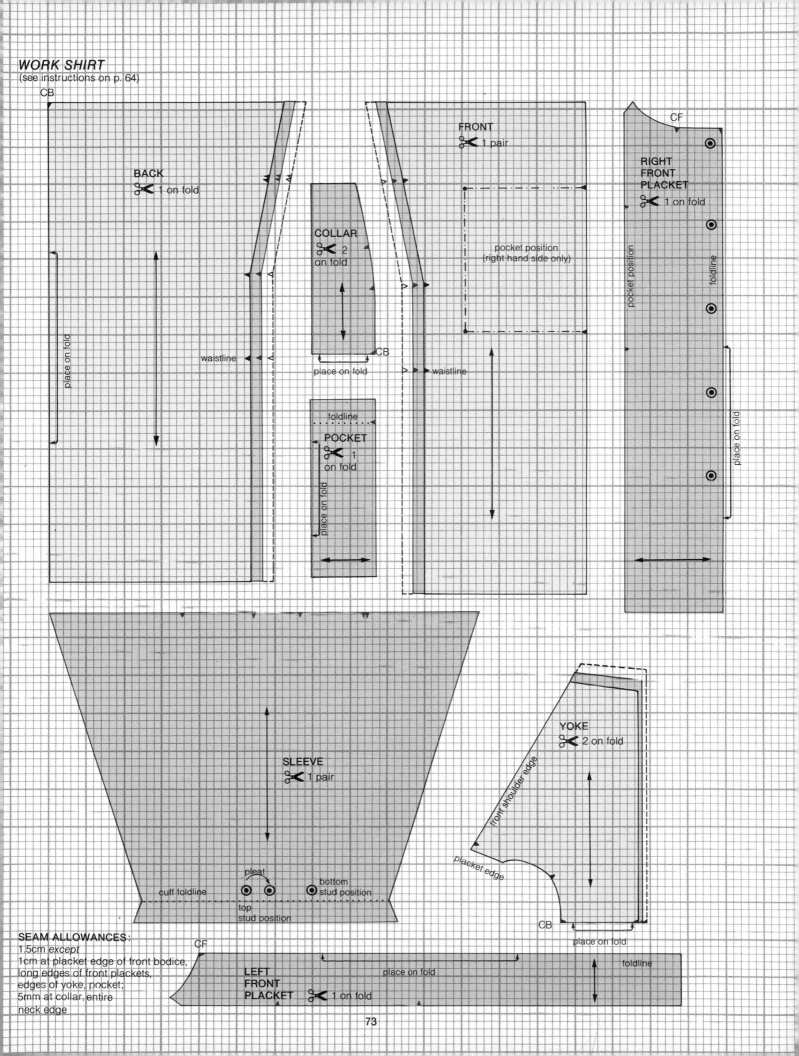

WORK SHIRT
(see instructions on p. 64)

CB

BACK
✂ 1 on fold

place on fold

waistline

FRONT
✂ 1 pair

COLLAR
✂ 2
on fold

place on fold

CB

waistline

pocket position
(right hand side only)

RIGHT
FRONT
PLACKET
✂ 1 on fold

CF

pocket position

foldline

place on fold

foldline

POCKET
✂ 1
on fold

place on fold

SLEEVE
✂ 1 pair

cuff foldline

pleat

bottom
stud position

top
stud position

YOKE
✂ 2 on fold

front shoulder edge

placket edge

CB

place on fold

SEAM ALLOWANCES:
1.5cm *except*
1cm at placket edge of front bodice,
long edges of front plackets,
edges of yoke, pocket;
5mm at collar, entire
neck edge

CF

LEFT
FRONT
PLACKET
✂ 1 on fold

place on fold

foldline

73

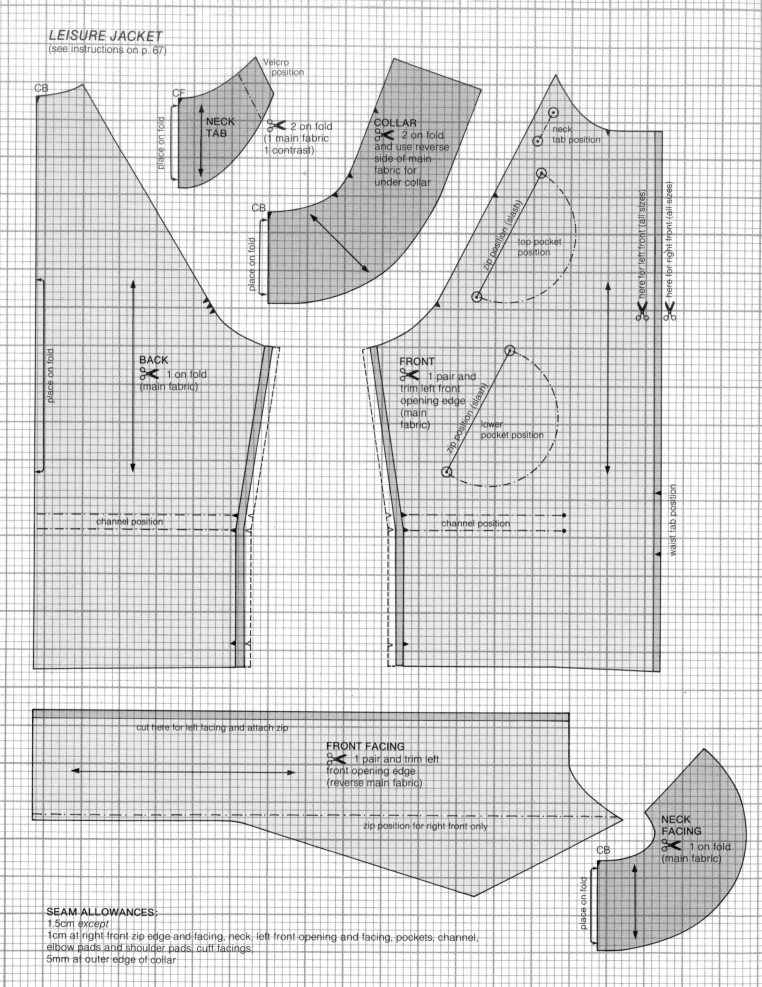

LEISURE JACKET
(see instructions on p. 67)

Velcro position

CB

CF

NECK TAB
✂ 2 on fold
(1 main fabric
1 contrast)

place on fold

COLLAR
✂ 2 on fold
and use reverse
side of main
fabric for
under collar

CB

place on fold

neck tab position

zip position (slash)

top pocket position

place here for left front (all sizes)

place here for right front (all sizes)

place on fold

BACK
✂ 1 on fold
(main fabric)

FRONT
✂ 1 pair and
trim left front
opening edge
(main fabric)

zip position (slash)

lower pocket position

channel position

channel position

waist tab position

cut here for left facing and attach zip

FRONT FACING
✂ 1 pair and trim left
front opening edge
(reverse main fabric)

zip position for right front only

CB

NECK FACING
✂ 1 on fold
(main fabric)

place on fold

SEAM ALLOWANCES:
1.5cm *except*
1cm at right front zip edge and facing, neck, left front opening and facing, pockets, channel,
elbow pads and shoulder pads, cuff facings;
5mm at outer edge of collar

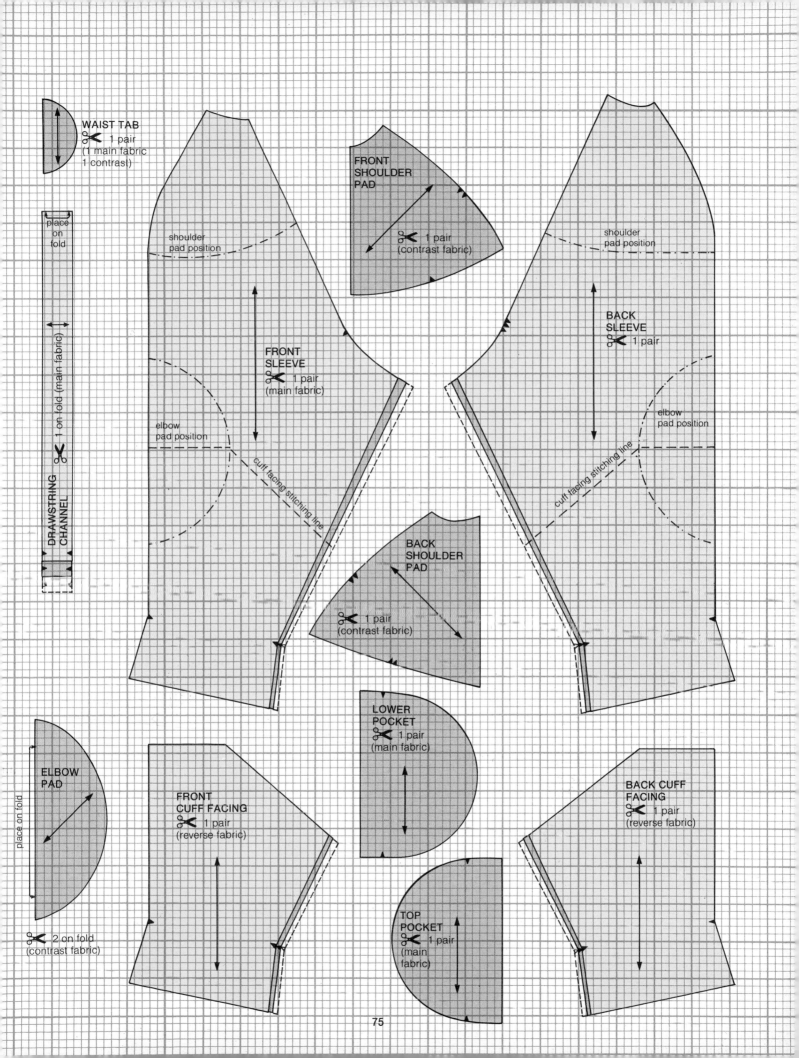

WAIST TAB
✂ 1 pair
(1 main fabric
1 contrast)

place on fold

1 on fold (main fabric)

DRAWSTRING CHANNEL

FRONT SHOULDER PAD
✂ 1 pair
(contrast fabric)

shoulder pad position

shoulder pad position

BACK SLEEVE
✂ 1 pair

FRONT SLEEVE
✂ 1 pair
(main fabric)

elbow pad position

elbow pad position

cuff facing stitching line

cuff facing stitching line

BACK SHOULDER PAD
✂ 1 pair
(contrast fabric)

ELBOW PAD

place on fold

✂ 2 on fold
(contrast fabric)

FRONT CUFF FACING
✂ 1 pair
(reverse fabric)

LOWER POCKET
✂ 1 pair
(main fabric)

TOP POCKET
✂ 1 pair
(main fabric)

BACK CUFF FACING
✂ 1 pair
(reverse fabric)

75

Fabric suggestions – *try a
patterned fine wool/angora
jersey for a softer effect.*

Tie-Neck Dress

A loose winter dress which fastens at the front with three buttons and an attached necktie. The sleeves and bodice are cut in one piece, and the dress has two patch pockets. It can be worn loose or belted at the waist and made in any medium-weight wool, silk or man-made equivalent fabric.

You will need:
2.70 of 150cm wide fabric
3 buttons

(*Note:* This pattern will not fit on 115cm wide fabric.)

1 With right sides together pin dress front pieces to dress back piece at shoulder seam, extending down top of arm. Stitch, neaten seam allowances separately and press open.

Pockets

2 Turn in 1cm to wrong side along top edges of pockets and stitch. Then turn 3cm self-facing at top of each pocket piece back along foldline, so that right sides come together and stitch down each side to hold. Neaten three remaining raw edges of each pocket. Turn facings to right side and press. Edgestitch on inside of pockets close to inner folded edges of facings, across top of pockets. Press pockets, pressing in 1.5cm seam allowance around remaining three neatened sides of pocket to wrong side. Pin pockets in position on each front dress piece where marked on pattern. Edgestitch all round the three sides, stitching in a "V" at top edges of pocket to strengthen

3 With right sides of both front pieces together, pin centre-front seam from left front slash point to hem. Stitch seam and neaton seam allowances together. Neaten left front self-facing edge and fold facing back along foldline, so that right sides come together. Stitch across facing

at neck edge, through facing and dress front. Turn to right side, press and slipstitch facing to left front down inner neatened edge, from neck to bottom of facing.

4 Neaten inner raw edge of right front self-facing. Lay front of dress flat on table or ironing board and set front pleat and right front opening edge in position (see fig. 1) by folding from foldline to hem notch, so that inner seamed edge of pleat faces towards right side seam. Pin pleat and facing in position. Press and then topstitch down right front through facing, stitching 3cm in from opening edge, starting at neck edge and stitching down and round in a curve at bottom of opening to (**a**) (stitching through pleat underneath at this point to hold pleat in position). ⊒

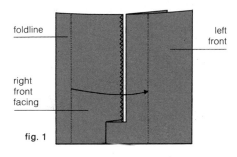

foldline

left front

right front facing

fig. 1

5 With right sides together pin dress front to dress back at underarm and side seams. Stitch seams from cuff edges round to underarm point and down to hem at each side. Neaten seam allowances separately and press open.

Necktie

6 With right sides together pin centre-back of tie to centre-back of dress. Pin necktie around neck edge. Stitch between inner edge of left facing and folded edge of right facing, clip seam allowances and press upwards. Press in 1cm to wrong side along remaining long raw edge of tie directly opposite neck edge. Then fold tie in half lengthways so that right sides are facing and pin down short ends and along remaining long edges to either side of neck edge allowing 1cm seam allowance. Stitch, stopping stitching at each front opening edge (see fig. 2). Trim seam allowances and turn tie to right side. Pin and tack remaining turned in edge of tie over stitching line around neck, so that seam allowances are enclosed. On right side of dress, stitch just below tie, directly over original stitching line, all round neck edge, catching folded inner edge of tie in stitching. ⊒

Cuff

7 With right sides together align notched edges of one cuff piece. Pin seam, stitch and press seam allowances open. With right sides together slip cuff over sleeve and pin raw edge of cuff to cuff edge of sleeve, matching underarm seam of sleeve with cuff seam. Stitch cuff to sleeve all round this edge. Press in 1cm to wrong side around remaining raw edge of cuff and pin folded edge in position directly over original seamline, on inside of sleeve. Slipstitch folded edge to sleeve. Press and roll cuff back on itself on right side. Repeat for other cuff.

To finish

8 *Hem:* Adjust length of hem if necessary allowing 2cm for hem. Trim centre-front seam allowance within hem. Turn up 1cm to wrong side around hem edge and stitch. Turn up a further centimetre and pin in position. Edge-stitch around inner folded edge of hem through to right side. Stitch through back of pleat at hem edge to hold pleat in position. ⊒

9 Mark positions for three buttonholes on right front opening edge, starting 1.5cm down from neck edge, 1.5cm in from fold of opening edge and 10cm apart. Stitch buttonholes and sew on buttons to match on left front opening edge. Press. ⊒

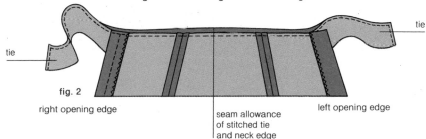

tie

tie

fig. 2

right opening edge

seam allowance of stitched tie and neck edge

left opening edge

(see pattern charts on pp. 88, 89)

Sweater and Skirt

Using heavy-rib, knitted wool fabric you can sew a sweater. The sweater shown here is loose-fitting and has a deep roll collar and front "V" inset. The cuffs and bottom of the sweater are held in by stretching bands of the knitted fabric to form tighter welts, which are sewn to the looser sleeves and bodice. The matching skirt is pleated into an elasticated waistband.

You will need:

For the sweater:
1.80m of 150cm wide fabric *or*
2.00m of 130cm wide fabric

For the skirt:
1.90m of 150cm wide fabric *or*
1.90m of 130cm wide fabric
51 (55, 59)cm × 2cm of waist elastic
2 hanging loops

Notes on sewing rib jersey

(a) A heavy rib jersey, such as the one illustrated, stretches when taken off the roll and hung. It is therefore advisable to allow for approximately 5cm "drop" after making up, and to allow the skirt to hang for a day before deciding on the hem length required.

(b) Consult your machine handbook for the most suitable method of stitching jersey with your particular machine.

(c) Ideally use a stitch which both stitches the seam and neatens the seam edges in one operation. If, however, your sewing machine does not have this stitch, use a fine zigzag for seaming and then zigzag neaten seam edges.

(d) 5mm seam allowances are included throughout for all seams. Seam allowances should be trimmed where necessary after sewing, and neatened together. Take care when cutting out to keep notches within 5mm seam allowances.

Sweater

1 With right sides together, pin the front inset in position in the front piece, slashing seam allowances carefully at the centre-front "V" point of front bodice, to ease. Strengthen around the "V" with hand stitches if necessary, stitching seam allowances flat.

2 With right sides together, pin the front shoulder edges of the sleeves to the front bodice, matching notches. Stitch each shoulder seam and neaten seam allowances together. Then pin back shoulder edges of sleeves to back bodice at shoulders, matching notches. Stitch and neaten seam allowances together.

3 Turn sweater so right sides come together, and align underarm seams of sleeves and side seams of front and back bodice pieces. Pin seams and stitch underarm and side seam in one operation. Neaten seam allowances together, and repeat for other side.

Roll collar

4 Fold collar piece in half so right sides come together and align centre-back seam edges. Pin seam, stitch and neaten seam allowances. Turn collar back to right side and fold collar in half so that *wrong* sides come together and both raw neck edges align. Staystitch the two raw edges together to hold. Pin collar to neck edge of sweater, aligning seam with centre-back notch and placing right side of underneath half of collar against right side of sweater. Tack in position, then stitch through all thicknesses. Neaten all seam allowances together.

Cuffs

5 Fold cuff so right sides come together and underarm seam edges align. Pin seam and stitch. Neaten seam allowances together and turn cuff to right side. Fold cuff in half so wrong sides come together and remaining raw edges align. Staystitch around the two raw edges to hold together. Position cuff around cuff edge of sleeve , right sides together, stretching cuff and aligning underarm seams and raw edges.

Stitch cuff to cuff edge of sleeve and neaten all seam allowances together. Repeat for other cuff and sleeve.

Hip-band

6 With right sides together pin side seams of hip-bands together. Stitch and neaten seam allowances together. Fold band in half so wrong sides come together and raw edges align. Neaten both raw edges together. Stitch hip-band to sweater in same way as cuffs, stretching it to fit bottom of sweater, matching seam allowances and neatening all seam allowances together. Press sweater carefully, pressing seam allowances flat.

Skirt

7 Pin pleats in position around top edge of front and back skirt pieces as marked on pattern. Staystitch across tops of pleats to hold, within seam allowances. With right sides together, pin front skirt piece to back skirt piece at side seams. Stitch both seams and neaten seam allowances together.

Waistband

8 Fold waistband in half so right sides come together and short seam edges align. Stitch this seam. Turn waistband to right side and fold in half so *wrong* sides come together and long raw edges align. Staystitch long seam edges together, leaving a 4cm gap for inserting elastic. Pin waistband around top of skirt so right side of outer side of waistband is against right side of skirt at waist edge and stretching waistband to fit skirt. Align the seam in the waistband with the left side seam of the skirt. Stitch waistband to skirt, leaving same 4cm gap unstitched for elastic, and attaching hanging loops at each side seam.

9 Thread appropriate length of elastic through waistband, securing ends together. Stitch unstitched section of waistband seam allowances together and then stitch to skirt. Neaten all seam allowances together.

To finish

10 Leave skirt to hang overnight. Adjust length of hem if necessary, allowing 4cm turn up. Neaten raw edge of hem and then turn up 4cm to wrong side. Pin in position, tack and then blind hem stitch hem edge to skirt.

11 Press skirt carefully, pressing all seam allowances flat.

Fabric suggestions – *use a striped, plain wool-knit, in contrasting directions for collar, cuffs and inset to give a striking, lively effect.*

(see pattern charts on pp. 83, 84, 85)

Coat-Dress, Skirt and Cowl

Coat-Dress

A three-quarter length jersey coat-dress which buttons down the front and has an overlapping flap detail at the right front opening edge. Two different colours of fine wool jersey have been used for contrast effect at the front and back.

You will need:
1.90m of 150cm wide main fabric
1.10m of 150cm wide contrast fabric *or*
2.20m of 115cm wide main fabric
1.10m of 115cm wide contrast fabric
6 buttons
(For self-colour dress use
2.20m of 150cm wide fabric *or*
2.90m of 115cm wide fabric)

Fabric suggestions – for a more striking contrast effect use red and black jersey – alternating sleeves, back, fronts and pockets if you wish.

(*Note:* A good quality, fine-knit wool jersey will not require neatening around raw seam edges. For the garments illustrated it should be sufficient merely to press seam allowances open, leaving seam edges raw.)

1 *Front flap:* Fold front flap piece in half lengthways along foldline, so right sides come together. Stitch across top edge through both thicknesses. Turn flap to right side, press folded edge and then staystitch the two long remaining raw edges together to hold, within seam allowance. Set flap to one side.

Pockets

2 Turn self-facing back along foldline at top of pocket, so right sides come together. Stitch down fold at both sides to hold. Trim corners and turn pocket facing back to right side and press. Turn in seam allowance around three remaining raw edges and press in position. Topstitch on right side, across top of pocket through pocket and facing, 3cm down from top folded edge of pocket. Repeat for other pocket. Pin both pockets in position on dress fronts, following positions marked on pattern. Edge-stitch around the three turned in edges of pockets, through pocket and dress, stitching in a "V" at both top edges of pockets to strengthen.

Sleeves

3 With right sides together and matching notches, pin one front sleeve piece to corresponding back sleeve piece down upper arm seam. Stitch seam and press seam allowances open, clipping curves if necessary. With right sides facing, pin back shoulder edge of back sleeve to shoulder edge of dress back, matching notches. Stitch and press seam allowances open. Then pin front shoulder edge of sleeve to shoulder edge of dress front. Stitch and press seam allowances open. Repeat for other sleeve. Turn dress so right sides of front and back come together and pin underarm and side seams together down each side. Stitch entire seam on both sides, breaking stitching at underarm points. Press seam allowances open.

4 Pin flap in position against right front of dress, aligning notches in right front opening edge, so that it lies 1.5cm down from neck edge, and all raw edges at front align. Stitch flap to dress front (see fig. 1). Then lay right front facing strip over flap and dress front, right sides together and aligning long raw edges of dress and facing. Pin in position down front opening edge and then stitch from neck to hem. Repeat for left dress front and facing (but without flap). Stitch across hems of both facings 4cm from hem edge, through facing and dress front. Trim corners and turn facings to right side. 🗕

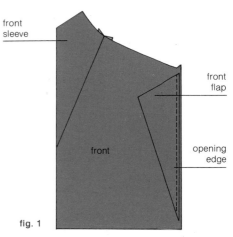

front sleeve

front flap

front

opening edge

fig. 1

5 With right sides together pin neck facing to neck edge of dress, matching notches and seamlines. Stitch 5mm in from neck edge. Clip seam allowances, leaving 5mm free at each front edge of facing for seam allowance (see fig. 2). Turn neck facing to right side and press in position. Tuck in seam allowance at front edges of neck facing and slipstitch tucked in edge to front facing. 🗕

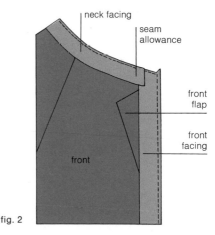

neck facing

seam allowance

front flap

front facing

front

fig. 2

6 Tack inner edges of neck and front facings to dress all the way round. Adjust length of hem if necessary allowing 4cm turn up. Then turn up hem along hem foldline and pin and tack in position, tucking hem under facing at front edges. On right side of dress, topstitch 3cm in from edge, starting at left side seam. Topstitch up left front opening edge, around neck, down right front opening edge and back round hem to left side seam. Press dress thoroughly. Hand stitch inside edge of front facing at hem to hem.

81

(see pattern charts on pp. 85, 86, 87)

Cuffs

7 Fold cuff facing piece in half so right sides come together and align short edges. Stitch short edges together, and press seam allowances open. Pin cuff to sleeve edge, right sides together, matching underarm seam and notches. Stitch all round cuff edge. Trim and clip seam allowances. Press facing back against inside of sleeve and pin inner edge in position against sleeve. On right side of sleeve, topstitch 3cm in from cuff edge through sleeve and facing, all round cuff. Repeat for other cuff and sleeve. ⊟

8 Make six buttonholes at positions marked on right dress front (see pp. 154–5). Sew on buttons, directly opposite buttonholes on left dress front, where marked. Additionally, you can sew a small popper under the corner of the flap and the under piece of the popper to left dress front to hold flap in position. Press dress thoroughly.

Cowl

This simple, useful garment is made from a double length of material, sewn together to form a circle. Made here in jersey to co-ordinate with the coat-dress and skirt, it can be worn in a variety of ways for decoration or warmth. It can be wrapped single or double around the neck as a cowl inside the coat dress. It can be worn over the head as a hood and held with a pin or brooch at the neck. Or you can twist it around your waist as a cummerbund. Alternatively wear it as a sash over one shoulder to break up a self-colour or self-pattern dress.

You will need:
1.00m of 150cm wide fabric *or*
1.40m of 115cm wide fabric

1 Fold cowl piece so right sides are facing and short edges and notches align. Stitch seam and press seam allowances open. Turn to right side.

2 Pull one raw end of tube over the other, so finished right sides come together, seamlines match and both remaining raw edges align (see figs. 1 and 2). Pin raw edges together and then stitch all round leaving a 10cm gap through which to turn cowl. Turn cowl to right side and slipstitch across gap. ⊟

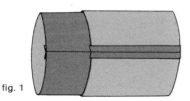

fig. 1

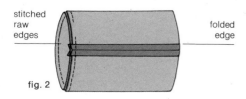

stitched raw edges

folded edge

fig. 2

Skirt

A straight jersey skirt with centre-back split and elasticated waist.

You will need:
90cm of 150cm wide fabric *or*
90cm of 115cm wide fabric
51 (55, 59)cm × 2.5cm of waist elastic
2 hanging loops

1 *Back vent:* With right sides facing, pin back skirt pieces together down centre-back seam. Stitch seam from waist edge down to (**a**). Press seam allowances open. Fold back left vent facing down seamline and press in position. Pin vent facing to skirt back. Clip across seam allowance of right back skirt, directly above vent and trim top corner of right vent (see fig. 1). Fold right vent facing back along foldline, press and pin fold in position. Lay skirt flat so right side faces uppermost and position right side of vent behind left side, so that vent lies flat. Hold all thicknesses with a pin at top of vent. Turn skirt to wrong side and tack through all thicknesses of vent, 1.5cm from top. Turn skirt back to right side and topstitch across top of vent, stitching from centre-back seam across to point 5mm in from inner edge of vent, following angle at top of vent (see fig. 2). Pull threads through to wrong side and tie off. ⊟

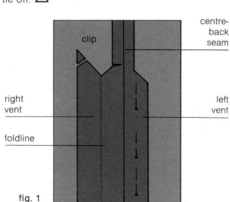

clip

centre-back seam

right vent

left vent

foldline

fig. 1

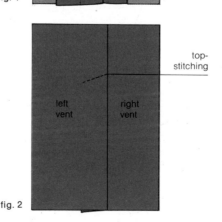

top-stitching

left vent

right vent

fig. 2

2 Pin back skirt piece to front skirt piece at side seams, with right sides together. Stitch seam and press seam allowances open.

3 *Elastic channel:* Turn over waist edge along foldline at top of skirt so wrong sides come together and pin in position. Starting at centre-back seam, stitch fold in place from inside, stitching 3cm down from fold of waist edge and 1cm up from inner raw edge. Stitch all the way round, inserting a hanging loop at each side seam and leaving a 2cm gap in stitching for inserting elastic. Thread length of elastic through channel and secure ends. Stitch across gap, joining original line of stitching.

4 *Hem:* Adjust hem length if necessary allowing 4cm turn up. Turn back vents so right sides come together and align lower hem edges. Stitch across lower edges of vents, 4cm in from raw hem edge. Trim corners and turn vents back to right side. Turn up remaining hem along hemline, allowing 4cm turn up. Pin and tack edge of hem in position against skirt. On right side of skirt topstitch down left vent only, starting at stitching line across top of vent and stitching 3cm in from edge of vent. Stitch down to point 3cm above hemline, pivot and topstitch around hem edge, 3cm in from hem edge (see fig. 3). Continue stitching all round, finishing at folded edge of right vent (do not topstitch up right vent). Blind hem stitch inner edge of right vent to skirt from top of vent to hem. Hand stitch inner raw edges of vent at hem to hem.

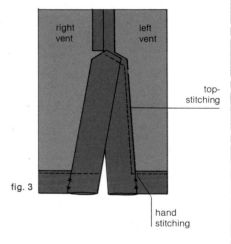

right vent

left vent

top-stitching

fig. 3

hand stitching

SKIRT
(see instructions on p. 79)

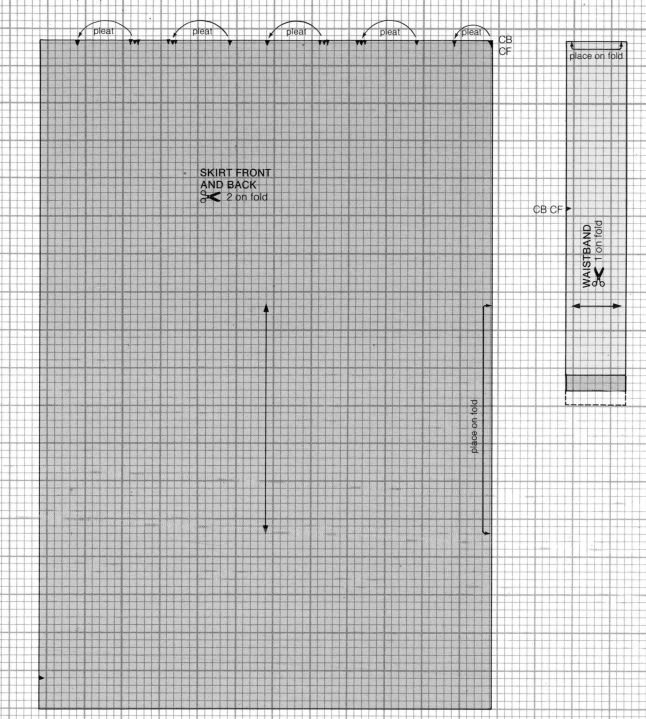

pleat pleat pleat pleat pleat CB
CF

SKIRT FRONT
AND BACK
✂ 2 on fold

place on fold

CB CF ►

place on fold

WAISTBAND
1 on fold

place on fold

SEAM ALLOWANCES:
5mm throughout

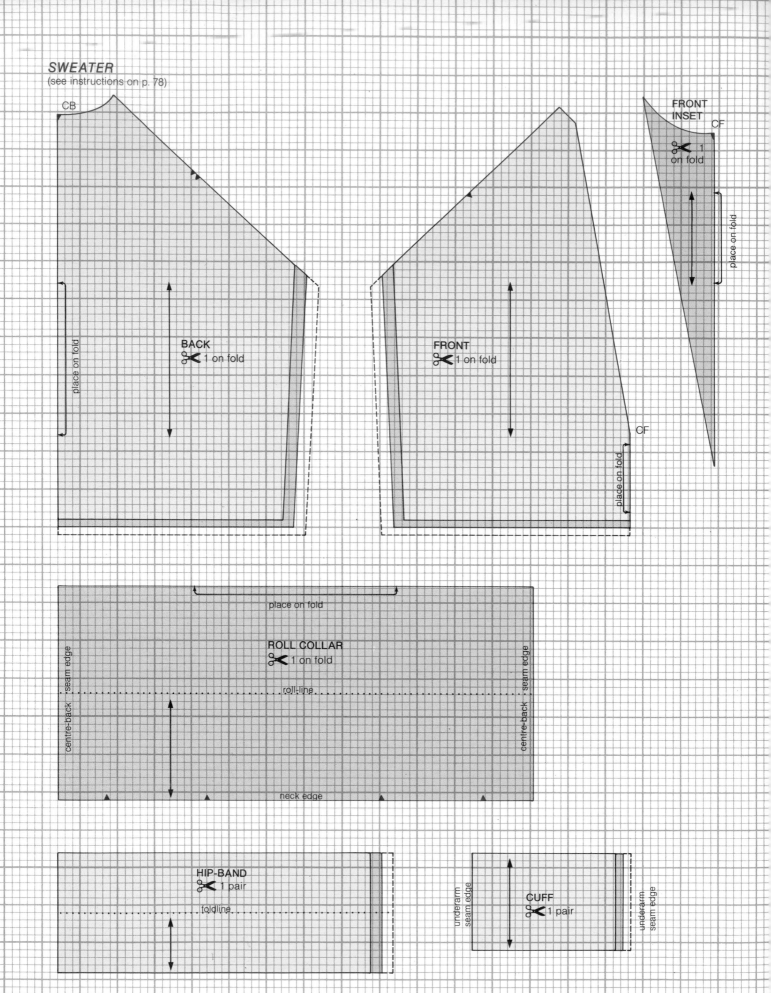

SWEATER
(see instructions on p. 78)

CB

BACK
✂ 1 on fold

place on fold

FRONT
✂ 1 on fold

place on fold

CF

FRONT INSET
CF
✂ 1 on fold

place on fold

ROLL COLLAR
✂ 1 on fold

place on fold

seam edge

centre-back

roll-line

centre-back · seam edge

neck edge

HIP-BAND
✂ 1 pair

foldline

CUFF
✂ 1 pair

underarm seam edge

underarm seam edge

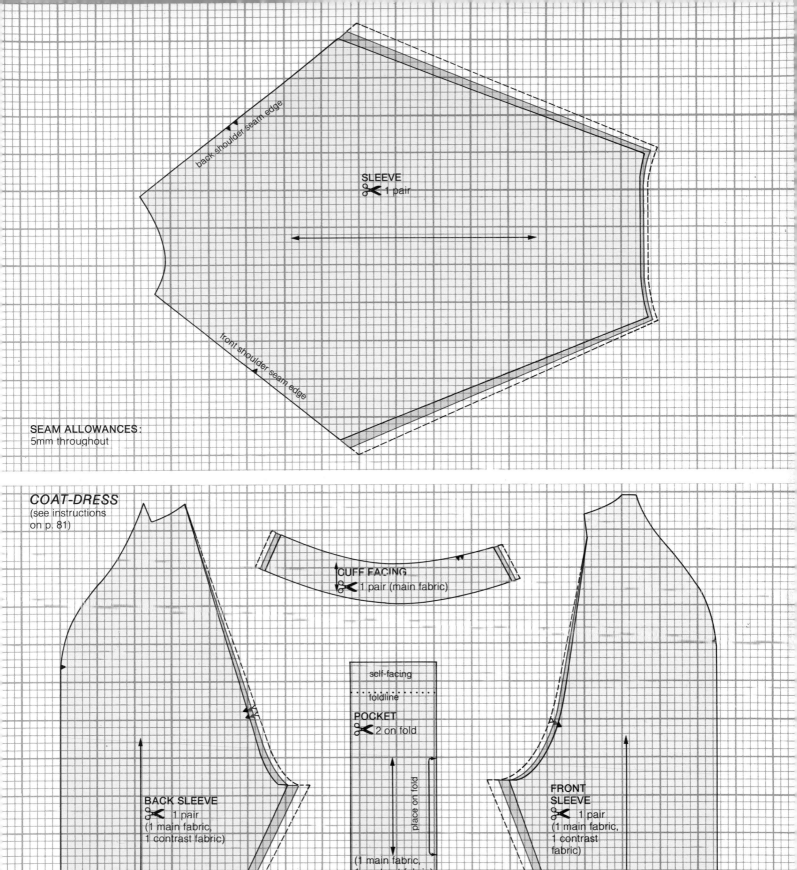

SLEEVE
✂ 1 pair

back shoulder seam edge

front shoulder seam edge

SEAM ALLOWANCES:
5mm throughout

COAT-DRESS
(see instructions
on p. 81)

CUFF FACING
✂ 1 pair (main fabric)

self-facing

·········foldline

POCKET
✂ 2 on fold

place on fold

(1 main fabric,
1 contrast fabric)

BACK SLEEVE
✂ 1 pair
(1 main fabric,
1 contrast fabric)

FRONT
SLEEVE
✂ 1 pair
(1 main fabric,
1 contrast
fabric)

SEAM ALLOWANCES:
1.5cm *except*
1cm at front opening edge of dress, front neck facing edge,
flap and front facing;
5mm at neck edge, cuff edge

*(continued
overleaf)*

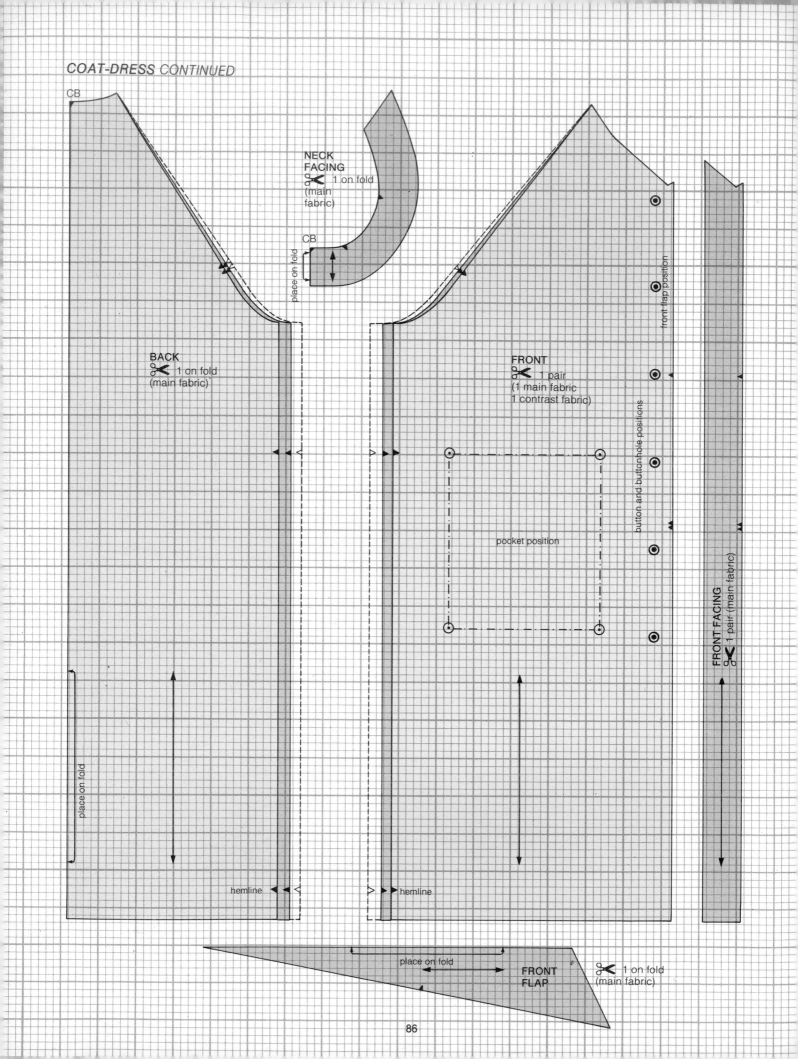

CB

NECK
FACING
✂ 1 on fold
(main
fabric)

CB

place on fold

BACK
✂ 1 on fold
(main fabric)

FRONT
✂ 1 pair
(1 main fabric
1 contrast fabric)

front flap position

button and buttonhole positions

pocket position

FRONT FACING
✂ 1 pair (main fabric)

place on fold

place on fold

hemline

hemline

place on fold

FRONT
FLAP

✂ 1 on fold
(main fabric)

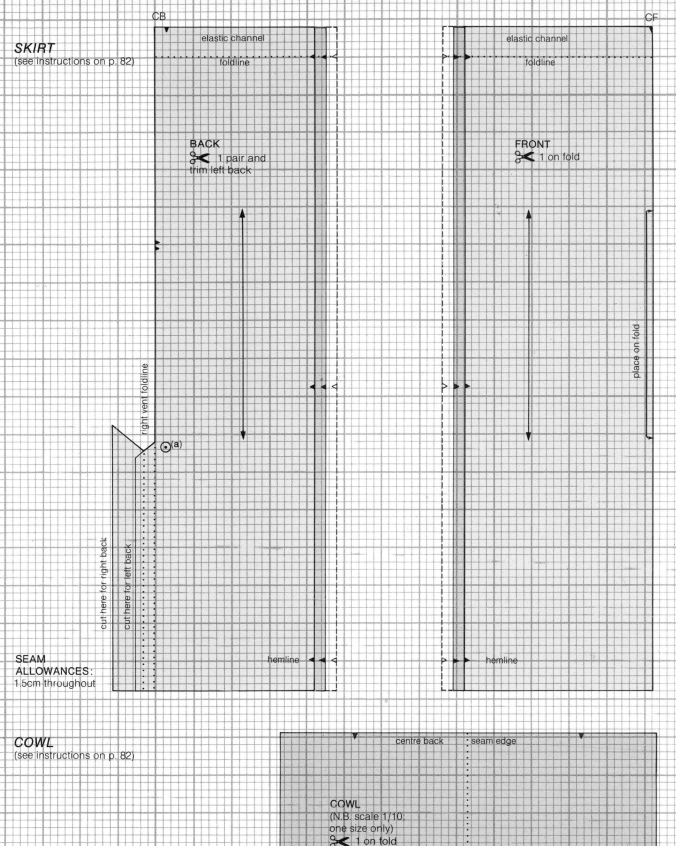

SKIRT
(see instructions on p. 82)

CB

elastic channel

foldline

BACK
✂ 1 pair and
trim left back

right vent foldline

⊙(a)

cut here for right back

cut here for left back

SEAM
ALLOWANCES:
1.5cm throughout

hemline

CF

elastic channel

foldline

FRONT
✂ 1 on fold

place on fold

hemline

COWL
(see instructions on p. 82)

centre back   seam edge

COWL
(N.B. scale 1/10;
one size only)
✂ 1 on fold

foldline

place on fold

SEAM ALLOWANCES:
1.5cm throughout

87

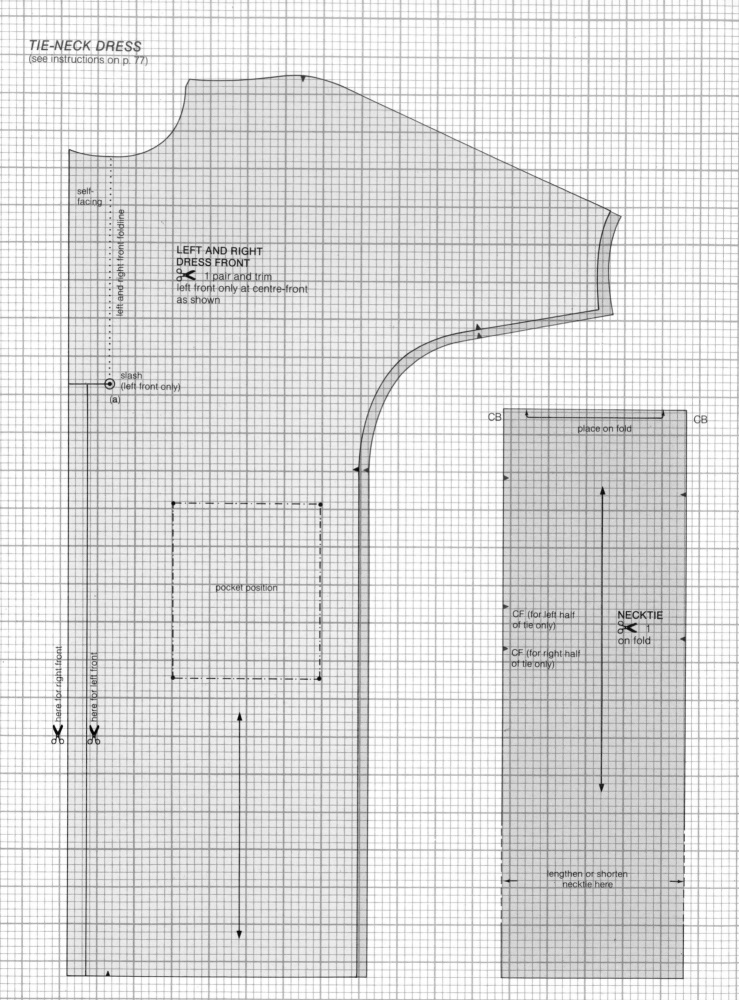

TIE-NECK DRESS
(see instructions on p. 77)

self-facing

left and right front foldline

LEFT AND RIGHT
DRESS FRONT
✂ 1 pair and trim
left front only at centre-front
as shown

slash
(left front only)
(a)

here for right front

here for left front

pocket position

CB   place on fold   CB

CF (for left half
of tie only)

CF (for right half
of tie only)

NECKTIE
✂ 1
on fold

lengthen or shorten
necktie here

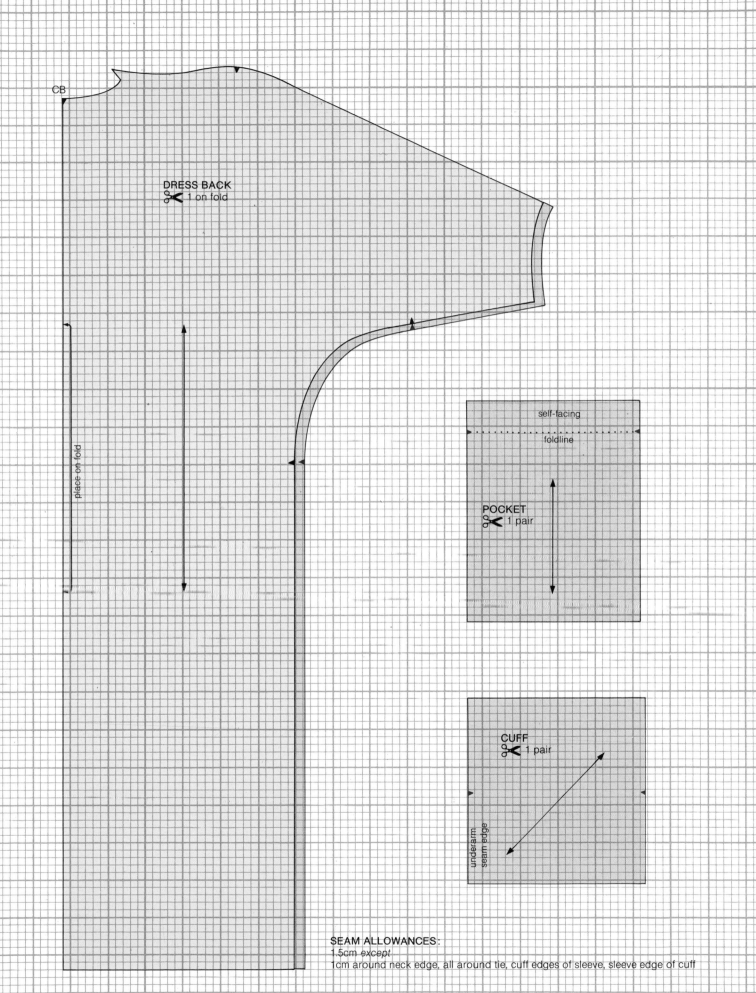

CB

DRESS BACK
✂ 1 on fold

place on fold

self-facing

foldline

POCKET
✂ 1 pair

CUFF
✂ 1 pair

underarm
seam edge

SEAM ALLOWANCES:
1.5cm *except*
1cm around neck edge, all around tie, cuff edges of sleeve, sleeve edge of cuff

3/4 Length Coat, Skirt and

This combination of simple but effective winter staples has been made up in co-ordinating fabrics to give a complete winter outfit. However, the individual garments are versatile and by using different fabrics and textures can be incorporated in many of the other outfits in the book.

Fabric suggestions – *try similarly co-ordinating fabrics in peacock and purple shades for a gentler effect.*

Raglan-Sleeved Blouse

(see pattern charts on pp. 104, 109, 110, 112, 113)

Coat

An unlined winter coat falling to just above the knee. The wide cowl neck wraps round to a side opening which can be fastened with a button and loop if you wish. All seams are flat-felled inside to neaten and the hem and edges machine hemmed, making the coat quick and easy to make.

You will need:
2.80m of 150cm wide fabric *or*
3.50m of 115cm wide fabric
1 button (or hook and eye)

(*Note:* Allow more fabric for checks and plaids.)

1 With right sides together pin back sleeve pieces to coat back at shoulder seams. Stitch both seams, trim seam allowances of coat back, and flat-fell neaten the seam towards back (see p. 146).

2 Pin front sleeve pieces to back sleeve pieces, right sides together, at upper arm seam. Stitch and flat-fell neaten seam towards back.

3 With right sides together pin coat fronts to sleeve fronts at shoulder seams. Stitch and flat-fell neaten seams towards front.

4 Turn coat so right sides of front and back come together and align underarm seam edges and side seam edges. Pin and then stitch seams from cuff down to hem, pivoting at underarm points. Stitch around underarm points again to strengthen. Flat-fell neaten seam allowances towards back.

Collar

5 If the fabric you are using is reversible pin front collar pieces to back collar pieces at shoulder seams, with reverse sides facing and matching notches. Stitch seams as far as (**b**) and flat-fell neaten them towards back. Pin collar around neckline so the underneath side of the collar is against the right side of the coat and shoulder seams of coat and collar align. Stitch collar to neck edge and flat-fell neaten seam allowances downwards, towards hem.

6 To neaten hem, front opening and collar, turn in 5mm and then 1cm to wrong side all round raw edges. This stitching line is visible on the right side of the jacket so keep it parallel to the edge. If your fabric is very bulky it may be easier to tack the folded edge in position first. Start at left side seam hem edge and stitch close to inner folded edge, round to left front opening edge. Then continue stitching up the front opening edge making sure the corner of the hem and front opening edge is neat and secure. Continue neatening up and around collar, folding raw edges of collar over to right, upper side of collar to form a contrasting binding. Make sure the front corners of the collar are neatly turned in (press and trim underneath very slightly if necessary). Neaten down right front opening edge and remainder of hem to meet left side seam. ⏹

Cuffs

7 If you are using reversible material fold cuff pieces so that reverse sides of fabric come together and pin underarm seam. Stitch under-arm seams and flat-fell neaten towards back (matching sleeve underarm seams). Pin cuff around cuff edge of sleeve, finished, reverse side of cuff against right side of sleeve. Stitch cuffs to sleeves and flat-fell neaten seams towards sleeves. Turn in and stitch remaining raw edge of cuffs as for collar and turn finished cuff back against sleeve so that cuff seam is covered by turned back cuff.

Pockets

8 Turn under 1cm to wrong side at opening edge of pocket and stitch close to fold, to hold. Fold pocket self-facing to right side along fold-line as marked on pattern and stitch across both ends to hold. Turn facing back to right side and press. Hand stitch inner folded edge of facing to pocket. Turn in 1.5cm to wrong side around raw curved edge, clipping where necessary and tacking in position 5mm in from folded edge. Press and trim seam allowance to 1cm (see fig. 1). Pin pocket in position on coat front matching pattern if necessary. Starting at (**a**) on pocket opening edge, edgestitch all round folded edge of pocket through pocket and coat, as far as top of pocket opening, stitching in small "V" as you start and finish, to strengthen (see fig. 2). Then topstitch 1cm in from edgestitching all round pocket, leaving opening free. Pull threads through to inside and tie off.

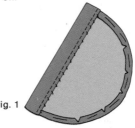

fig. 1

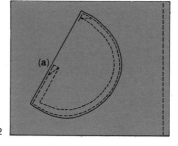

fig. 2

9 Sew a buttonhole loop and button at front neck edge under collar, overlapping right front over left (or sew on a hook and eye). Press coat thoroughly.

Skirt

A versatile straight, lined skirt, made here to co-ordinate with the coat and blouse.

You will need:
80cm of 150cm wide fabric *or*
80cm of 115cm wide fabric
80cm of 115cm wide lining
70cm × 2.5cm of waistband stiffening
2 hanging loops
20cm zip   1 hook and eye *or* button

1 Sew darts in front and back skirt pieces where marked and press towards side seams.

2 Place right sides of front and both back skirt pieces together and pin side seams. Stitch both side seams from waist edge to hem. Pin centre-back seam from notch marking bottom of zip to hem and stitch. Tack remaining seam along zip opening edge together. Neaten all seam allowances (including zip seam allowance) separately and press open.

3 Position zip behind tacked centre-back seam so that right side of zip and skirt face upwards, and set head of zip 1cm down from waist edge of skirt. Pin and then tack zip in position. Hand or machine stitch down each side of zip, 5mm in from zip teeth. Remove tacking stitches and press.

4 Repeat steps 1 and 2 for lining. Position lining inside skirt, placing wrong side of skirt against wrong side of lining and matching side seams and dart positions. Pin around waist edge and then tack. Open up tacked section of centre-back lining seam and pin folded edges of lining to each side of zip, a few millimetres in from teeth. Hand stitch folded edge of lining to zip down both sides.

5 Fold waistband in half lengthways so right sides come together and stitch across both short ends. Turn to right side. Place raw edge of outer side of waistband against waist edge of skirt, right sides together, matching centre-back and centre-front points, and overlapping extension of waistband at right centre-back as notched. Pin in position and stitch all round waist edge, allowing 1cm seam allowance. Turn waistband to wrong side and stitch across lower edges of right centre-back extension, allowing 1cm seam allowance. Trim, then turn waistband back to right side and press seam allowances upwards, away from skirt. Insert waistband stiffening inside waistband, tacking it in position against outer side if necessary. Press seam allowance along remaining raw edge of waistband to inside and set folded edge so that it slightly overlaps original stitching line. Tack in position, inserting skirt loops at each side seam. On right side of skirt, stitch just under waistband on skirt, directly over original seam, catching inner folded edge of waistband underneath in topstitching. ⏹

To finish

6 Sew hook and eye (or buttonhole and button) to centre-back of waistband, positioning right waistband extension under left waistband edge.

7 *Hem:* Adjust length of hem, if necessary, allowing a 2.5cm turn up. Neaten around raw edge of hem and turn up 2.5cm to wrong side. Pin in position and hand hem stitch all round. Adjust hem of lining if necessary. Turn up 5mm to wrong side and stitch all round. Turn up a further centimetre to wrong side and edgestitch close to folded edge through to right side of lining. Press skirt thoroughly.

Blouse

A long-sleeved collarless blouse which makes use of different colourways in the three front and back panels. The blouse fastens at the front with buttons down the opening edge of the centre panel. Make it in any light- to medium-weight fabric to co-ordinate with the straight skirt illustrated, or many of the separates in the book.

> **You will need:**
> 1.50m of 150cm wide main fabric
> 70cm of 150cm wide contrast fabric *or*
> 1.70m of 115cm wide main fabric
> 70cm of 115cm wide contrast fabric
> (For self-fabric blouse use 1.70m of 150cm *or* 2.00m of 115cm wide fabric)
> 6 buttons

Bodice

1 With right sides facing pin both back pieces to centre-back panel, matching notches. Stitch both seams, neaten seam allowances together and press towards centre-back. Edgestitch close to seam on right side of centre-back panel, down both sides, from neck to hem. Press.

2 With right sides together, pin one centre-front panel to left front, matching notches. Stitch, neaten seam allowances together and press towards centre-front. Press in 1cm to wrong side down remaining long raw edge of panel and tack this folded edge to hold. Repeat for other centre-front panel and right front.

Sleeves

3 Pin back shoulder edge of left sleeve to left back shoulder edge, right sides together and matching notches. Stitch, neaten seam allowances together and press towards sleeve. Edgestitch on sleeve, close to seam from neck to underarm point, through seam allowances. Repeat for right sleeve.

4 With right sides together pin left front to left sleeve at shoulder seam, matching notches. Stitch, neaten and edgestitch as step 3, and repeat for right sleeve.

5 Stitch shoulder darts in neck edge of right and left sleeves, aligning raw edges of each dart with right sides together and stitching from neck edge to **(a)** marked on pattern, allowing 1.5cm seam allowance. Neaten seam allowances separately and press darts open.

6 Fold blouse so right sides of front and back come together and align underarm seam edges, and side seam edges. Pin left underarm seam and side seam together and stitch entire seam, pivoting at underarm point. Neaten seam allowances separately and press open. Repeat for right underarm and side seam.

7 With right sides together, pin neck facing around neck edge, matching centre-back and shoulder seam notches. Stitch, allowing 5mm seam allowances, stitching from inner edge of left centre-front panel to inner edge of right centre-front panel. Spread blouse and neck facing so right sides of both face uppermost and seam allowances underneath lie against facing. Understitch on facing, close to seam all round neck edge, catching in seam allowances under-

neath. Clip seam allowances and trim. Turn under 5mm to wrong side along remaining raw curved edge of facing and press in position around inside of neck.

8 With right side outermost, turn left centre panel back on itself along foldline so right sides come together and tacked folded inner edge meets seamline. Pin the two layers of centre panel together at neck edge and stitch across from foldline to inner edge of panel, allowing 5mm seam allowance, so that seam meets finished neck edge (see fig. 1). Repeat for right centre panel.

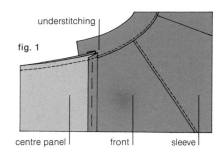

understitching

fig. 1

centre panel | front | sleeve

9 With right sides still together stitch across right and left centre panels at hem in same way, allowing 1.5cm seam allowance. Turn both centre panels to right side and press, pressing folds in position down front opening edges.

10 Tuck raw short ends of neck facing under tacked inner edges of left and right centre panels, and hold in position with a pin (see fig. 2). Tack and then stitch neck facing to blouse, stitching close to inner folded edge, through to right side, all round neck edge between inner edges of centre panels.

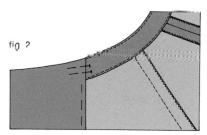

fig. 2

11 Neaten raw hem edge between inner edges of centre panels. Turn up 1.5cm at hem edge to wrong side. Press and pin in position. Stitch hem to blouse 5mm in from neatened edge, all round hem between centre panels.

12 Pin and tack inner tacked edges of left and right centre panels directly over original seamlines, to cover all seam allowances. Turn blouse to right side and edgestitch down left centre panel, close to seam, from neck to hem edge, catching in tacked edge underneath. Repeat for right centre panel.

13 Then edgestitch all the way round blouse on right side, starting at left side seam, edgestitching close to hem edge round to right front opening edge of right centre panel. Pivot needle here and stitch up right front opening edge, around neck edge and down left front opening edge, around hem to meet starting point. Press.

Cuffs

14 Fold cuff facing in half so right sides come together and short edges align. Stitch short edges together and press seam allowances open. Turn in 5mm to wrong side around curved unnotched edge of facing and press. Tack pressed edge to hold. Repeat for other cuff facing.

15 Pin cuff facing to cuff, right sides together and matching underarm seams. Stitch cuff facing to cuff all round, allowing 1cm seam allowance. Spread cuff and facing so both face uppermost and seam allowances underneath lie against facing. Understitch on facing, close to seam all round cuff. Repeat for other cuff.

16 Turn facing back to inside of sleeve and pin in position. Edgestitch close to inner folded edge of facing, through to right side. Then edgestitch around lower edge of cuff on right side. Repeat for other cuff.

To finish

17 Make five buttonholes on front opening edge of right centre panel and one at top inner edge of panel, where marked. Sew on buttons on left centre panel, opposite button-holes.

Double Breasted Jacket,

Jacket

A double breasted, collarless winter jacket, falling to waist length. It has epaulettes at the shoulders and two pleats at the side back hem, held with buttons. The jacket is fully lined.

You will need:
1.30m of 150cm wide fabric *or*
1.90m of 115cm wide fabric
1.20m of 115cm wide lining
60cm of interfacing
12 × 2.5cm or 2cm buttons
1 medium-sized popper

Bodice

1 Attach interfacing to front self-facings and epaulette pieces.

2 Stitch darts in back shoulder edges and press them towards armholes.

3 With right sides together, pin front bodice pieces to back bodice piece at shoulder seams. Stitch and press seam allowances open.

4 With right sides together, pin back neck facing to front self-facings at shoulder seams. Stitch and press open.

5 *Epaulettes:* Fold one epaulette piece in half lengthways so that right sides come together. Stitch down long side and round pointed end as far as folded edge, leaving short square end open. Trim, turn and press. Topstitch, 5mm in, around the three finished edges, pivoting at corners. Repeat for other epaulette piece.

6 Position epaulettes on shoulders, aligning raw square ends of epaulettes with raw neck edge and matching centre of epaulettes with shoulder seamlines. The points of the epaulettes should lie outwards directly over seamlines. Pin in position and staystitch raw square end to neck edge on both sides.

7 Following instructions on p. 154 make four bound buttonholes at positions marked on opening edge of right front bodice only. If the fabric you are using is a loose weave, reinforce the area around the buttonholes with a small rectangle of iron-on interfacing, applied to the wrong side of right front bodice, or use a contrasting or co-ordinating lighter weave fabric for binding the buttonholes.

8 With right sides together pin back neck facing around neck edge of bodice matching centre-back notches. Align shoulder seams of bodice and facing and continue pinning front self-facing in position against front bodice, folding self-facing against bodice at front opening edges, following foldline marked on pattern. Pin through facing and bodice to hold fold of opening edge in position. Stitch all round neck edge. Trim seam allowance of facing, clipping curves. Open out facing and bodice so that right sides of both face uppermost and seam allowances underneath lie against facing. Understitch on facing (see p. 148) around neck edge, close to seam, starting and finishing understitching about 5cm inside corner of front opening edge. Turn facing to inside and press around neckline so facings lie flat against bodice.

9 With right sides together pin front bodice to back bodice at side seams. Stitch and press seam allowances open.

10 Turn left facing against left front bodice so that right sides come together following foldline of opening edge. Align raw hem edges and pin across through both thicknesses from opening edge to inner edge of facing. Stitch 1cm up from lower raw edges, leaving 1cm free at inner raw edge of facing for attaching lining. Trim seam allowances, and turn to right side. Repeat for right front bodice and facing. ⊿

Sleeves

11 Stitch sleeve darts in position and press towards back underarm seam edge. Fold left sleeve so right sides come together and underarm seam edges align. Pin underarm seams, stitch and press seam allowances open. Repeat for right sleeve. Pin sleeves into armholes, right sides together, matching side seams with underarm seams and notches at front and back, and easing sleeve head to fit armhole if necessary. Stitch around armholes and press seam allowances towards sleeves.

Lining

12 Stitch darts in shoulders of back lining piece. Press darts towards armholes. With right sides facing pin front lining pieces to back lining piece at shoulder seams. Stitch and press seam allowances open. Press bust pleats in position on front pieces, folding pleats downwards and staystitching across ends of pleats,

Blouse and Sixties Pants

within seam allowance, to hold. Pin front and back lining pieces together at side seams, with right sides together. Stitch and press seam allowances open. Pin pleat in position at centre-back neck edge, so that it lies towards right back and staystitch in position. Stitch darts in wrong sides of sleeve pieces and press towards back underarm seam edge. Fold sleeves so right sides come together and pin underarm seams. Stitch and press seam allowances open. Pin lining sleeves into armholes, with right sides together and matching side seams with underarm seams and notches at front and back. Ease sleeve heads to fit armhole if necessary. Stitch around armholes and press seam allowances towards sleeves.

13 Position lining inside jacket with wrong sides of lining and jacket facing each other. Place lining sleeves inside jacket sleeves. Hold lining and jacket sleeve together with pins, aligning underarm seams. Then pull pinned sleeve of lining and jacket inside out, so right side of lining is outermost. Making sure lining and sleeve are still anchored with a pin about 10cm in from cuff edge at underarm seams, and taking care not to twist lining, take out remaining pins around cuff edge. Then turn

(see pattern charts on pp. 103, 104, 105, 111)

jacket cuff edge in 3.5cm to wrong side. Pin in position and slipstitch this inner edge to main sleeve so that stitches do not show on right side (see fig. 1). Then turn edge of lining under 1cm to wrong side and pin folded edge in position over slipstitched edge overlapping lining by 1cm. Slipstitch folded edge of lining to turnback of cuff with small neat stitches (see fig. 2). Repeat for other sleeve.

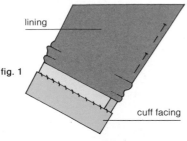

fig. 1

lining

cuff facing

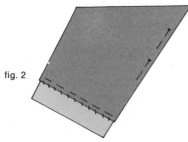

fig. 2

14 With sleeve linings in position, turn jacket and lining so that *wrong* sides of both are outermost, and *right* sides are together. Beginning at centre-back point, pin right side of lining to right side of jacket facing along inner edge of neck facing, allowing 1cm seam allowance. Continue pinning front facing edge of lining to each inner edge of front jacket facing, down to hem on both sides. Stitch lining to facing all round, leaving 1cm free at each hem edge.

15 Loosely hand stitch underarm point of lining to underarm point of jacket, allowing 1.5cm "give" in lining. Turn jacket so that lining and jacket are right way out and lining is inside jacket.

16 Open jacket and turn up 4cm to inside along hem edge of jacket. Pin in position and slipstitch raw hem edge to jacket so that stitches do not show on right side. Turn under 1cm to wrong side along raw hem edge of lining and pin this folded edge over hem of jacket, so that it overlaps hem edge by 1cm (excess lining will then form a fold around hem). Hand slipstitch lining to hem of jacket. Hand stitch small section of inner edge of facing to hem on both sides which is not covered by lining.

To finish

17 Press jacket, press hem fold around cuffs and bottom of jacket and corresponding hem folds of lining in place. Then topstitch on right side of jacket 5mm in from edge, from hem of left front opening edge, up around neckline and back down right front opening edge to hemline.

18 *Buttonholes:* Tack in a rectangle around each of the four buttonholes through all thicknesses (see fig. 3). Then carefully cut the facing behind each buttonhole, directly over the opening of each buttonhole, cutting in the same way as for buttonholes, snipping a "V"-shape at the ends of each cutting line. Tuck under the cut edges and "V"s around the back of each buttonhole and hand stitch folded edges to back of buttonhole (see fig. 4). Repeat for remaining three buttonholes. Remove tacking.

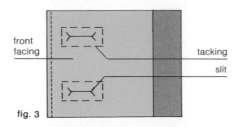

front facing

tacking

slit

fig. 3

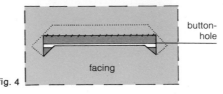

button-hole

facing

fig. 4

19 Sew a button to each epaulette, stitching through shoulder and epaulette. Sew four buttons on left front to line up with buttonholes and then four more on right front, opposite buttonholes as marked on pattern. Sew top half of popper under top button on *right* front. Sew under half of popper directly below on left front opening edge.

20 At back hem of jacket measure 8.5cm in from side seams towards centre-back, and mark point with a pin. Fold this point back towards side seam to a point 1cm in from side seam on jacket back to form a pleat in hem edge. Hold pleat in position with a button, stitched through all thicknesses. Repeat for other side of back hem edge.

Blouse

A long-sleeved winter blouse with roll collar and centre-back button fastening. Shown here in a lighter weight tweed to co-ordinate with the jacket and pants it can be made in any medium-weight fabric for day or evening.

You will need:
1.50m of 150cm wide fabric *or*
1.70m of 115cm wide fabric
5 buttons

Bodice

1 Sew darts in both back bodice pieces. Tie off thread ends and press each dart towards armhole edge.

2 With right sides together pin back bodice pieces to front bodice piece at shoulder seams. Stitch, neaten seam allowances separately and press open.

3 With right sides still together pin front and back bodice pieces together at side seams. Stitch, neaten seam allowances separately and press open.

Collar

4 Fold roll collar piece in half lengthways along foldline so that right sides come to-

gether. Stitch across both ends, allowing 3cm seam allowance. Then trim away seam allowance of one side of collar to 5mm, leaving other side of seam allowance to form a self-interfacing (see fig. 1). Turn collar to right side and press fold in position.

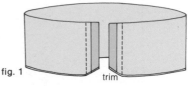

fig. 1

trim

5 Neaten raw edges down both sides of centre-back opening from neck to hem. Following foldline down each back piece, turn back 3cm so *right* sides come together and stitch across fold at hem edge, 3cm from raw hem edge, on both sides, to neaten facing hem edge. Trim across seam allowance at bottom corners and turn self-facing back along foldline so *wrong* sides come together. Press in position down foldline and pin. Then stitch 1cm in from neatened edge on inside, through to right side, from neck to hem. Repeat for other side of back opening.

6 Pin side of collar with trimmed seam allowances to neck edge, right sides together and aligning notches in raw collar edge with centre-front, side seams and centre-back. Stitch this side of collar to neck edge of bodice, leaving other side of collar free. Clip seam allowances around neck edge and press upwards away from bodice.

7 Neaten remaining long raw edge of collar and pin in position over original seam around neck edge so that raw edge overlaps seam by 1cm (see fig. 2). Pin and tack in position along seamline. Turn to right side and stitch along neck seamline from right centre-back opening edge round to left centre-back opening edge, through all thicknesses. Press collar carefully.

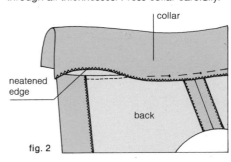

collar

neatened edge

back

fig. 2

8 Neaten hem edge and turn up 3cm to inside, following notches. Press, pin and tack in position. Topstitch all round hem on right side, 2cm up from folded hem edge, through all thicknesses.

Sleeves

9 Fold left sleeve piece so right sides come together and, aligning raw edges, pin underarm seam. Stitch, neaten seam allowances separately and press open. Repeat for right sleeve piece.

10 *Cuffs:* With right sides together, align short underarm seam edges of left cuff facing and stitch. Press seam allowances open. With right sides together, pin left cuff facing around cuff edge of left sleeve, matching notches and underarm seams. Stitch around cuff edge, trim cuff seam allowances and open out facing

and sleeves so that right sides of both face upwards and seam allowances underneath lie against facing. Understitch around facing, close to seam, through all seam allowances (see p. 148). Neaten remaining raw edge of facing and then press facing back against inside of sleeve. Pin and tack neatened edge in position against sleeve. On right side of sleeve, topstitch all round, 2cm in from cuff edge through sleeve and facing. Repeat for right cuff and facing.

11 Pin left sleeve into left armhole, with right sides together, easing sleeve head if necessary. Stitch, trim seam allowances around armhole to 1cm and neaten together. Press them towards bodice and then edgestitch on bodice close to seam, all around armhole, stitching through seam allowances. Repeat for right sleeve.

To finish

12 Make five buttonholes at positions marked on left back bodice, along topstitching line. Attach buttons to right back bodice along topstitching line.

Pants

Tight fitting ankle-length sixties-style pants, with centre-back zip opening. Make them in firm cotton, or in a slightly stretchy, medium-weight fabric.

You will need:
1.20m of 150cm wide fabric *or*
1.90m of 115cm wide fabric
20cm zip
70cm × 2.5cm of waistband stiffening
1 hook and eye (*or* button)

---

1 Stitch darts in both back pants pieces, pressing them out towards side seams. Staystitch across tops of darts. Pin pleats in position at waist edge of both front pants pieces. Staystitch across pleats to hold.

2 Placing right sides together, pin left front leg piece to left back leg piece down outside leg seam. Stitch, neaten seam allowances separately and press open. Repeat for left inside leg seam. Sew inside and outside leg seams of right leg in the same way.

3 With right sides facing pin left leg to right leg along centre-front seam, around crotch and up centre-back seam as far as (**a**). Stitch seam and then stitch again to strengthen. Neaten seam allowances separately and press open.

4 Tack remaining unstitched section of centre-back seam together following seamline. Press

seam open and position zip directly behind seamline, setting head of zip 1cm down from waist edge. Pin zip in position down each side following instructions on p. 156 for centred zip. Stitch zip into opening by hand, stitching up each side of zip from bottom of opening, 5mm from zip teeth. Press and remove tacking stitches (see fig. 1).

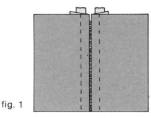

fig. 1

5 Fold waistband in half lengthways so that right sides come together and stitch down both short ends. Turn to right side and pin raw edge of outer side to right side of waist edge, aligning raw edges and overlapping waistband at right centre-back. Stitch all round allowing 1cm seam allowance. Press seam allowances around waist edge upwards, away from pants. Press 1cm in to wrong side along remaining long raw edge. Insert waistband stiffening into waistband, behind seam allowance, tacking in position to hold if necessary. Fold over remaining turned in edge of inner side so that it just covers original line of stitching. Pin in position, slightly overlapping original seam and tucking in 1cm seam allowance at lower edges of unstitched extension of waistband. Insert hanging loops at each side seam and tack all round. Slipstitch tucked in edges together along bottom of extension. On right side of waistband, starting at left centre-back, stitch round to right centre-back, stitching just under waistband on pants, directly over original seam, catching folded edge underneath in stitching (see fig. 2)

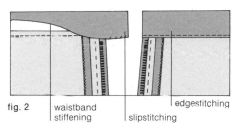

fig. 2 | waistband stiffening | slipstitching | edgestitching

To finish

6 Sew hook and eye to waistband at centre-back opening (or make buttonhole and sew on button).

7 Neaten raw hem edges around both ankles. Turn up 4cm to wrong side and pin in position. Stitch hem by hand around both ankles.

Tailored Jacket and Straight Skirt

Skirt

A straight lined skirt, falling to the knee with centre-back zip and darted waist. This skirt is a fashion staple and can be made in almost any fabric and lengthened or shortened accordingly.

You will need:
80cm of 150cm wide fabric *or*
80cm of 115cm wide fabric
80cm of 115cm wide lining
70cm × 2.5cm of waistband stiffening
2 hanging loops
20cm zip
1 hook and eye (*or* button)

Follow the pattern chart on p. 104 and the pattern instructions on p. 92. The skirt illustrated here is cut 6cm shorter, but made up and lined in exactly the same way.

Jacket

A classic tailored jacket with "rolled" collar and revers. The jacket is fully lined and fastens with a single button at the waist. It can be made in any medium-weight wool for winter or a linen or heavy silk for summer.

You will need:
1.60m of 150cm wide fabric *or*
2.10m of 115cm wide fabric
1.30m of 115cm wide lining
70cm of interfacing (see *Note*)
2 shoulder pads
10cm of domette (see *Note*)
1 button

(*Note:* This jacket requires simple tailoring materials and techniques. The revers and collar, hem and cuffs are all interfaced. The type of interfacing required will depend on the weave and weight of the fabric you choose, but it is advisable to use natural fibre interfacings such as cotton, linen or wool canvas. These can be ironed-on or sewn on to the relevant fabric pieces. Applying interfacing, "rolling" revers, using domette and shoulder pads are explained in the Overcoat pattern on p. 100.)

1 With right sides together, pin both back pieces together at centre-back seam, matching notches. Stitch and press seam allowances open. Again with right sides together, pin side panel pieces to either side of joined back pieces matching notches. Stitch and press seam allowances open. Then pin front pieces

to side panels, right sides together and matching notches. Stitch and press seam allowances open.

2 With right sides together pin jacket front to jacket back at shoulder seams, easing slightly to fit. Stitch seams and press seam allowances open. Stitch darts in each front piece following marks on pattern. Starting at the hem edge, slash each sewn dart open to within about 5cm from top of dart, so that seam allowances lie evenly to either side of slash. Press seam allowances around darts open.

3 Attach interfacing to wrong side of front facings and back neck facing. With right sides together, stitch under collar pieces together at centre-back seam. Press seam allowances open and trim. Then attach interfacing to wrong side of under collar.

4 Staystitch around jacket neck edge, within seam allowance, from (a) to (a), to strengthen. With right sides together pin joined, interfaced under collar to neck edge, matching notches and (a) and (b) points (see fig. 1). Stitch under collar to jacket between (b) points, clipping seam allowance at each (a) point to ease.

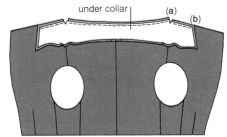

under collar (a) (b)

fig. 1

5 With right sides together pin front facings to back neck facing at shoulder seams. Stitch and press seam allowances open.

6 With right sides together pin top collar to joined facing around neck edge, matching notches. Stitch from left (b) point to right (b) point, clipping collar and facing seam allowance at (a) points to ease. Clip curved seam allowances around neck edge and press seam allowances open. With right sides together and aligning seamlines and notches, lay joined top collar and facing over under collar and jacket. Pin together all the way round collar and facing, aligning all seam edges. Continue pinning down each front facing, and across hem edges of facings. Starting at inner hem edge of left facing, stitch facing and top collar to jacket all the way round, allowing 1cm seam allowance. Stitch up left front opening edge and around rever points, pivot needle at (a), then stitch around collar edge and back down right front opening edge, finishing at inner hem edge of right facing. Clip curves and trim corners and seam allowances of under collar.

7 Turn collar and facing to right side and position facing against inside of jacket. Set "roll" around neck edge by bending top collar and facing over under collar and jacket so they slightly overlap under collar and jacket front at seam and tack in position about 1.5cm in from seamed edge, all round collar and revers. Lift up back neck facing and loosely slipstitch neck seams of top collar and under collar together to hold in position. Press facings back against inside of jacket.

Sleeves

8 On left upper sleeve piece, ease slightly between notches in back seam edge at elbow point as marked. With right sides together and matching notches pin upper sleeve piece to under sleeve piece at back seamline. Stitch and press seam allowances open. Attach cuff interfacing strips to wrong side of entire cuff edge, so that one long edge aligns with raw cuff edge and the other overlaps cuff foldline by 1.5cm. Stretch slightly between notches at elbow position of upper sleeve at front seamline. Then fold sleeve so right sides come together and front seam edges and notches align. Pin seam, stitch and press open. Ease around head of sleeve between notches. Repeat for right sleeve and cuff.

9 With right sides together and matching notches pin left sleeve into left armhole, aligning underarm notch of sleeve with underarm notch of bodice and adjusting ease on sleeve head to fit. Tack sleeve in position and then stitch all round. Stitch entire seam again 5mm inside first seam, within seam allowances, to strengthen. Trim seam allowances. Repeat for other sleeve.

10 *Domette:* Use pieces of domette to mould sleeve head around shoulder. Fold one piece of domette lengthways along foldline marked on pattern so that one half overlaps other half by 3cm. Hold fold in position with a pin. Then slipstitch folded edge to seam allowance around one shoulder of jacket so that longer half of the domette lies against the sleeve head (see fig. 2). Attach remaining piece of domette to other shoulder in same way.

11 *Shoulder pads:* Pin shoulder pads in position at each shoulder, so that long straight edge aligns with armhole seam and curved edge faces towards neck. Hand stitch straight edge of pads to top of armhole seams and hold point of inner curved edge to shoulder seam allowance with a few more hand stitches (see fig. 2).

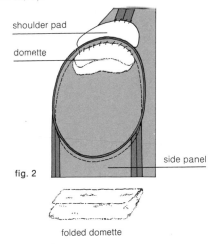

shoulder pad

domette

side panel

fig. 2

folded domette

12 *Cuffs:* Neaten cuff edge if necessary. Fold back cuff self-facing to wrong side along foldline and pin and tack in position. Slipstitch cuff edge to sleeve, so that stitches do not show on right side. Repeat for other cuff.

13 *Buttonhole:* Make buttonhole in right front bodice at position marked on pattern, following instructions on p. 154 for bound buttonhole (or make a hand-stitched or machine-stitched buttonhole if you prefer). Press buttonhole

thoroughly from wrong side and then press facing back in position behind buttonhole. Tack facing to jacket front in a rectangle around buttonhole and cut a corresponding slit in facing, directly behind buttonhole (see Double Breasted Jacket on p. 96) snipping in a "V" at each end of buttonhole. Fold back cut edges to wrong side and slipstitch folded edges to back of buttonhole to finish off.

14 Neaten raw hem edge if necessary. Attach long strip of interfacing to hem edge, positioning interfacing so that it overlaps the foldline of the hem by 1.5cm down one long edge and aligns with the hem edge at the other. Tuck the extra interfacing at each short end under the front facings, trimming away any excess interfacing at hem edge so that it fits neatly. Then turn up hem along foldline and press in position. Tack around hem edge, through both thicknesses, 1cm in from hem foldline. Loosely stitch hem to jacket by hand so that stitches do not show on right side.

15 Neaten inner raw edge of facing if necessary. Making sure that collar and revers lie correctly and that you have allowed sufficient "roll" by moulding them over your hand, pin inner edges of front facings to jacket from shoulderline to buttonhole position. Try on jacket again to check that facing does not pull, and then slipstitch inner edge of facing to jacket so that stitches do not show on right side.

Lining

16 Stitch darts in back lining piece as marked. Split dart as before and press seam allowances open. With right sides together and matching notches, pin front lining pieces to side panel lining pieces. Stitch and press seam allowances open. With right sides again together pin side panel lining pieces to back lining piece, matching notches. Stitch and press seam allowances open. Press pleat, as marked, in back lining piece and staystitch across top of pleat. Press pleats in shoulder edge of front lining and staystitch across. With right sides together pin front linings to back lining at shoulder seam edges. Stitch and press seam allowances open.

17 Make sleeve linings in same way as jacket sleeves (see step 8) easing at elbow points and sleeve head. Pin and stitch into armhole of lining as before (see step 9).

18 Press back 1cm to wrong side all round raw edges of lining (including cuffs), clipping curves to ease, and tack folded edge in position to hold if necessary. Position lining inside jacket so wrong sides of jacket and lining are facing, holding centre-back points and underarm points together with pins to begin with. Then pin folded edge of lining to jacket facing, matching seamlines and overlapping jacket facing by 1cm, leaving hem and cuffs unattached. Sew lining to facing by hand using small neat slipstitches. Try on jacket again at this point and check position of lining at hem and cuff edge, to ensure that lining does not pull jacket out of shape. Extra lining is allowed at cuff edge and hem, so that lining forms a small fold over the top of stitching when finished. Pin edge of lining in position allowing for fold and slipstitch to cuff and hem edges in same way as before.

19 Sew button on to left front of jacket opposite buttonhole. Remove tacking stitches around hem, collar, revers and cuffs and press jacket thoroughly.

(see pattern charts on pp. 104, 108, 109)

Overcoat

This classic warm overcoat has emphasized shoulders, patch pockets and back vent. The coat is fully lined, the revers and collar interfaced and the shoulders padded. Use any heavy-weight wool fabric, such as melton cloth or tweed.

You will need:
2.60m of 150cm wide fabric *or*
3.40m of 115cm wide fabric
2.00m of 115cm wide lining
1.30m of interfacing (see below)
3 buttons
1 pair of shoulder pads
10cm of domette (see below)

Notes on simple tailoring

Both the Tailored Jacket on p. 98 and the Overcoat require simple tailoring materials and techniques:

Interfacing is used to give extra body to collars and revers, as well as cuff, hem and pocket edges. As much of the professional finish depends on moulding the fabric, it is best to use a natural fibre interfacing such as cotton, linen or wool canvas, depending on the weight and weave of your fabric. Iron-on varieties of these interfacings are available, but if you choose this method of application, cut the pieces on the cross-grain where possible, so that the interfacing fabric gives when turned or folded. Also iron the interfacing on to the fabric over a tailor's ham so that the fabric bends in the way it will eventually bend on the garment.

Non iron-on interfacing should be attached to the collar and rever pieces with large tacking stitches (pad-stitches) which hold the entire piece of interfacing to the entire piece of fabric. Apply the interfacing to the wrong side of the fabric and roll the pieces of fabric and interfacing over your hand whilst tacking in place, so fabric and interfacing lie as they will in the finished garment. First, sew a line of tacking stitches through interfacing and fabric along the roll-line and then tack in place to either side of roll-line. Tack interfacing to wrong side of hem edges, cuff edges and facing edges with a line of long tacking stitches.

Domette is a fluffy wool fabric sold on the roll and is used to fill out sleeve heads so they gently curve beyond the shoulder seam and shoulder pad. It fits between the fabric and the lining of the sleeve and should be attached to the armhole seam. Instructions for applying it are given in the main text.

Shoulder pads can either be made of layers of fabric held together in a cotton or silk bag or a foam plastic equivalent. They vary in size, so choose one in proportion with your garment – you will need larger ones for the Overcoat than for the Tailored Jacket. The pad should be applied under the shoulder seam so that the long straight edge curves round and aligns with the top of the armhole seam and the point of the inner curve faces towards the neck edge and aligns with the shoulder seam. The pad is attached to the armhole seam allowance and shoulder seam allowance with hand stitches, and the pad and garment should be curved in the way they will be when worn as you sew them in place.

"Rolling" revers and collars merely means bending the double thicknesses over your hand as you hold them together so that inner and outer curves are accommodated. This prevents the collar or rever turning up at the edges after sewing. When topstitching the collar or rever, roll it first and tack around the edge, holding the two thicknesses together so that the upper side slightly overlaps the under side.

Back vent

1 With right sides together, and matching notches pin both back pieces together down centre-back seam from neck edge to point (c) at top of vent. Fold back left vent following seamline so that wrong sides come together, and pin both thicknesses together at top of vent to hold. Clip across seam allowance to (c) at top of right vent. Then fold right back in half so that wrong sides come together and hold fold in position with pins. Position right half of vent behind left half of vent, so that entire vent lies flat.
Hold in position with a pin.

and then tack across top of vent through all thicknesses, 1.5cm from top raw edge of vent (see fig. 1). Tack down each folded edge, 1.5cm in from fold, from top of vent to hem, to hold fold edges of vents in place. Press centre-back seam open and press vent from inside. Turn coat back to right side and topstitch across top of vent through all thicknesses starting at centre-back seam, 1.5cm down from top edge of vent, and stitching down at an angle parallel to top edge of vent. Stop topstitching at inner edge of vent. Pull threads through to wrong side at beginning and end of line of stitching and tie off.

2 With right sides together and matching notches, pin coat fronts to coat back at side seams. Stitch seams from underarm points to hem and press seam allowances open. Then pin coat fronts to back at shoulder seams, with right sides facing. Stitch seams and press seam allowances open.

Collar and revers

3 Attach interfacing to wrong side of front facings and revers. If you are not using iron-on interfacing, blind tack interfacing in position along roll-line indicated on pattern, taking care that tacking stitches are not visible on right

centre-back seam
right vent
left vent
tacking
fig. 1

side of facing. Then bend facing over your hand along roll-line and stitch interfacing to rever with irregular tacking stitches. Hold in position down inner edge of facing with a line of tacking stitches, again allowing for the "roll" of the rever. Attach interfacing to wrong side of back neck facing (tacking it in position if it is not iron-on, aligning neck edge of facing with neck edge of interfacing so that interfacing will be caught in neck seam). With right sides together stitch centre-back seam of under collar pieces, press seam open. Attach interfacing to wrong side, firstly with a line of tacking stitches along the roll-line (i.e. where the collar will bend) and then sewing irregular tacking stitches to either side allowing for "roll".

Fabric suggestions – *experiment
with different colourways in the
same fabric to give a softer, more
sophisticated line.*

4 Staystitch round neck edge of coat within
seam allowance between (**a**) points. With right
sides together pin and tack interfaced, joined
under collar to neck edge of coat, matching
notches. Stitch collar to neck edge, starting at
centre-back point and stitching out towards
one (**a**) point. Pivot needle here and clip seam
allowance at (**a**), then continue stitching round
neck edge of collar and coat to (**b**). Repeat for
other side of collar, again starting at centre-
back and stitching out to opposite (**a**) and (**b**)
points. Clip and trim seam allowances and
press open.

(see pattern charts on pp. 106, 107)

5 With right sides together pin front facing pieces to back neck facing at shoulder seams. Stitch seams and press seam allowances open. Then clip across seam allowances to (**a**) on facings, to ease.

6 With right sides together pin neck edge of top collar to neck edge of joined facing piece. Stitch collar to facing, starting at centre-back point, stitching out to (**a**) and then on to (**b**). Repeat for other side. Clip seam allowances to ease and press open. With right sides together, pin entire facing and top collar to coat and under collar, aligning raw edges and seamlines and matching notches. Pin and tack right down front opening edges and across lower hem edges of facings, as far as inner facing edge. You will need to ease facing with pins between rever points and buttonhole points, where facing is cut slightly larger to accommodate "roll". Then stitch from inner edge of left facing, 1cm in from seam edges, across hem, up front opening edge, around collar, back down right front opening edge and across right facing hem edge. Trim corners, clip curves and layer seam allowances all round if bulky.

7 Turn facing back against inside of coat, turning collar right side out at same time. Press facing in position against inside of coat, positioning it so that top collar and rever facing slightly overlap seam edge, moulding fabric over your hand to set "roll" in collar and revers. Tack 1.5cm in from edge, all round collar and revers to hold top collar and facing in position. Lift back neck facing and loosely slipstitch neck seams underneath together. Turn facing back against inside of coat. Starting at left hem edge topstitch on right side of coat 1cm in from edge of coat, up front opening edge to just below rever turn point. Stop topstitching here. Pull threads through to inside and tie off. Start topstitching again on right side of rever, continuing from point where you left off, and topstitch up around rever point, around collar and back down right rever point to rever turn point. Stop topstitching, pull threads through and tie off. Start again on right side of right front opening edges and continue down to hem.

Sleeves

8 Attach interfacing to wrong side of cuff edges of sleeve, aligning lower raw edges of interfacing and cuff. The interfacing should overlap the cuff foldline by 1.5cm at remaining long edge of interfacing. Fold sleeve lengthwise so right sides come together and sleeve seam edges align. Pin seam, easing with pins at elbow. Stitch seam, clip seam allowances at curve and press open. Stitch a line of easing stitches between notches around sleeve head, where marked on pattern. Repeat for other sleeve.

9 With right sides together, matching notches and pulling up ease stitches where necessary, pin left sleeve into left armhole. Stitch sleeve all round armhole and then stitch again for strength. Clip seam allowances where necessary. Repeat for right sleeve. Fold piece of domette lengthwise, so that one side is 3cm longer than the other (see fig. 2, p. 99). Hold fold in position with a pin. Align folded edge of domette with armhole seam so that longer side is against sleeve head and shorter side lies back against longer side (see fig. 2). Pin in position, and slipstitch folded edge to armhole seam around shoulder. Repeat for other shoulder. Then position a shoulder pad at each shoulder, so that the straight edge of the pad

aligns with the top armhole seam and the inner curved edge points towards neckline. Pin and then slipstitch straight edge to armhole seam allowance; catch point of inner curved edge of pad to shoulder seam allowance with a few hand stitches. Repeat for other shoulder pad and armhole.

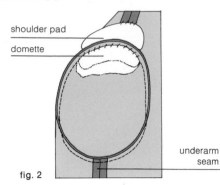

shoulder pad

domette

underarm seam

fig. 2

10 *Cuffs:* Try on coat to check sleeve length. Neaten around raw cuff edge if necessary and then turn up cuff edge to wrong side along foldline to form self-facing. Press fold of cuff in position and pin inner raw edge to sleeve. Blind hem stitch cuff edge to sleeve. Repeat for other cuff and sleeve.

11 *Buttonholes:* Make three buttonholes at positions marked on right coat front, following instructions for bound, hand-stitched, or machine-stitched buttonholes on pp. 154–5. (If your fabric has a loose weave attach a small rectangle of iron-on interfacing behind each buttonhole on wrong side of right front, to strengthen fabric before making buttonhole.)

12 *Hem:* Attach strips of interfacing to wrong side around hem edge placing one strip between vent and front facing on one side and other strip between vent and front facing on other side. Align one long edge of interfacing with hem edge; the other long edge should overlap hem foldline by 1.5cm. Tuck short ends of interfacing under vent and front facing, trimming away any excess interfacing at these points and tack interfacing in place. Neaten hem edge if necessary. Then press up hem along hemline, following line at hem of front facing, allowing a 4cm hem. Pin hem in position. Tuck hem under vent flap and front facing, trimming away excess material of hem inside vent and facing. Tack hem in position, 1.5cm in from fold of hemline, then blind hem stitch hem to coat all the way round. Hand stitch across inner raw edges of vent and front facing, where they cross hem turn up. Blind hem stitch remaining inner raw edges of vents to coat.

Pockets

13 Making sure that top collar and revers are correctly "rolled" (by bending them over your hand), blind hem stitch back neck facing and rever facing to coat, stitching down to a point about 15cm up from hem edges on both facings.

14 Attach trimmed interfacing pieces to wrong side of both pockets. Turn back self-facing along foldline so right sides come together. Stitch down each side of fold to hold. Turn back self-facing to right side and press in seam allowance to wrong side around remaining three sides of pocket, and tack in position. Then press in seam allowance around four sides of pocket lining and tack in position. Lay pocket flat with wrong side uppermost and

then lay pocket lining over pocket so wrong sides are facing. Align top edge of pocket lining so it just overlaps lower edge of pocket self-facing and pin in position. Then slipstitch folded edge of lining to back of pocket. Press pocket from wrong side.

15 Pin pockets in position against coat front following pocket positions marked on pattern. Then sew pockets securely to coat by hand, taking care to make stitches invisible and holding either side of top edge firmly. On right side of pocket, topstitch 1cm in from outer edge around side and lower edges of finished pocket through all thicknesses. Repeat for other pocket.

Lining

16 With right sides together, pin both back lining pieces together down centre-back seam from neck edge to (**c**). Stitch and press seam allowances open. Then pin back pleat at neck edge in position. Press and staystitch across top of pleat at neck edge to hold. Press pleats in position at shoulder edges of front lining pieces and staystitch across tops of pleats to hold. With right sides together pin front linings to back lining at shoulder and side seams. Stitch and press seam allowances open. Make up sleeve linings in same way as coat sleeves, easing around sleeve head. Pin sleeves into armholes, right sides together and matching notches. Stitch all round armholes and then stitch again, 5mm in from first seam, within seam allowance, to strengthen. Clip seam allowance and trim. Press in 1cm to wrong side all round entire raw edge of lining, including hem and cuffs, tacking to hold if necessary.

17 Place lining inside coat, so wrong sides come together, positioning sleeve linings inside coat sleeves. Hold lining to coat with pins at centre-back and underarm points. Then work out from centre-back neck edge, down each front facing, pinning folded edge of lining to inner edge of facing, matching seamlines and taking care lining does not pull coat out of shape. Then sew lining to coat by hand with small neat slipstitches, all round facings, stopping stitching about 5cm above hem, on both sides. At hem, pin folded edge of lining to inner edge of hem, so that excess lining forms a fold over hem. Slipstitch hem edge of lining to hem all round holding fold in place at front facing edge with a few stitches. Attach cuff lining edges to cuff in same way as hem so excess sleeve lining forms a fold over stitching. ◪

To finish

18 Attach three buttons to left coat front, opposite buttonholes, as marked on pattern.

19 Press coat thoroughly, pressing from the wrong side wherever possible. Press revers and collar over a tailor's ham, and use a sleeve board if you have one. Take care when pressing from the right side that you do not shine the fabric or cause seam allowances to show through. Ideally have the coat professionally pressed at a dry-cleaners.

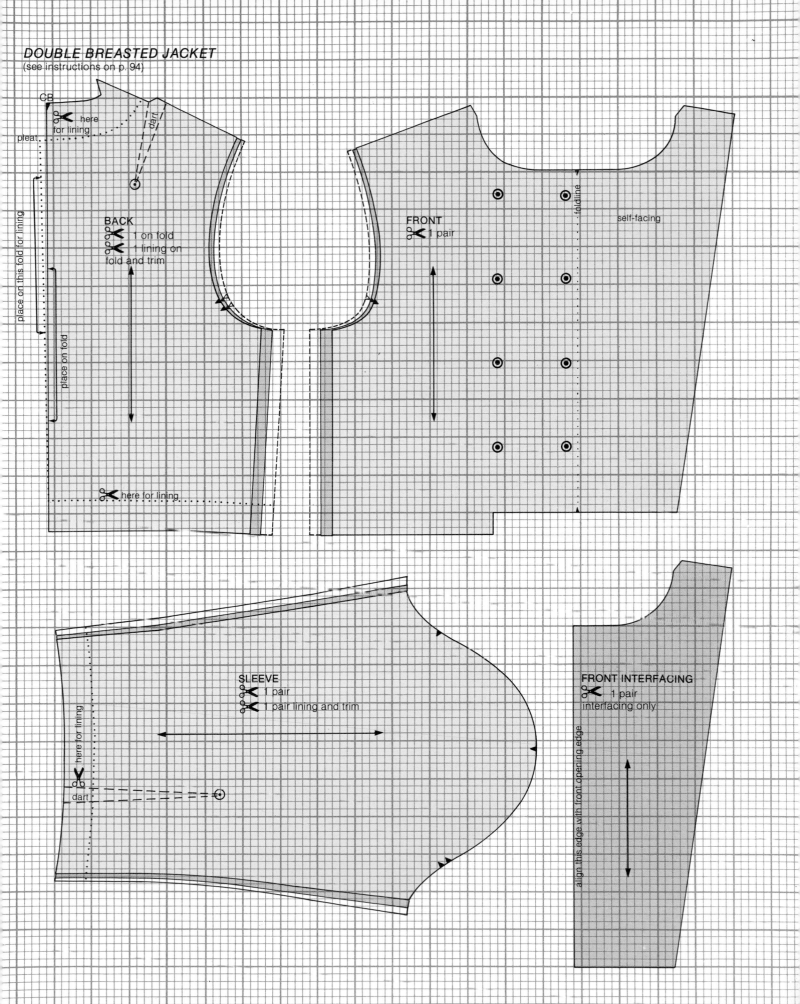

DOUBLE BREASTED JACKET
(see instructions on p. 94)

CB

✂ here
for lining

pleat

place on this fold for lining

place on fold

dart

BACK
✂ 1 on fold
✂ 1 lining on
fold and trim

✂ here for lining

FRONT
✂ 1 pair

foldline

self-facing

here for lining

dart

SLEEVE
✂ 1 pair
✂ 1 pair lining and trim

FRONT INTERFACING
✂ 1 pair
interfacing only

align this edge with front opening edge

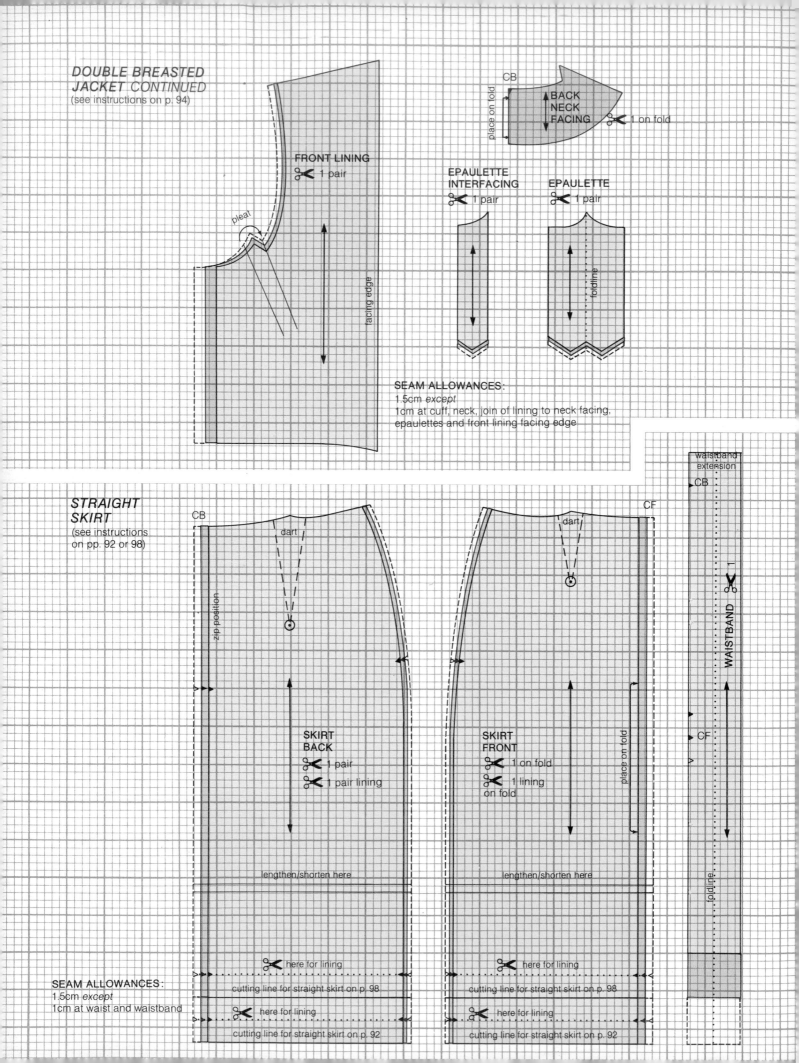

DOUBLE BREASTED JACKET CONTINUED

(see instructions on p. 94)

FRONT LINING
✂ 1 pair

pleat

facing edge

CB

place on fold

BACK NECK FACING
✂ 1 on fold

EPAULETTE INTERFACING
✂ 1 pair

EPAULETTE
✂ 1 pair

foldline

SEAM ALLOWANCES:
1.5cm *except*
1cm at cuff, neck, join of lining to neck facing, epaulettes and front lining facing edge

STRAIGHT SKIRT

(see instructions on pp. 92 or 98)

CB

dart

zip position

SKIRT BACK
✂ 1 pair
✂ 1 pair lining

CF

dart

SKIRT FRONT
✂ 1 on fold
✂ 1 lining on fold

place on fold

waistband extension

CB

WAISTBAND
✂ 1

CF

foldline

lengthen/shorten here

lengthen/shorten here

✂ here for lining

✂ here for lining

cutting line for straight skirt on p. 98

cutting line for straight skirt on p. 98

✂ here for lining

✂ here for lining

cutting line for straight skirt on p. 92

cutting line for straight skirt on p. 92

SEAM ALLOWANCES:
1.5cm *except*
1cm at waist and waistband

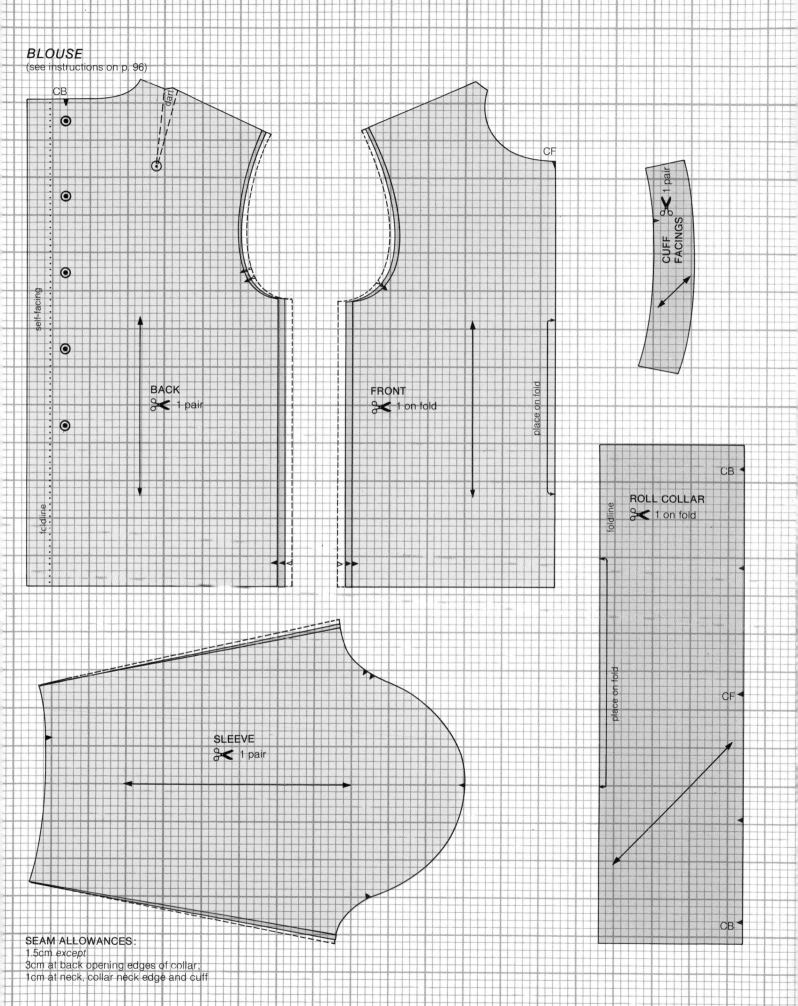

BLOUSE
(see instructions on p. 96)

CB

dart

self-facing

foldline

BACK
✂ 1 pair

FRONT
✂ 1 on fold

CF

place on fold

CUFF FACINGS
✂ 1 pair

CB

ROLL COLLAR
✂ 1 on fold

foldline

place on fold

CF

SLEEVE
✂ 1 pair

CB

SEAM ALLOWANCES:
1.5cm *except*
3cm at back opening edges of collar;
1cm at neck, collar neck edge and cuff

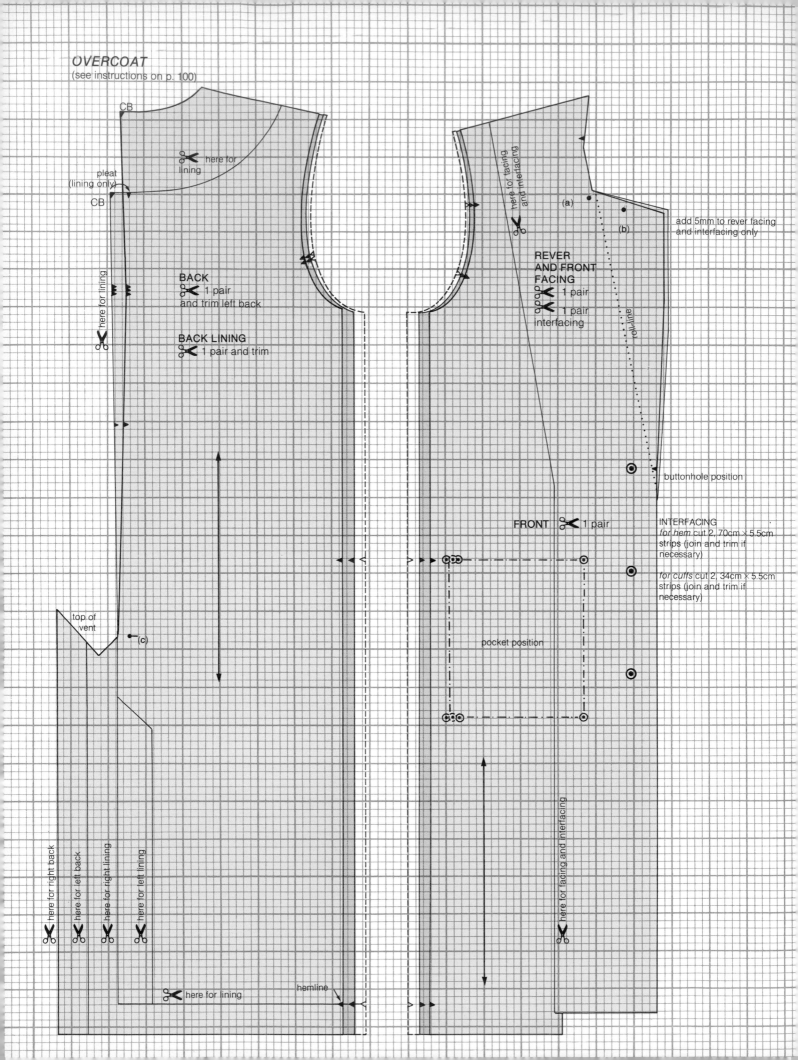

OVERCOAT
(see instructions on p. 100)

CB

✂ here for lining

pleat
(lining only)

CB

here for lining

BACK
✂ 1 pair
and trim left back

BACK LINING
✂ 1 pair and trim

here for facing
and interfacing

✂

(a)

(b)

add 5mm to rever facing
and interfacing only

**REVER
AND FRONT
FACING**
✂ 1 pair
✂ 1 pair
interfacing

roll-line

⊙ buttonhole position

FRONT ✂ 1 pair

INTERFACING
for hem cut 2, 70cm × 5.5cm
strips (join and trim if
necessary)

for cuffs cut 2, 34cm × 5.5cm
strips (join and trim if
necessary)

top of
vent

(c)

pocket position

here for right back
here for left back
here for right lining
here for left lining

here for facing and interfacing

✂ here for lining

hemline

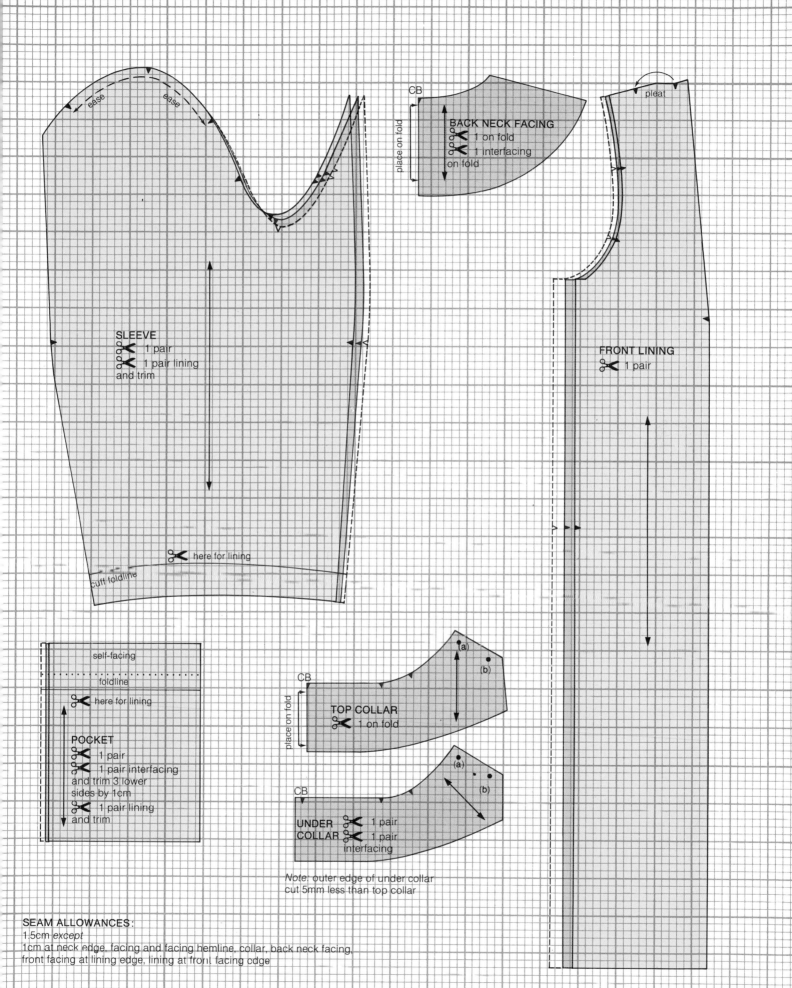

SLEEVE
✂ 1 pair
✂ 1 pair lining
and trim

ease   ease

✂ here for lining

cuff foldline

BACK NECK FACING
CB
place on fold
✂ 1 on fold
✂ 1 interfacing
on fold

pleat

FRONT LINING
✂ 1 pair

self-facing

foldline

✂ here for lining

POCKET
✂ 1 pair
✂ 1 pair interfacing
and trim 3 lower
sides by 1cm
✂ 1 pair lining
and trim

TOP COLLAR
CB
place on fold
✂ 1 on fold
(a)
(b)

UNDER COLLAR
CB
✂ 1 pair
✂ 1 pair
interfacing
(a)
(b)

Note: outer edge of under collar
cut 5mm less than top collar

SEAM ALLOWANCES:
1.5cm *except*
1cm at neck edge, facing and facing hemline, collar, back neck facing,
front facing at lining edge, lining at front facing edge

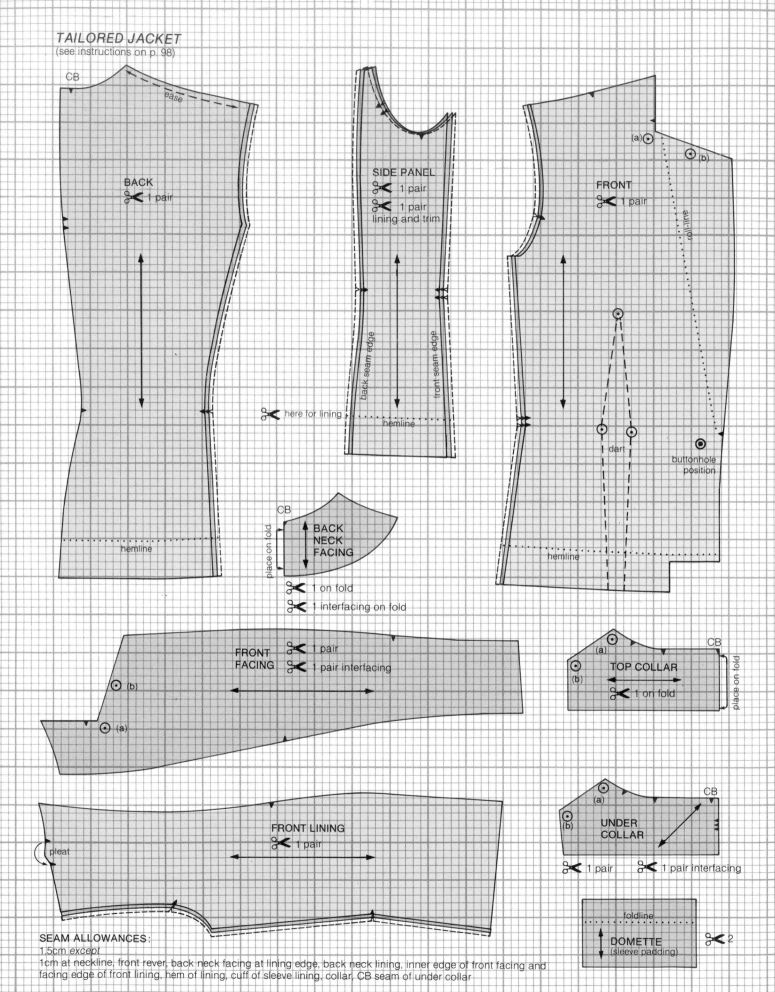

TAILORED JACKET
(see instructions on p. 98)

CB

ease

BACK
✂ 1 pair

hemline

SIDE PANEL
✂ 1 pair
✂ 1 pair
lining and trim

back seam edge

front-seam edge

✂ here for lining

hemline

FRONT
✂ 1 pair

(a)⊙
⊙(b)

roll-line

⊙

⊙

⊙ dart

⊙

buttonhole position

hemline

CB

place on fold

↕ BACK
NECK
FACING

✂ 1 on fold

✂ 1 interfacing on fold

FRONT
FACING ✂ 1 pair
        ✂ 1 pair interfacing

⊙ (b)

⊙ (a)

(a)⊙
(b)⊙

TOP COLLAR

CB

place on fold

✂ 1 on fold

FRONT LINING
✂ 1 pair

pleat

(a)⊙
(b)⊙

UNDER
COLLAR

CB

✂ 1 pair   ✂ 1 pair interfacing

foldline

DOMETTE
(sleeve padding)   ✂ 2

SEAM ALLOWANCES:
1.5cm *except*
1cm at neckline, front rever, back neck facing at lining edge, back neck lining, inner edge of front facing and facing edge of front lining, hem of lining, cuff of sleeve lining, collar, CB seam of under collar

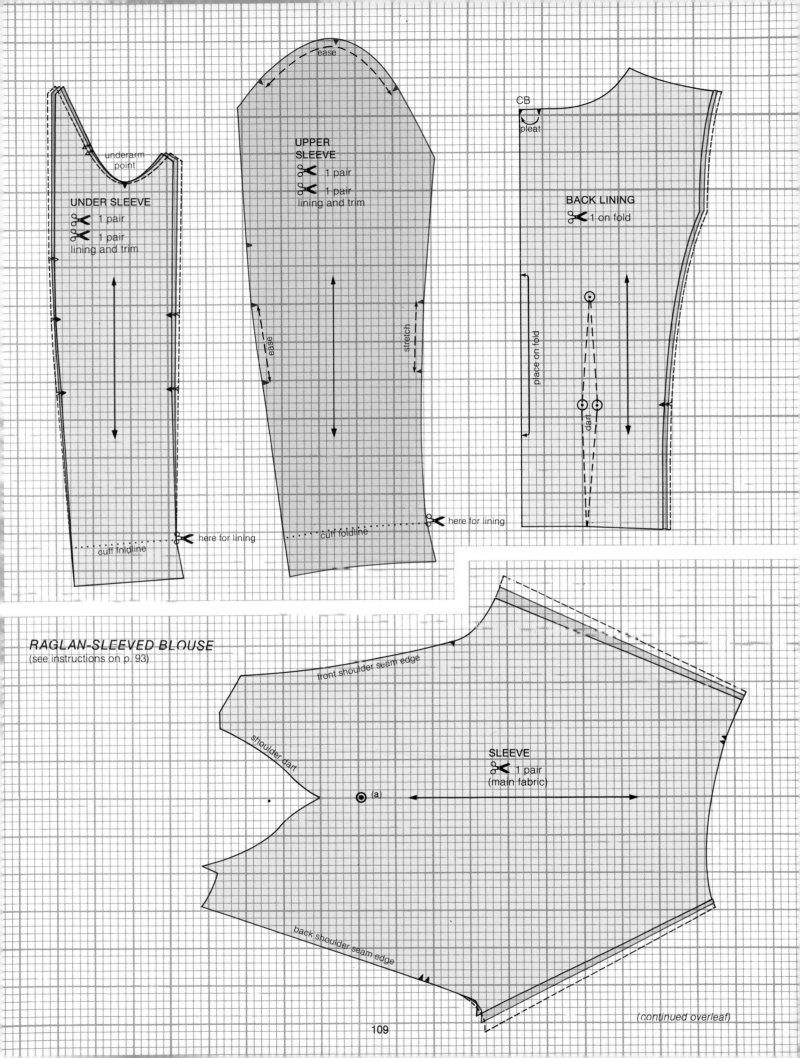

UNDER SLEEVE
✂ 1 pair
✂ 1 pair
lining and trim

underarm point

ease

cuff foldline

here for lining

UPPER SLEEVE
✂ 1 pair
✂ 1 pair
lining and trim

ease

stretch

cuff foldline

here for lining

CB
pleat

BACK LINING
✂ 1 on fold

place on fold

dart

RAGLAN-SLEEVED BLOUSE
(see instructions on p. 93)

front shoulder seam edge

shoulder dart

SLEEVE
✂ 1 pair
(main fabric)

(a)

back shoulder seam edge

109

(continued overleaf)

RAGLAN-SLEEVED BLOUSE CONTINUED

(see instructions on p. 93)

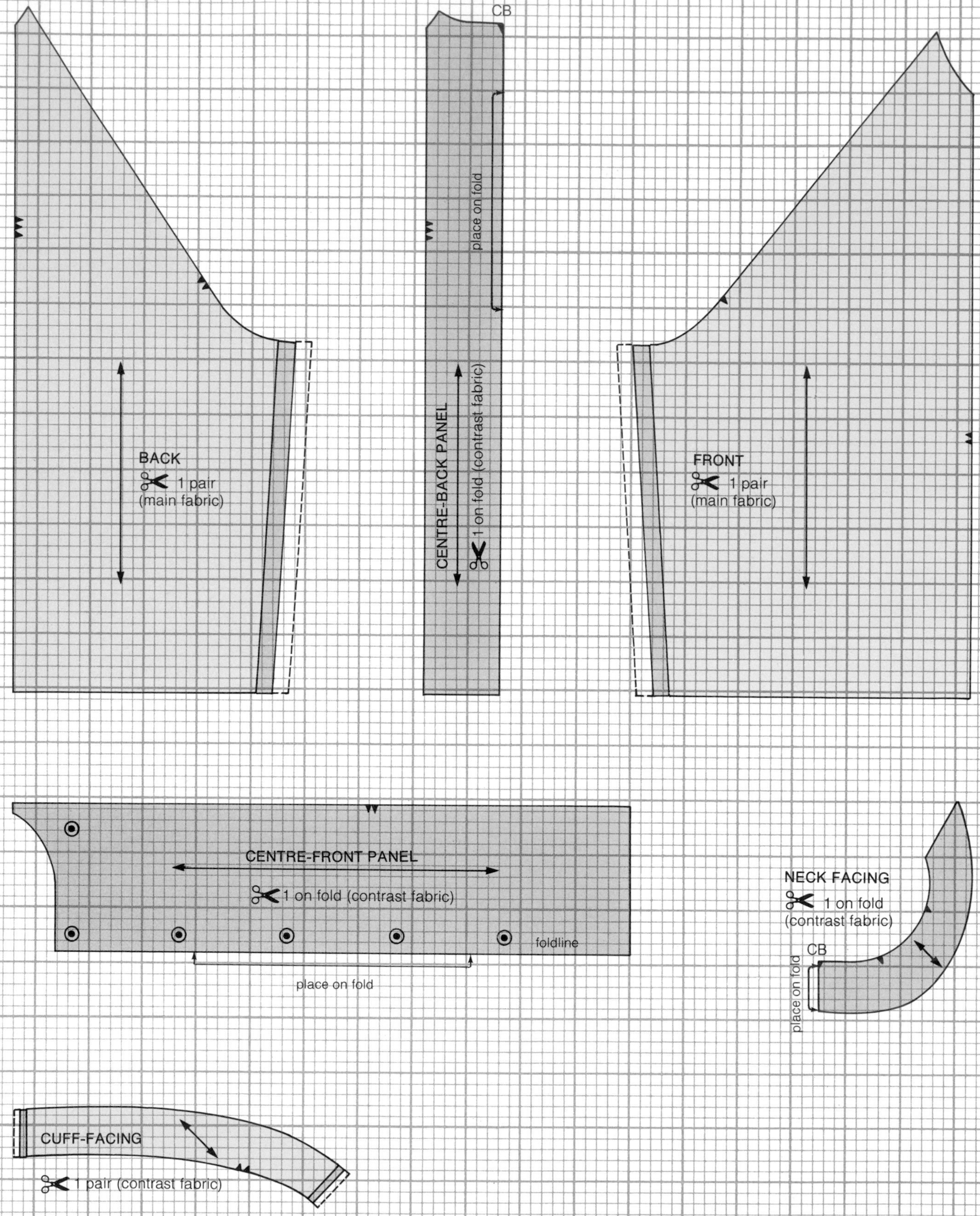
CB
place on fold
CENTRE-BACK PANEL
1 on fold (contrast fabric)
BACK
1 pair
(main fabric)
FRONT
1 pair
(main fabric)
CENTRE-FRONT PANEL
1 on fold (contrast fabric)
foldline
place on fold
NECK FACING
1 on fold
(contrast fabric)
CB
place on fold
CUFF-FACING
1 pair (contrast fabric)

SEAM ALLOWANCES:
1.5cm *except*
1cm at front and back and centre-front and centre-back panel edges, cuff edge of sleeve, front edge of neck facing
5mm at neck edge

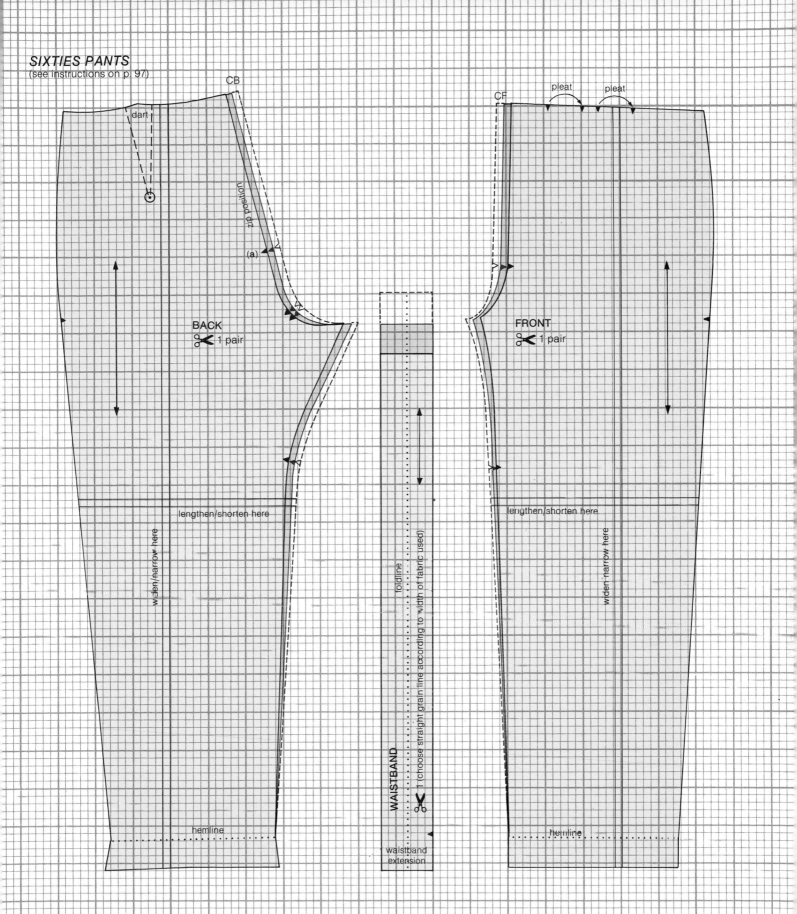

SIXTIES PANTS
(see instructions on p. 97)

CB

dart

zip position

(a)

BACK
✂ 1 pair

FRONT
✂ 1 pair

CF

pleat   pleat

lengthen/shorten here

lengthen/shorten here

widen/narrow here

widen/narrow here

foldline

WAISTBAND

✂

I choose straight grain line according to "width of fabric used)

waistband
extension

hemline

hemline

SEAM ALLOWANCES:
1.5cm *except*
1cm at waist edge and waistband

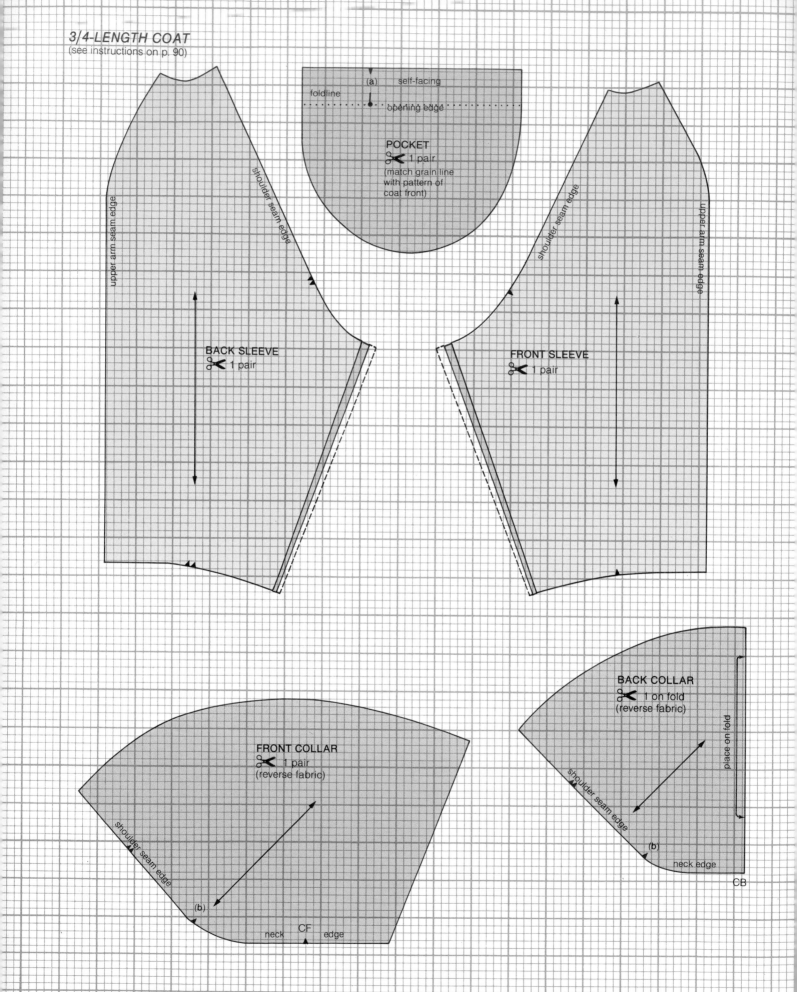

3/4-LENGTH COAT
(see instructions on p. 90)

POCKET
✂ 1 pair
(match grain line with pattern of coat front)

(a) self-facing
foldline
opening edge

upper arm seam edge

shoulder seam edge

BACK SLEEVE
✂ 1 pair

FRONT SLEEVE
✂ 1 pair

shoulder seam edge

upper arm seam edge

FRONT COLLAR
✂ 1 pair
(reverse fabric)

shoulder seam edge

(b)

neck   CF   edge

BACK COLLAR
✂ 1 on fold
(reverse fabric)

place on fold

shoulder seam edge

(b)

neck edge

CB

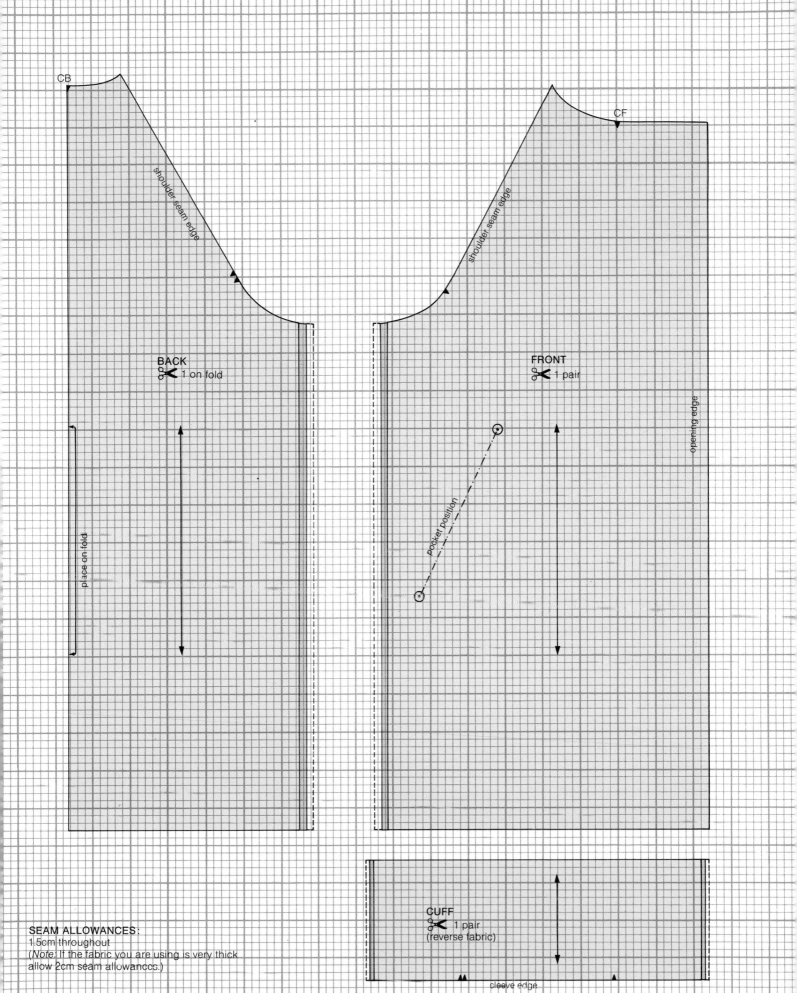

CB

shoulder seam edge

CF

shoulder seam edge

BACK
✂ 1 on fold

FRONT
✂ 1 pair

opening edge

place on fold

pocket position

CUFF
✂ 1 pair
(reverse fabric)

SEAM ALLOWANCES:
1.5cm throughout
(*Note:* If the fabric you are using is very thick allow 2cm seam allowances.)

sleeve edge

113

Cocktail Dress

A close-fitting knee-length evening dress, with deep front neckline and zipped back. The pattern is cut so that the dress moulds around you – the sleeves and bodice are cut in one piece and joined to an underarm and bodice gusset which lend a perfect fit. The shoulders are wide and padded, the skirt darted and narrow. Ideal in any evening fabric – cut the pattern twice if a lining is required.

You will need:
1.90m of 150cm wide fabric *or*
2.80m of 115cm wide fabric
60cm zip
1 pair of lightweight shoulder pads
1 hook and eye

Skirt

1 Stitch darts in back skirt pieces where marked and press towards side seams. With right sides facing, place both back skirt pieces together and pin centre-back seam from hem as far as (**a**). Stitch seam, neaten seam allowances of entire seam separately and press open. Stitch darts in front skirt piece where marked and press towards side seams. With right sides together pin front skirt piece to back skirt piece at side seams. Stitch both side seams, neaten seam allowances separately and press open. Set skirt to one side.

Bodice

2 Stitch darts as marked in each front bodice piece. Press darts towards side seams.

3 With right sides together pin sleeve gusset to bodice gusset along curved underarm seam, matching notches and easing curves, clipping seam allowances if necessary. Stitch seam with bodice gusset uppermost for ease of stitching. Clip curves, trim seam allowances to 5mm and neaten together and press towards sleeve gusset. Repeat for other sleeve gusset and bodice gusset.

4 With right sides together pin one bodice gusset to one front bodice piece at front side seam edge, matching notches, and easing around curve. Then continue pinning joined sleeve gusset to sleeve of front bodice, slashing seam allowances of bodice at underarm point, matching notches and pinning down to cuff edge. Stitch entire seam, then stitch again around underarm point of front bodice to strengthen. Repeat for other front bodice piece and bodice and sleeve gussets. Neaten all seam allowances separately and press open.

5 With right sides together pin left front bodice pieces to left back bodice at shoulder and upper arm seam. Stitch seam from neck to cuff, neaten seam allowances separately and press open. Repeat for right front and back bodice pieces.

6 With right sides still together pin left bodice and sleeve gusset pieces to left back bodice, matching notches and again slashing seam allowance at underarm point. Stitch entire seam from waist edge, around underarm point to cuff edge. Strengthen underarm seam as before. Neaten seam allowances separately and press open. Repeat for right back bodice.

7 With right sides together pin front neck facings to back neck facings at shoulder seams. Stitch, then press seam allowances open. With right sides together pin left facing to left bodice piece, matching notches and shoulder seams and pinning from waist edge around shoulder to centre-back edge. Stitch, allowing 5mm seam allowance, and repeat for right bodice and facing. Open out facing and bodice so that right sides of both face upper-most and seam allowances underneath lie against facing. Understitch on facing all round (see p. 148) close to seam, stitching through all seam allowances. Repeat for other facing. Clip curves and turn facings to inside. Neaten long inner raw edge of facings. Press, then hand stitch inner facing shoulder seam allowance to shoulder of bodice.

8 Neaten both centre-back seam edges and press 2.5cm seam allowance to wrong side down both sides. Hold front bodice pieces together at centre-front point with a pin. With right sides together, pin bodice to skirt matching centre-front points and centre-back edges. Stitch all round. Trim seam allowances to 1cm. Pin right side of bias strip to seam allowance around waist edge (see fig. 1) starting and finishing 1cm in from centre-back folded edge. Stitch to seam allowance, allowing 1cm seam allowance and stitching directly over waist seamline. Press 1cm in to wrong side along remaining long raw edge of strip. Then fold the strip over the waist seam allowances, so the seam allowances are enclosed. Stitch along folded edge, through all thicknesses, following original seamline. Press bound seam allowance upwards. Press 2.5cm centre-back self-facing to wrong side again, covering waist seam allowance and hand stitch inner edge of facing to binding at waistline. Set zip in position behind opening, and pin down each side, tucking under any excess tape at neck edge if necessary. Tack zip in place and try on to check fit (adjustments can be made by altering centre-back seam allowance). Hand stitch zip into dress (see p. 156). Fold facing over top of zip at neck edge (tucking in seam allowance) and hand stitch short centre-back edge of facing to zip tape just inside zip teeth. Sew hook and eye to either side of centre-back neck edge. ⏢

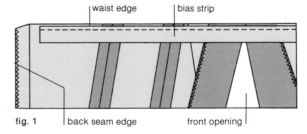

fig. 1   waist edge   bias strip   back seam edge   front opening

Shoulder pads

9 Fold shoulder pad bag piece in half diagonally. Insert shoulder pad between the two sides so that the straight outer edge of the shoulder pad aligns with the fold of the bag and hold in position with pins. Stitch around the two raw edges, through both thicknesses of fabric to enclose pad (see fig. 2). Neaten raw edges together. Pin pads in position at shoulder so that the point of the bag aligns with the shoulder seam about 5.5cm in from neck edge. Hand stitch pad to shoulder seam allowance, so it lies evenly to either side of seam. Repeat for other shoulder pad.

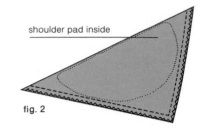

shoulder pad inside

fig. 2

To finish

10 *Hem:* Adjust hem length if necessary, allowing for a 3cm deep hem. Neaten raw hem edge and press under 3cm to wrong side. Pin in position and stitch neatened hem edge to dress by hand. ⏢

11 *Cuffs:* Neaten raw cuff edges and turn up, following foldline on pattern. Pin in position and stitch to sleeve by hand. ⏢

12 Hand stitch front bodice pieces together at centre-front from waistline to about 2cm above waistline, to cover bound seam allowances, stitching from inside of dress. ⏢

Fabric suggestions – try a heavy Chinese brocade which will "mould" in the same way.

114

(see pattern charts on pp. 125, 126)

Evening Shift and Sash

Shift

A very loose and simple to make shift. It is cut very wide, with short sleeves and is tied at the waist with a matching sash.

You will need:
2.50m of 150cm wide main fabric
90cm of 150cm wide contrast fabric *or*
2.50m of 115cm wide main fabric
90cm of 115cm wide contrast fabric
(If you are making the contrasting sash there is sufficient extra fabric to cut the sleeves from the sash fabric allowance. In this case you do not need the extra 50cm of contrast fabric allowed here.)

(*Note:* For very lightweight fabrics such as silk, crepe de chine, or similar fabric, all seams can be neatened by flat-felling, see p. 146.)

1 With right sides facing, pin dress front to dress back at shoulder seams and side seams. Stitch, neaten seam allowances separately and press open.

2 Pin bias strip around neck edge, right sides together and aligning raw edges. Stitch around neck edge of dress allowing a 1cm seam allowance and tucking in and trimming raw short ends of strip at beginning and end to neaten. Trim seam allowances to 5mm and press binding and seam allowances away from dress. Understitch on binding close to seamline, stitching through seam allowances, all round neck edge. Turn in 1cm to wrong side around remaining long raw edge of binding and pin folded edge in position against inside of dress. Edgestitch close to inner folded edge of binding all round neck edge, through to right side.

Sleeves

3 Fold one sleeve so that right sides come together, aligning underarm seam edges and pin seam. Stitch, neaten seam allowances separately and press open. Turn in 5mm to wrong side around cuff edge and stitch. Turn in a further centimetre, clipping into corner of "V" shape at underarm seam to ease, and stitch close to inner folded edge, through to right side all round cuff of sleeve. Repeat for other sleeve.

4 With right sides together and matching notches, pin right sleeve into right armhole, aligning underarm seams. Stitch all round armhole, neaten seam allowances together and press towards cuff. Repeat for other sleeve.

To finish

5 Adjust hem length if necessary, then turn under 5mm to wrong side around hem edge and stitch. Turn under a further centimetre and stitch close to inner folded edge through to right side all round hem. (For heavier weight fabric, you may find it better just to neaten the raw hem edge at first and then turn up 1.5cm to wrong side and stitch in position.) ⊿

Sash

A simple sash which hangs over one shoulder and ties around the hip. It is made out of two lengths of material which form the shoulder and hip-bands; the shoulder-band is pleated into the hip-band. Made up here to match the shift, it would also be very effective made in lightweight jersey-knit fabric.

You will need:
1.50m of 150cm wide fabric *or*
1.90m of 115cm wide fabric

1 Neaten all raw edges of both pieces of fabric by turning in 5mm to wrong side and stitching. Then turn in a further centimetre to wrong side, all the way round and stitch close to inner folded edge, through to right side. Press.

2 On shoulder-band pleat both short ends of the band following marks on pattern so that band measures about 15cm wide. Staystitch across pleats to hold in position. ⊿

3 Place hip-band flat with right side facing uppermost and measure 53cm in from left end and mark point with a pin. Then measure 40cm in from right end and mark with another pin. Using pins as a guide, place one pleated end of shoulder-band underneath hip-band, right side of shoulder-band against wrong side of hip-band and aligning outer edge of pleats with 53cm pin (see fig. 1). Overlap the pleated edge and the top edge of the hip-band 1.5cm and pin the two pieces together along the pleated edge. Taking care not to twist the shoulder band, attach the other pleated end in the same way, aligning the outer edge with the 40cm pin, right side of pleated end against wrong side of hip-band and overlapping edge of pleated end 1.5cm. Pin in position and then stitch both pleated ends of shoulder-band to hip-band, backstitching at beginning and end of stitching line to strengthen. Press sash.

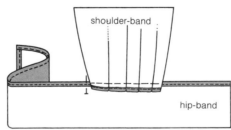

fig. 1

Fabric suggestions – *try a traditional flower-printed imitation silk for a gentler, more classic look, or a rich-textured gold and black woven fabric for more dressy evening wear.*

 (see pattern charts on pp. 122, 123)

Fabric suggestions – *use crisp fabrics such as pure silk taffeta or imitation moiré silk in plain strong colours for a similarly stunning effect.*

Ball Gown

A classic full-length ball gown with a very full skirt, gathered into a fitted bodice. The bodice is cut on the cross-grain to give a perfect fit without using boning and has pleated straps over each shoulder. The decorative bow is optional and can be worn as shown or perhaps pinned at the back waist. Alternatively gather up the front hem of the skirt at one point and hold the gathers with the bow.

You will need:
5.50m of 150cm wide fabric *or*
5.90m of 115cm wide fabric
30cm zip
1 small hook and eye

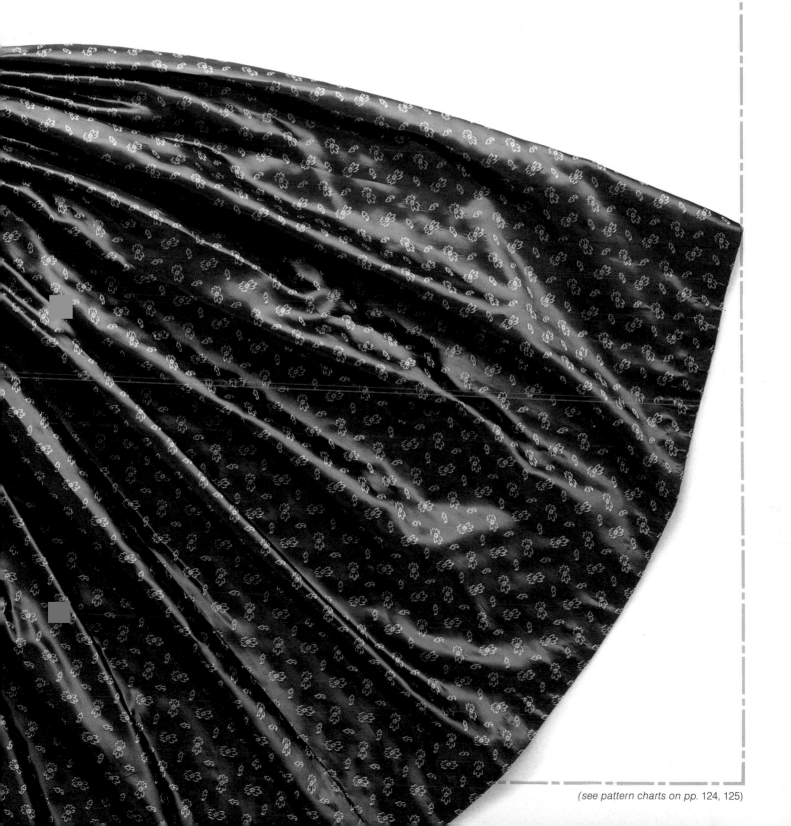

(see pattern charts on pp. 124, 125)

Bodice

1 Stitch darts where marked in front bodice. Press the two upper darts downwards towards the waist and neaten seam allowances of lower waist darts separately and press open.

2 With right sides together, pin both back bodice pieces to front bodice piece at side seams. Stitch, neaten seam allowances separately and press open. Neaten seam edge down either side of centre-back seam. (*Note:* if you find your fabric stretches a lot where cut on the cross, tape the side seams by stitching seam binding directly over the original seam – see p. 147.)

3 *Pleated panel:* Pin pleats in position on panel as marked so they face downwards, and staystitch across both pleated ends, to hold. Press.

4 *Shoulder straps:* Fold each strap piece in half lengthways so that right sides come together and align curved seam edge. Stitch down long curved seam on both straps, and turn to right side. Press each strap and staystitch across the two raw ends of each strap.

5 Pin pleats in position at each end of strap as marked on pattern, so that they lie towards centre-front and centre-back. Staystitch again across pleats, within seam allowances, to hold (see fig. 1). ⊐

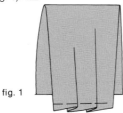

fig. 1

6 With right sides together, position pleated panel against top of bodice, matching notches at front, side and back. Stitch pleated panel to bodice stitching from left centre-back top edge round to right centre-back top edge. Stitch again for strength within seam allowance and press seam allowances upwards towards neck. Position back edge of shoulder strap against top edge of pleated panel, right sides together, placing it between notches on panel, aligning raw edges of end of strap and top of panel and making sure pleats face towards centre-back. Pin in position and stitch across. Repeat for other shoulder strap (see fig. 2). Stitch again, within seam allowances across pleated ends of strap and back bodice seam allowances to hold. Position front edge of shoulder straps in the same way, following notches and aligning raw pleated edges of straps and top edge of panel. Pin and tack front edge of both straps in position but do not stitch them yet.

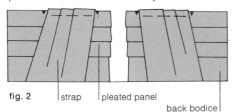

fig. 2 |strap |pleated panel
            back bodice

7 *Facing:* With right sides together, pin front facing to back facings at side seams. Stitch seams and press seam allowances open. Position facing around top edge of pleated panel, matching notches and side seams and aligning

all raw edges, right sides together. The shoulder strap ends should be sandwiched between the pleated panel and the facings. Pin and tack facing to bodice. Try bodice on at this point to make sure straps are the correct length and that they lie flat. Make any adjustments necessary to the front edges of the shoulder straps, re-tacking the straps and facing in position after altering. Turn bodice to wrong side again, so wrong side of bodice and facing are outermost and straps are again sandwiched. Stitch facing to bodice all around top edge of pleated panel. Turn up 1.5cm to wrong side at lower edge of facing at left centre-back opening edge. Then stitch down from top edge, to lower edge of facing, 1.5cm in from centre-back opening edge catching turned up edge in stitching to hold facing and back bodice together (see fig. 3). Repeat for right centre-back opening and facing. Spread bodice and facing so right sides of both face uppermost and seam allowances underneath lie against facing. Understitch on facing (see p. 148) close to seam all around top of bodice, stitching through seam allowances. Trim seam allowances. Turn under 1.5cm to wrong side all round lower raw edge of facing. Fold facing back against inside of dress, positioning lower folded edge directly over original lower seamline of pleated panel and bodice. Pin facing in position and hand-stitch to inside of bodice. ⊐

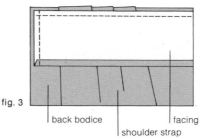

fig. 3 |back bodice |facing
              |shoulder strap

8 To hold pleats in pleated panel permanently in position, lift each pleat up and hand stitch with small back stitches along the underneath fold of each pleat, from left centre-back edge right round to right centre-back edge (see fig. 4). Catch the facing underneath in your back stitches and make sure the stitches are covered by the pleat. Repeat for other two pleats. Then press pleats firmly in position.

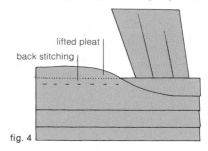

lifted pleat
back stitching

fig. 4

Skirt

9 With right sides together pin centre-back seam of centre-back skirt panel. Stitch from zip notch down to hem. Neaten seam allowances separately and press open. With right sides together pin back edge of each side panel to either side of centre-back panel. Stitch seams, neaten seam allowances separately and press open. Then pin centre-front panel to front edges of side panels, right sides together. Stitch seams, neaten seam allowances separately and press open.

10 Sew a double line of gather stitching around top waist edge of skirt, within seam allowances, breaking lines of stitching at seams for ease of gathering. With right sides together pin centre-back opening edges of skirt to centre-back opening edges of bodice. Then pin centres of skirt side panels to side seams of bodice and centre-front of front panel to centre-front notch of bodice. Gather

up each panel to fit waist edge of bodice (approx 20cm), gathering either side of seamed back panel separately. With right sides still together pin gathered edges in position on bodice, so that they lie evenly all round waist edge. Stitch skirt to bodice, starting at right centre-back and stitching round to left centre-back. Stitch again 3mm in from first line of stitching, within seam allowance. Trim seam allowances to 1cm. Place long edge of bias strip against waist seam allowance, so that right side of strip lies against waist seam allowance and all raw edges align (see fig. 5). Pin in position and then stitch, allowing 1cm seam allowance. Press in 1cm to wrong side along remaining long raw edge of strip and fold strip over seam allowance, pinning folded edge in position directly over first line of stitching. Edgestitch close to folded edge of strip all round waist, stitching through all thicknesses so waist seam allowances are enclosed in binding strip. Trim away any excess strip at centre-back and press upwards.

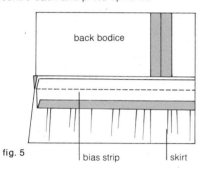

fig. 5   bias strip   skirt   back bodice

11 Turn back centre-back opening seam allowance and stitch both sides to binding with a few hand stitches to hold at waist point. Pin zip in position down centre-back opening, positioning it as a centred zip. Sew in zip by hand (see p. 156). Sew small hook and eye to top of centre-back opening so hook is concealed.

12 Adjust hem length if necessary allowing a 4cm turn up. Turn in 5mm to wrong side all round raw hem edge and stitch. Turn up 3.5cm more to wrong side and pin in position. Stitch hem to skirt by hand.

Bow

13 With right sides facing, pin both bow pieces together. Stitch all round edge leaving 5cm unstitched at centre of one long edge, through which to turn. Trim seam allowances and turn bow to right side. Press and slipstitch un-stitched gap together. Fold shorter ends of bow back on themselves, behind centre of bow. Tack in position. Pin folds in position at centre of bow piece as marked on pattern.

14 Fold bow knot piece in half lengthways so right sides come together and stitch around the three sides leaving a gap in the long seam through which to turn. Turn knot piece to right side, press and slipstitch gap together. Wrap knot piece around folded bow piece, holding short ends of knot together at back of bow with a pin. Slipstitch the two short ends together behind bow, stitching through bow also to hold knot in position.

Attaching the bow

(a)
Pin bow to join of left front shoulder strap and pleated panel. Hand stitch it to the dress, stitching from the back of the bow, catching bow and bow knot in stitches so that bow is firmly attached.

(b)
Hand stitch bow to dress directly over one of the darts at the front waist.

(c)
Gather up the skirt at the hem by sewing a line of gathering stitches up the seam of the front panel and side panel, starting at hem and stitching up to a point about 35cm above hem edge. Pull up the line of gather stitching and hold securely with hand stitches. Sew bow firmly in position over gathered up section of skirt.

(d)
Sew pieces of Velcro to either side of the centre-back opening at the waist. Sew corresponding pieces of Velcro to the back of the bow and fix bow in position after fastening the dress.

(a)

(b)

(c)

(d)

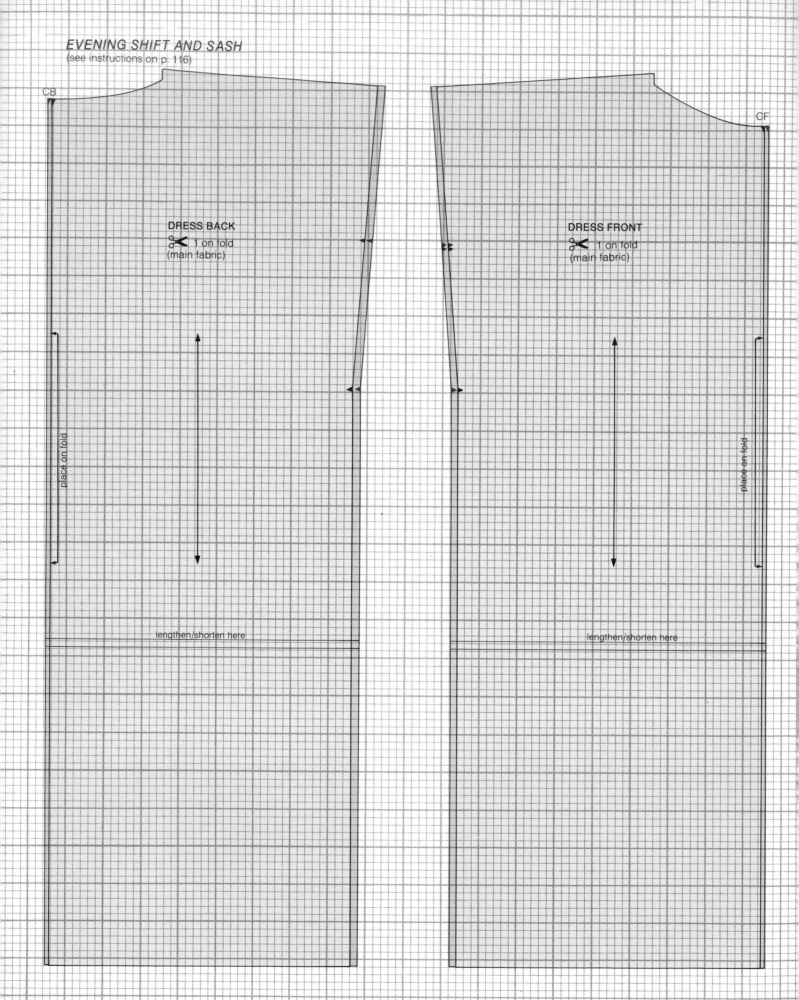

EVENING SHIFT AND SASH
(see instructions on p. 116)

CB

DRESS BACK
✂ 1 on fold
(main fabric)

place on fold

lengthen/shorten here

CF

DRESS FRONT
✂ 1 on fold
(main fabric)

place on fold

lengthen/shorten here

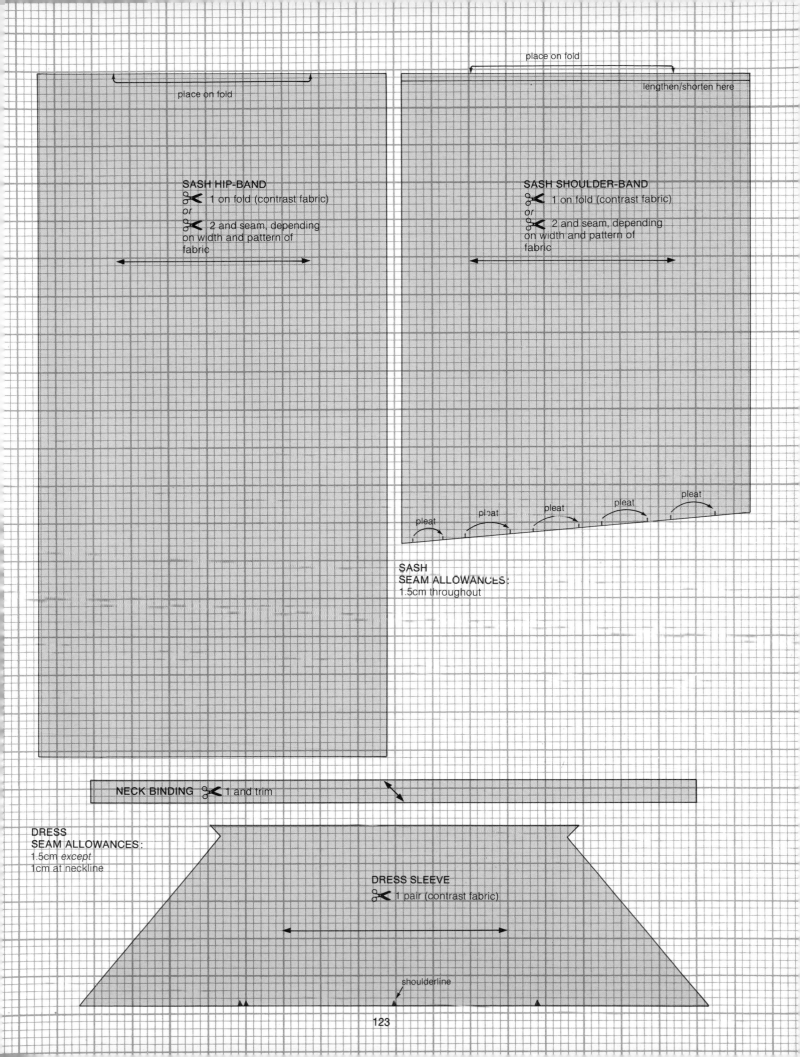

place on fold

place on fold

lengthen/shorten here

SASH HIP-BAND
✂ 1 on fold (contrast fabric)

or

✂ 2 and seam, depending on width and pattern of fabric

SASH SHOULDER-BAND
✂ 1 on fold (contrast fabric)

or

✂ 2 and seam, depending on width and pattern of fabric

pleat pleat pleat pleat pleat

SASH
SEAM ALLOWANCES:
1.5cm throughout

NECK BINDING ✂ 1 and trim

DRESS
SEAM ALLOWANCES:
1.5cm *except*
1cm at neckline

DRESS SLEEVE
✂ 1 pair (contrast fabric)

shoulderline

BALL GOWN
(see instructions on p. 119)

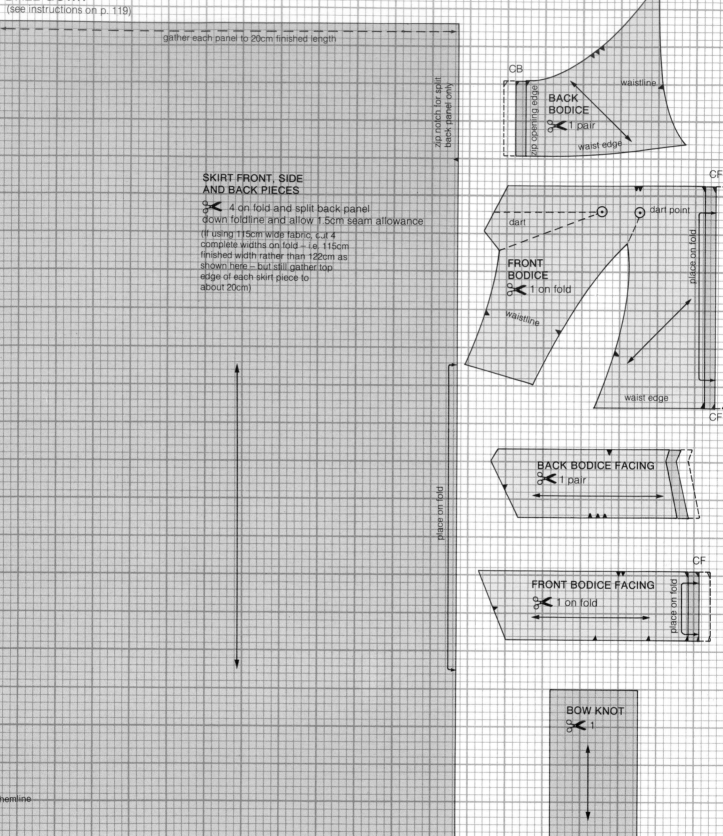

gather each panel to 20cm finished length

zip notch for split back panel only

**SKIRT FRONT, SIDE
AND BACK PIECES**

✂️ 4 on fold and split back panel
down foldline and allow 1.5cm seam allowance

(If using 115cm wide fabric, cut 4
complete widths on fold – i.e. 115cm
finished width rather than 122cm as
shown here – but still gather top
edge of each skirt piece to
about 20cm)

place on fold

hemline

CB

zip opening edge

**BACK
BODICE**

✂️ 1 pair

waistline

waist edge

CF

dart   dart point

**FRONT
BODICE**

✂️ 1 on fold

waistline

place on fold

waist edge

CF

BACK BODICE FACING

✂️ 1 pair

CF

FRONT BODICE FACING

✂️ 1 on fold

place on fold

BOW KNOT

✂️ 1

SEAM ALLOWANCES:
1.5cm *except*
3cm fitting allowance at front edge of shoulder strap

BIAS STRIP
cut 1, 80cm × 4cm for binding waist seam allowance

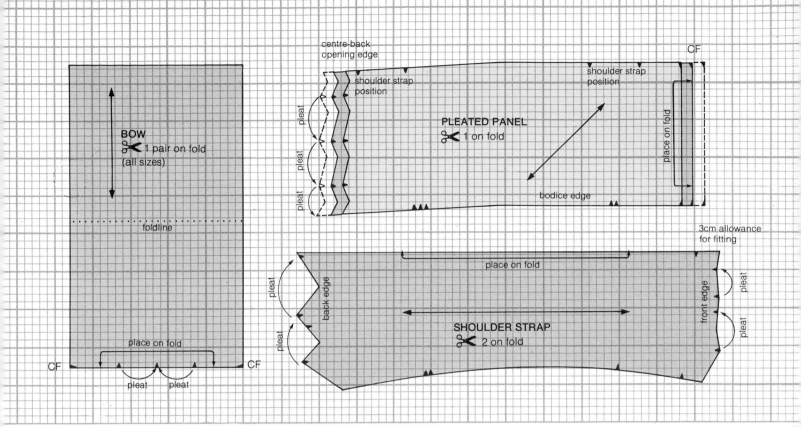

BOW
✂ 1 pair on fold
(all sizes)

foldline

place on fold

CF   CF

pleat   pleat

centre-back
opening edge

shoulder strap
position

pleat

pleat

pleat

PLEATED PANEL
✂ 1 on fold

shoulder strap
position

place on fold

bodice edge

CF

3cm allowance
for fitting

pleat

back edge

place on fold

SHOULDER STRAP
✂ 2 on fold

front edge

pleat

pleat

pleat

pleat

COCKTAIL DRESS
(see instructions on p. 114)

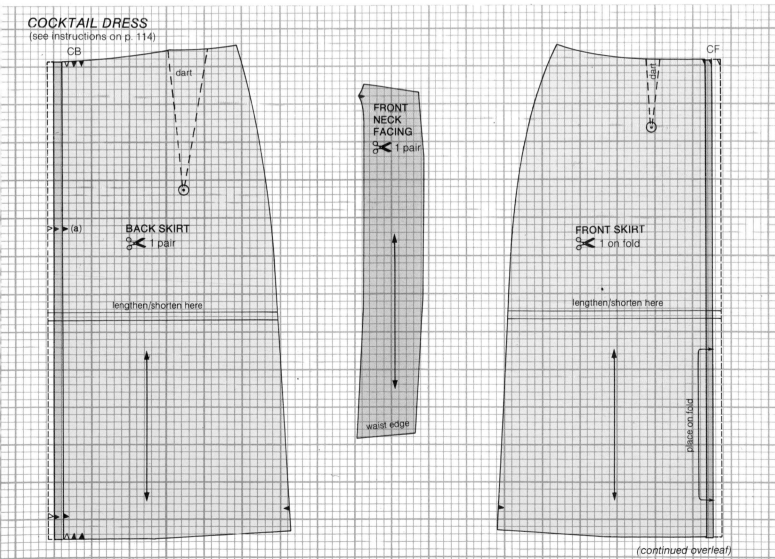

CB

dart

▷ ▶ ▶ (a)

BACK SKIRT
✂ 1 pair

lengthen/shorten here

FRONT
NECK
FACING
✂ 1 pair

waist edge

CF

dart

FRONT SKIRT
✂ 1 on fold

lengthen/shorten here

place on fold

(continued overleaf)

125

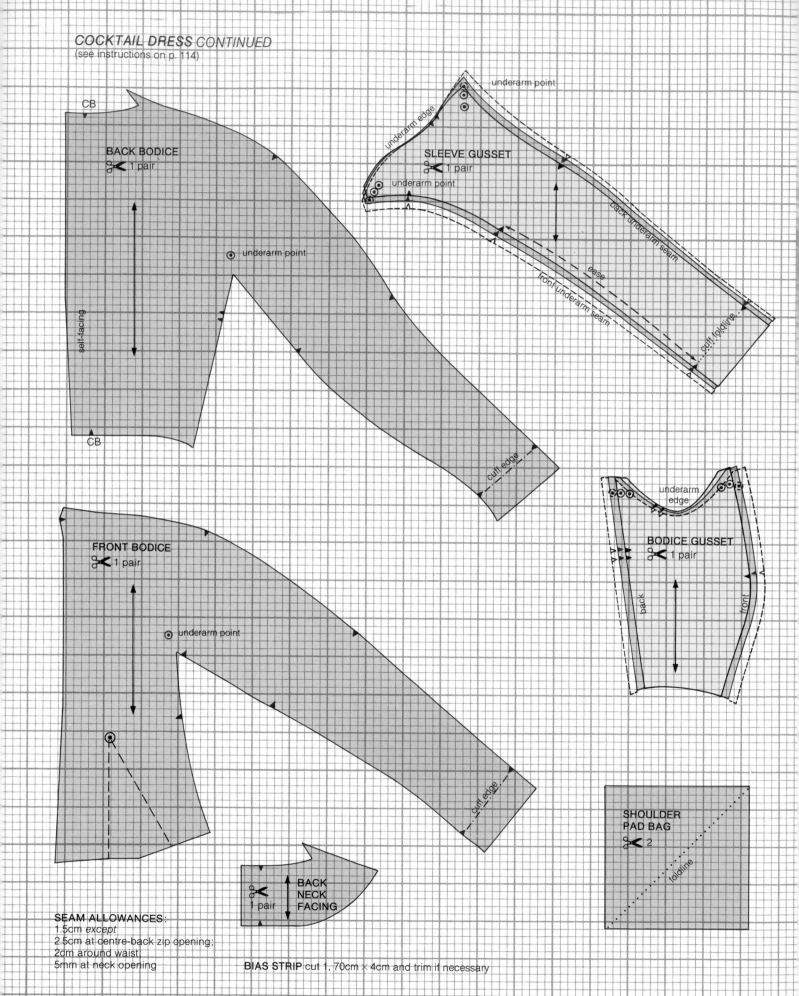

BACK BODICE
✂ 1 pair

CB

self-facing

⊙ underarm point

CB

FRONT BODICE
✂ 1 pair

⊙ underarm point

SLEEVE GUSSET
✂ 1 pair

underarm point

underarm edge

underarm point

back underarm seam

ease

front underarm seam

cuff foldline

cuff edge

cuff edge

BODICE GUSSET
✂ 1 pair

underarm edge

back

front

SHOULDER PAD BAG
✂ 2

foldline

BACK NECK FACING
✂ 1 pair

SEAM ALLOWANCES:
1.5cm *except*
2.5cm at centre-back zip opening;
2cm around waist
5mm at neck opening

BIAS STRIP cut 1, 70cm × 4cm and trim if necessary

Accessories

Waist Tie/Scarf

You will need:
40cm of 150cm wide fabric *or*
40cm of 130cm wide fabric (as illustrated)
(The tie would not be long enough if made in 115cm wide fabric.)

1 Fold strip of fabric in half lengthways, so right sides are facing and pin raw edges together. Stitch round the three pinned sides, allowing a 1cm seam allowance and leaving a 5cm gap in the centre of the longest side, through which to turn tie. Turn tie, press, and slipstitch gap together. Press.

Hip Belt

You will need:
70cm of 150cm wide fabric *or*
70cm of 115cm wide fabric (includes self-lining)
10cm of Velcro

1 With right sides together pin both belt pieces together (or belt and lining), matching centre-back notches. Stitch the two pieces together, leaving a 5cm gap at the centre-back of the waist edge, through which to turn belt.

2 Trim and clip seam allowances and turn belt to right side. Slipstitch centre-back opening together. Press belt and then edgestitch all round, starting and finishing edgestitching at centre-back waist edge.

3 Cut two strips of Velcro to fit pointed left end of belt (see fig. 1). (You may find it easier to stitch the two pieces of Velcro together before applying them, by overlapping the borders of

the Velcro where they meet and stitching through both borders to hold.) Pin Velcro in position underneath pointed left end of finished belt. Join opposite pieces of Velcro for right end of belt in the same way so they exactly match original left pieces. Set Velcro for right front to one side.

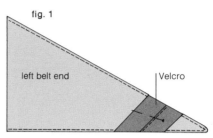

fig. 1

left belt end — Velcro

4 Stitch around edges of Velcro on left end to hold in position, stitching through all thicknesses and pivoting at corners.

5 Wrap belt around hips and pin Velcro for right front in position on right side of right front end, so that it exactly matches left end. Stitch in position, stitching all round edges through both thicknesses of belt (see fig. 2). Press belt thoroughly.

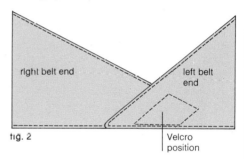

right belt end — *left belt end*

fig. 2 — Velcro position

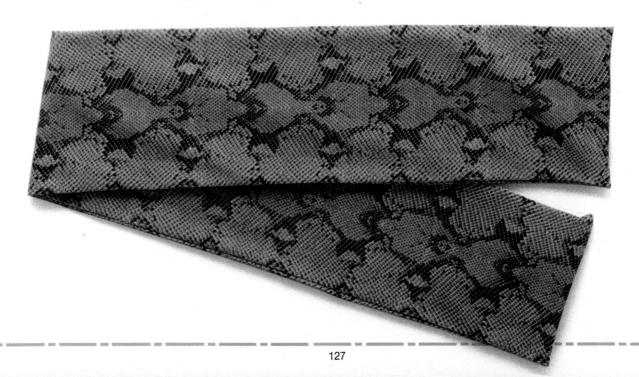

Bag

You will need:
60cm of 150cm wide main fabric *or*
70cm of 115cm wide main fabric
40cm of 150cm *or* 115cm wide contrast
  fabric
3m × 3cm of webbing tape

Pocket

1 Neaten top edge of pocket and fold over
4cm to wrong side. Pin in position. Stitch fold in
position 1cm from inner raw edge. Then edgestitch along top folded edge of pocket.

2 Press in 1.5cm to wrong side along lower
edge of pocket and tack folded edge to hold if
necessary. Then pin pocket in position on front
of bag where marked, pinning down the two
sides and along lower edge. Staystitch the two
sides to main bag piece and edgestitch along
lower edge through pocket and bag piece.

3 With right sides together and aligning raw
edges, pin one side panel to one side of bag
front from top to bottom of panel, catching
pocket seam allowance in seam. Continue
pinning around base of main bag piece, clipping seam allowances at corners to ease if
necessary, and continue pinning up to top
edge of bag back (see fig. 1). Stitch entire seam
and neaten seam allowances together. Repeat
for other panel and opposite side of bag.

4 Neaten all round top raw edge of bag. Then
press in 4cm to wrong side along foldline
marked on pattern to form self-facing and pin
in position. Stitch through both thicknesses
1cm in from raw edge of self-facing all round
bag. Then edgestitch all round top folded edge
of bag.

5 With right side of bag outermost, topstitch
down seams of panel and bag, 1cm in from
seamed edges, stitching from top of bag to
bottom of pocket (see fig. 2) stitching through
all thicknesses. Repeat for three remaining
seams.

6 With right sides together, join short ends of
webbing together. Neaten seam allowances
together. Lay bag flat and with right sides still
outermost, pin "handles" in position where
marked. Start at the underneath left hand side
of the bag, positioning the join of the webbing
against this point. Pin the webbing out to either
side, pinning around bottom and up front and
back sides of bag. Loop webbing round to
form two handles of equal length at top and
then pin the webbing to the front, back and
underneath of the opposite side of the bag in
the same way. Adjust pins if necessary to
ensure handles are the same length. Edgestitch down both sides of tape where pinned to
bag, stitching through tape and bag to hold.
The stitching divides the front pocket into three.

fig. 2

fig. 1

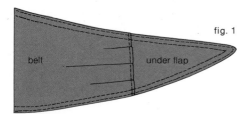

fig. 1

belt   under flap

Hat

You will need:
20cm of 150cm *or* 115cm wide main fabric
60cm of 150cm *or* 115cm wide contrast
   fabric
(Use stretch fabric only)

1 Place two domed hat pieces together, so right sides are facing and pin together down one curved seam. Repeat for other two domed pieces. Then place the two joined pieces together so right sides are facing and remaining long curved seam edges align. Pin and stitch the two pieces together down the two seams to form complete dome. Clip seam allowances and press open.

2 Repeat step 1 for lining and then position lining inside hat so wrong sides come together and seams align. Pin lower raw edges of lining and hat together and staystitch all round, within seam allowance, to hold. Hand stitch the lining to the hat invisibly at the top centre point to hold. Set dome aside.

3 With right sides facing pin the short ends of the hat band together. Stitch and press seam allowances open. Then fold band in half lengthways along foldline marked on pattern, so *wrong* sides come together. Pin the two raw edges together, matching seamlines and stay-stitch all round to hold. Pin band around dome, right sides of band against hat lining and aligning all raw, staystitched edges (see fig. 1). Align seam of band with one seamline of dome. Stitch band to dome all round. Neaten seam allowances together and press towards dome.

hat band

hat dome

fig. 1

4 Turn hat so right side is outermost and fold band in half, back against dome, covering seam allowances. Invisibly slipstitch band to dome if necessary.

Clip Belt

This belt is made out of good-quality imitation leather and fastened at the waist with a standard dog-clip from a pet store or D.I.Y. store. You may use real leather if you have access to skins – use fine skin and self-line it.

You will need:
60cm of 150cm wide fabric *or*
60cm of 90cm wide fabric (includes self-
   lining)
7cm dog clip and ring

1 If using fine or imitation leather, place both belt pieces together (or belt and lining), so right sides are facing. Pin both pieces together along top and bottom long curved edges leaving short ends open. Stitch and turn belt to right side. Edgestitch the two seamed curved edges. Then topstitch 5mm in from edge-stitching.

2 With right sides together, pin the two pieces of one under flap together around the three edges of the point leaving the other end open. Stitch, trim corners and turn to right side. Repeat for other under flap pieces.

3 Pin pleats in position at each end of main belt, pleating upwards. Staystitch across pleats, within seam allowances, to hold.

4 To make loops to hold clip and ring, fold in 1cm to wrong side down each long edge of the loop piece, and then fold loop piece in half again lengthways so both folded edges align. Hold in position with pins and then edgestitch through all thicknesses to hold. Edgestitch other long edge of loop. Cut the finished strip in half to make the two loop pieces.

5 Position pleated right end of belt over raw edges of end of right under flap, so that seam allowances overlap, then stitch (see fig. 1). Edgestitch and topstitch all round right under flap as for main belt. Then position clip loop, bending it in half and threading it through ring of dog clip and pinning it to the centre of the under flap and belt seam (see fig. 2). Stitch through ends of loop and belt to hold.

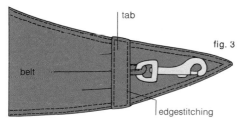

loop   clip   fig. 2

belt

under flap

6 Trim pleated seam allowance of right end of belt as close to seam as possible. Turn in seam allowances around one tab piece, holding in position with tacking if necessary to form a 1.5cm strip when finished. Then pin in position over seam between right end and under flap to cover seam entirely (see fig. 3). Edgestitch all round tab, through all thicknesses, to hold in position.

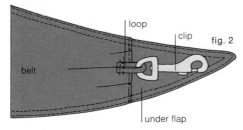

tab   fig. 3

belt

edgestitching

7 Repeat steps 5 and 6 for left end and under flap, inserting ring in place of dog clip. Neaten all seam allowances inside with hand stitches or glue.

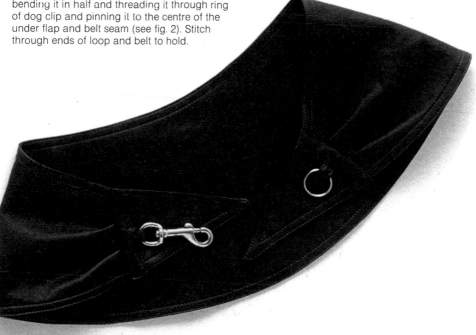

(see pattern charts on pp. 130, 131)

BAG
(see instructions on p. 128)

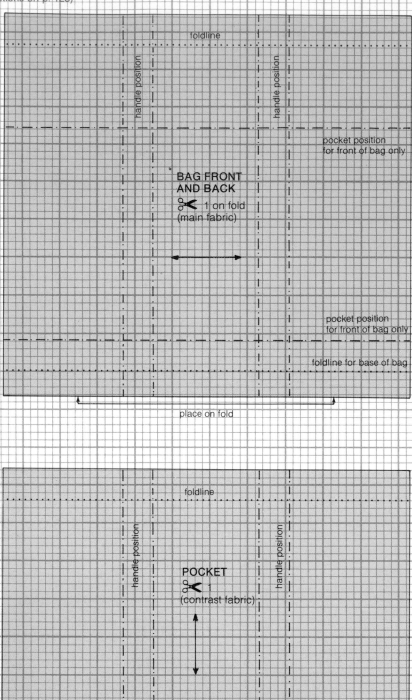

foldline

handle position

handle position

pocket position
for front of bag only

**BAG FRONT
AND BACK**
✂ 1 on fold
(main fabric)

pocket position
for front of bag only

foldline for base of bag

place on fold

foldline

SIDE PANEL
✂ 1 pair
(main fabric)

foldline

handle position

handle position

POCKET
✂ 1
(contrast fabric)

SEAM ALLOWANCES:
1.5cm throughout

WAIST TIE/SCARF
(see instructions on p. 127)

cut a strip 150cm (130cm) by 40cm

SEAM ALLOWANCES:
1cm throughout

HAT
(see instructions on p. 129)

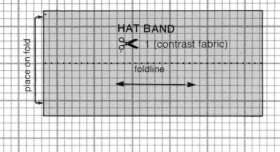

HAT BAND
✂ 1 (contrast fabric)

place on fold

foldline

HAT DOME

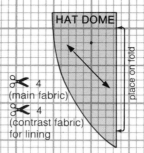

place on fold

✂ 4
(main fabric)
✂ 4
(contrast fabric)
for lining

SEAM ALLOWANCES:
1cm throughout

HIP BELT
(see instructions on p. 127)

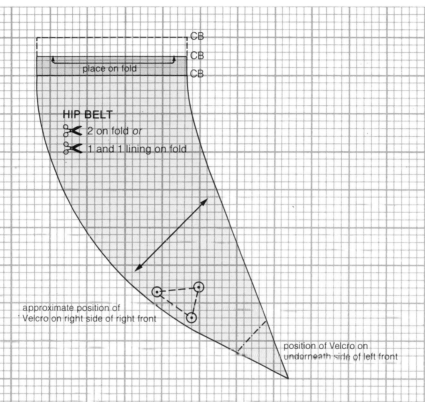

CB
CB
place on fold
CB

HIP BELT
✂ 2 on fold or
✂ 1 and 1 lining on fold

approximate position of
Velcro on right side of right front

position of Velcro on
underneath side of left front

SEAM ALLOWANCES:
5mm throughout

CLIP BELT
(see instructions on p. 129)

CB
CB
place on fold
CB

BELT
✂ 2 on fold or
✂ 1 and 1 lining on fold

UNDER FLAP
✂ 2 pairs or
✂ 1 pair and 1 pair lining

TAB
✂ 1 pair

LOOP
✂ 1

pleat
pleat

SEAM ALLOWANCES:
1cm down long edges of loop
5mm tab, under flap and main belt

Garment Outlines

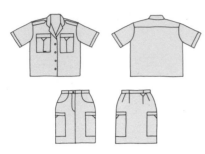

Safari Jacket p. 11, *p. 19*
Safari Skirt p. 12, *p. 20*

Shorts p. 14, *p. 21*
Vest p. 14, *p. 18*

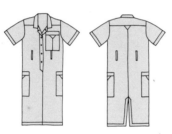

Safari Dress p. 16, *p. 22*

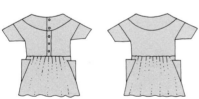

Cowl-Neck Dress p. 25, *p. 36*

Sundress p. 26, *p. 38*
Short-Sleeved Top p. 27, *p. 37*

Tunic Top p. 28, *p. 40*
Skirt p. 29, *p. 41*

Sleeveless Top p. 30, *p. 42*
Sarong Skirt p. 30, *p. 43*

Vest p. 14, *p. 18*
Pants p. 32, *p. 35*

Bikini p. 33, *p. 43*
Kanga p. 33, *p. 43*

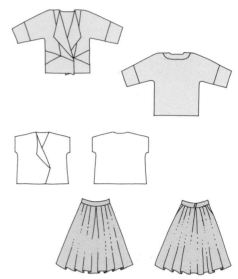

Summer Jacket p. 46, *p. 52*   Top p. 46, *p. 57*
Skirt p. 47, *p. 54*

Summer Dress p. 48, *p. 56*

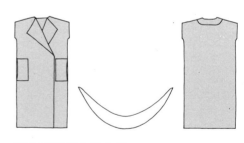

Wrapover Dress p. 50, *p. 58*
Tie Belt p. 51, *p. 58*

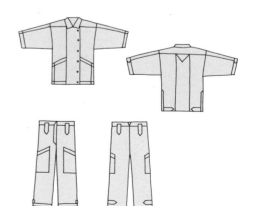

Denim Jacket p. 60, *p. 70*
Denim Pants p. 62, *p. 71*

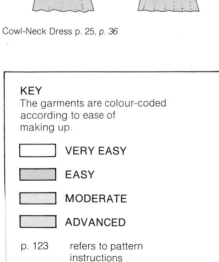

KEY
The garments are colour-coded according to ease of making up.

☐	VERY EASY
☐	EASY
☐	MODERATE
☐	ADVANCED

p. 123   refers to pattern instructions

p. 123   refers to *pattern charts*

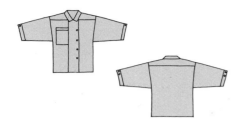

Work Shirt p. 64, *p. 73*

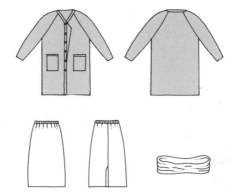

Coat-Dress p. 81, *p. 85*   Skirt p. 82, *p. 87*
Cowl p. 82, *p. 87*

Tailored Jacket p. 98, *p. 108*
Straight Skirt p. 98, *p. 104*

Leisure Jacket p. 66, *p. 74*
Full Skirt p. 68, *p. 69*

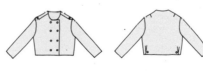

¾-Length Coat p. 92, *p. 112*   Raglan-
Sleeved Blouse p. 93, *p. 109*   Skirt p. 92, *p. 104*

Overcoat p. 100, *p. 106*

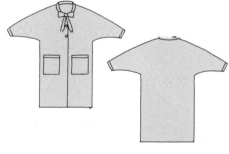

Tie-Neck Dress p. 77, *p. 88*

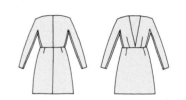

Cocktail Dress p. 114, *p. 125*

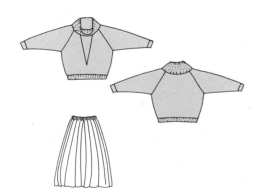

Sweater p. 78, *p. 84*
Skirt p. 78, *p. 83*

Double Breasted Jacket p. 94, *p. 103*
Blouse p. 96, *p. 105*   Sixties Pants p. 97, *p. 111*

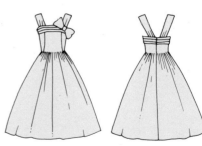

Evening Shift p. 116, *p. 122*
Sash p. 116, *p. 123*

Ball Gown p. 119, *p. 124*

MIX AND MATCH CHART

Use this chart to devise alternative outfits, using your own choice of fabric. ● indicates a possible combination.

KEY

- VERY EASY
- EASY
- MODERATE
- ADVANCED

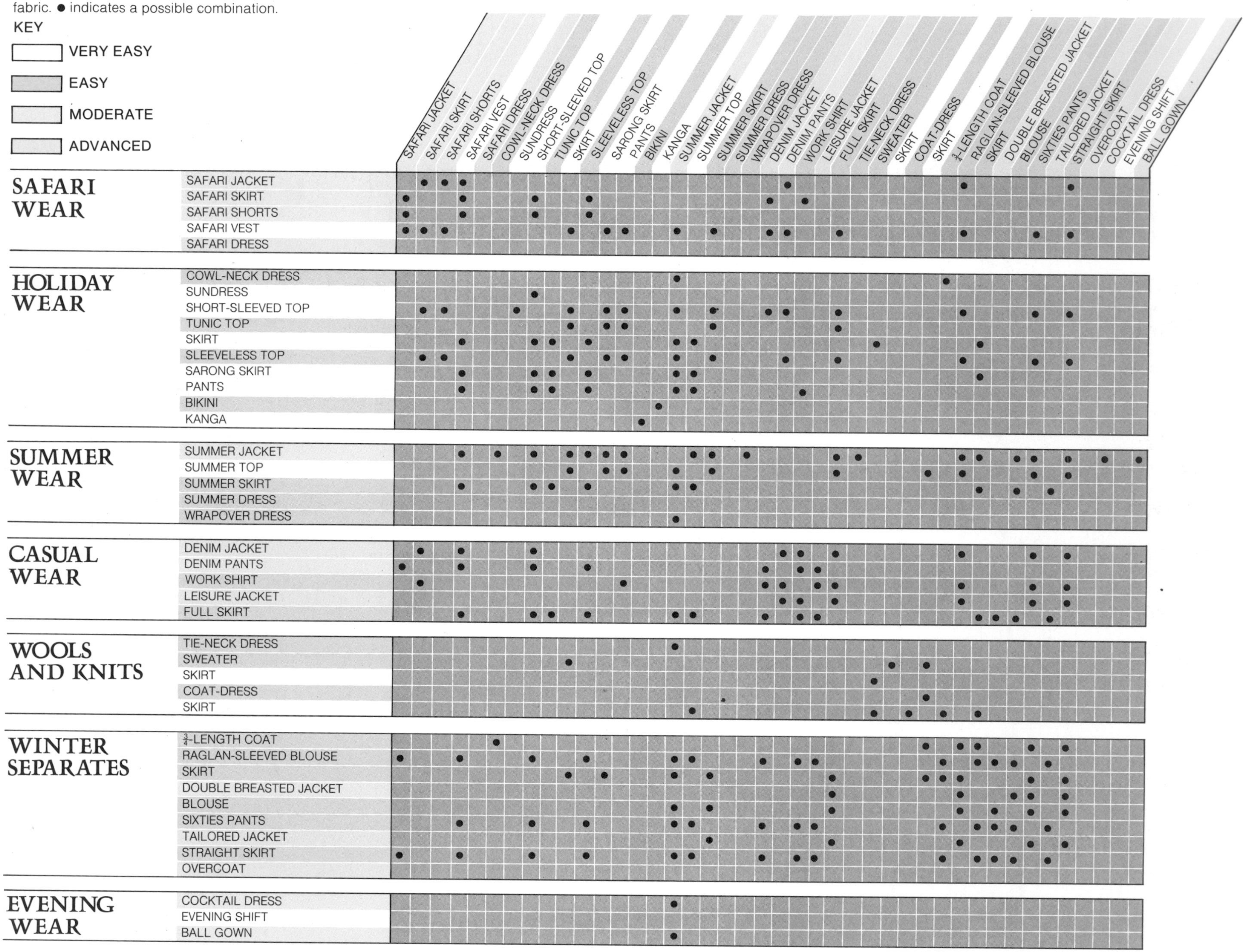
SAFARI JACKET
SAFARI SKIRT
SAFARI SHORTS
SAFARI VEST
SAFARI DRESS
COWL-NECK DRESS
SUNDRESS
SHORT-SLEEVED TOP
TUNIC TOP
SKIRT
SLEEVELESS TOP
SARONG SKIRT
PANTS
BIKINI
KANGA
SUMMER JACKET
SUMMER TOP
SUMMER SKIRT
SUMMER DRESS
WRAPOVER DRESS
DENIM JACKET
DENIM PANTS
WORK SHIRT
LEISURE JACKET
FULL SKIRT
TIE-NECK DRESS
SWEATER
SKIRT
COAT-DRESS
SKIRT
¾-LENGTH COAT
RAGLAN-SLEEVED BLOUSE
SKIRT
DOUBLE BREASTED JACKET
BLOUSE
SIXTIES PANTS
TAILORED JACKET
STRAIGHT SKIRT
OVERCOAT
COCKTAIL DRESS
EVENING SHIFT
BALL GOWN
SAFARI WEAR
SAFARI JACKET
SAFARI SKIRT
SAFARI SHORTS
SAFARI VEST
SAFARI DRESS
HOLIDAY WEAR
COWL-NECK DRESS
SUNDRESS
SHORT-SLEEVED TOP
TUNIC TOP
SKIRT
SLEEVELESS TOP
SARONG SKIRT
PANTS
BIKINI
KANGA
SUMMER WEAR
SUMMER JACKET
SUMMER TOP
SUMMER SKIRT
SUMMER DRESS
WRAPOVER DRESS
CASUAL WEAR
DENIM JACKET
DENIM PANTS
WORK SHIRT
LEISURE JACKET
FULL SKIRT
WOOLS AND KNITS
TIE-NECK DRESS
SWEATER
SKIRT
COAT-DRESS
SKIRT
WINTER SEPARATES
¾-LENGTH COAT
RAGLAN-SLEEVED BLOUSE
SKIRT
DOUBLE BREASTED JACKET
BLOUSE
SIXTIES PANTS
TAILORED JACKET
STRAIGHT SKIRT
OVERCOAT
EVENING WEAR
COCKTAIL DRESS
EVENING SHIFT
BALL GOWN

Sewing Techniques

EQUIPMENT

Basic equipment

You need a small amount of basic equipment:

Pattern paper
All the patterns in this book are given in chart form on a grid. If you use pattern paper marked in a 1cm scale it is very easy to transfer the patterns to the paper since each small square on the pattern charts represents 1cm.

Metre rule
Essential for transferring the pattern from the chart to the pattern paper, and useful for taking straight measurements or marking hems. Metal or plastic rules are more durable than wood – the edge of a wooden rule is easily damaged, and a rough wooden edge can damage your fabric.

Tailor's chalk
This is needed for drawing around the pattern pieces prior to cutting out, and for marking dart and pocket positions on the fabric. It comes in a variety of colours, the most common being white and black. Use white on dark fabrics and black on light ones.

Scissors
Good quality, sharp scissors are essential. Dressmaking shears, with angled handles and blades of 12–15cm are best for cutting fabric. The angled handles allow you to cut but still leave the fabric flat. Keep them sharp, and use them only for fabric. Use a different pair of all-purpose scissors for cutting paper patterns as paper will readily blunt scissor blades. A small pair of embroidery scissors with sharp points are useful for trimming, snipping threads and cutting buttonholes.

Needles and pins
Choose needles according to the fabric used – use a fine needle for lightweight fabric, and a sturdier one for heavy-weight fabric.

Pins vary in length and quality – buy the best you can afford and always have plenty. Keep them handy in a pin cushion. Bulky fabrics require longer pins.

Tape measure
A tape measure, preferably marked with centimetres and inches, is essential for taking body measurements.

Sewing machine
Sewing machines fall into two categories:
Straight-stitch machines, which sew in a straight line forwards or backwards, and only the stitch length can be adjusted.
Swing-needle machines, where the needle can swing from side to side in a variety of widths to produce stitches such as zigzag, simple embroidery and buttonhole, as well as straight-stitch. Both stitch length and stitch width can be regulated. In more advanced swing-needle machines three-step zigzag stitches can be made as well as a wide range of decorative stitches.

Iron and ironing board
As pressing is an essential dressmaking technique you will need an ironing board always at hand. Buy the best iron you can afford and make sure the temperature dial and thermostat are reliable. A steam/dry iron is best, although a dry iron and spray are usually adequate.

Depending on the fabric used, you may also need a pressing cloth.

Optional equipment

Although not essential, these items are useful as time-saving aids:

Bodkin
Used for threading elastic through a channel.

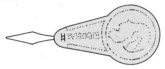

Needle threader
Helpful if you have difficulty threading needles.

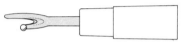

Seam ripper
Used for unpicking stitches, or ripping seams.

Thimble
Can make hand sewing more comfortable and efficient. Particularly useful for thick fabrics.

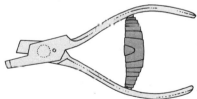

Notchers
A special gadget to cut notches in paper pattern pieces.

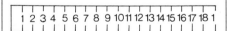

Half-metre rule
Handy for drawing short lines.

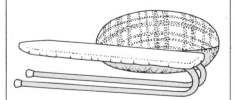

Tailor's ham
Useful for pressing curved areas.

Sleeve board
Makes pressing sleeves much easier.

Fabric

Choose good quality fabric as this will make the task of sewing much easier. Make sure that the weave is firm and that the threads do not shift when they are stretched. The weave should be even, so check it against the light for any unusually thick or thin areas, or holes. The dye should be even and look fresh and patterns should be uniform.

Most of the garments in this book have been made up in natural fibres: cotton, silk, linen and wool. However you can achieve just as good a result from good quality synthetics, or mixtures of pure and synthetic fibres. For example, the garments on p. 117 are made from rayon.

If you are a newcomer to dressmaking, start of with light- to medium-weight, non-slip fabrics such as cotton, brushed rayon, light wool, polyester or mixtures of these, since these are easy to handle. Avoid very lightweight fabrics such as chiffon or georgette and also heavy-weight, loosely-woven fabrics such as tweeds. Also avoid knitted or textured fabrics, fabrics with large patterns or with a nap (such as corduroy or velvet) where the pile runs in one direction only.

Types of fabric

Fabric is formed using a variety of techniques. Weaving, knitting, felting and netting are the four basic ways of constructing fabric from which other types are formed. Woven or knitted fabrics are most commonly used in dressmaking.

Woven This is the most common method of forming fabric, whereby two sets of yarn are worked at right angles to each other. Warp yarns are stretched lengthwise on the loom and are raised and lowered by movable frames. This allows weft yarns to be inserted crosswise by shuttles. All woven fabric has a selvedge.

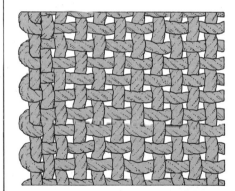

Knitted This method uses machines to produce a fabric of interlocking loops. Weft and warp knitting are the two basic techniques. Weft fabric is constructed with one continuous yarn forming loops crosswise. Stretch is greater across the fabric than down it. Although comfortable to wear, this fabric is prone to running and sagging. Warp knit fabric is made by forming loops lengthwise. Each yarn is controlled by its own needle. It follows a zigzag course, interlocking each loop with its neighbour down the length of the fabric. This produces durable run-proof fabric.

Haberdashery

Threads

Choose thread according to the type of fabric being used. Use synthetic threads with man-made fibres and mercerized cotton or silk thread with cotton, linen or wool. Choose thread which is one shade darker than your fabric because thread appears lighter when worked on a garment.

All types of thread are graded; the higher the number on the label, the finer the thread. When stitched, the thread should be well set into the fabric to give a firm long-lasting seam. If the thread is too heavy for the fabric it will remain on the surface and wear out quickly, reducing the durability of your garment.

Use proper tacking thread for tacking – the loose twist allows easy breaking.

Bindings and tapes

Bias binding used for neatening edges and seams.

Paris binding used for neatening edges and seams.

Seam binding used for neatening seams.

Cotton or linen tape used for loops, ties and for strengthening seams and openings.

Petersham used around waistlines for stiffening.

Elastic comes in various widths for different purposes.

Belt/waistband stiffening extra-firm stiffening which will withstand bending.

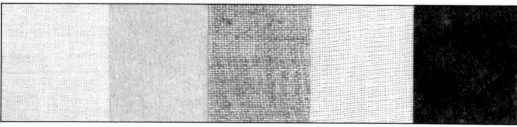

Interfacing comes in two types – woven and non woven. Both are available in fusible, "iron-on" versions where one side is coated with adhesive, so that the interfacing can be simply ironed on to the fabric.

Fastenings

Zips come in a wide range of weights – lightweight nylon zips have plastic teeth, cotton zips have metal teeth.

Velcro, a hook and loop fastener, consists of two strips of tape (one covered with tiny hooks, the other with tiny loops) which interlock on contact and come apart when pulled firmly.

Buttons The range of buttons available today is infinite. Buttons can be flat, with two or four holes, or shanked. Remember to remove leather or antique buttons before cleaning.

Press-studs There are two different types of press-studs: traditional sew-on poppers, made from metal or plastic, and metal snap fasteners which are attached through the fabric by means of a special tool.

Hooks and eyes/bars These are used to hold together openings which meet edge to edge.

MACHINE SEWING
Types of stitches

A well maintained machine will produce perfect stitches providing you use the right needle and thread for the fabric, with the correct tension.

The basic machine stitch is a straight stitch. Use a short stitch length for sewing seams and a long stitch length for easing and gathering. Adjust length by moving the stitch length regulator higher or lower.

Most modern machines are capable of forming more elaborate stitches. Use a wide zigzag for neatening raw edges and a narrow zigzag for stitching knitted fabric. Satin stitch – a wide zigzag with a short stitch length – is used for buttonholes.

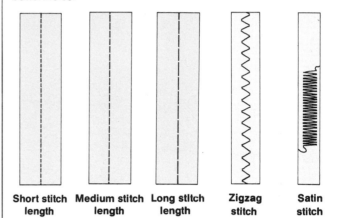

| Short stitch length | Medium stitch length | Long stitch length | Zigzag stitch | Satin stitch |

Needle selection

The size and type of point should be considered when selecting needles. Sizes range from 9 to 18 (the lower the number the finer the needle). To prevent damage to lightweight fabric use a fine needle. A heavier fabric will require a thicker needle to prevent needle deflection or breakage. For lightweight fabric such as cotton, fine wool or silk, use a size 9 or 11. For medium-weight fabric such as corduroy, suiting wool, linen or velvet use size 11 or 14, and for heavy-weight fabric such as coating, terry cloth or leather use size 16 or 18.

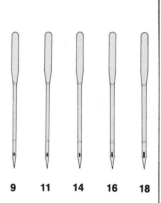

9   11   14   16   18

A sharp-point needle is recommended for woven fabrics

A ball-point needle should be used for knitted fabrics

A wedge-point needle is needed for leathers and vinyls

The type of point is also very important. A sharp-point needle is most commonly used and is recommended for all types of woven fabric. A ball-point needle has a rounded tip and is used when sewing knitted fabric because the point slides between the yarns instead of piercing them. A wedge-point needle is designed specifically for leathers and vinyls to minimize the risk of fabric splitting. Change your needle frequently, especially when sewing man-made fabrics.

HAND SEWING

The amount of hand sewing that has to be done on these garments has been kept to a minimum, however there are a few occasions when it is essential.

Tacking stitch

Tacking is used to hold fabric together temporarily. Use light-coloured or tacking thread for this.

Make even stitches about 6mm to 10mm long. When easing one layer of fabric against another, hold the layer to be eased on top and gather this top layer of fabric gently as you stitch.

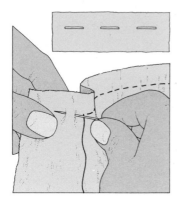

Back stitch

Back stitch is useful for making strong seams and for finishing off a line of machine or hand stitching. The stitches on the front of the work are small and appear continuous.

Make a small stitch back from left to right. Then make a double length stitch forwards on the wrong side of the work so the needle emerges a stitch's length in front of the first one.

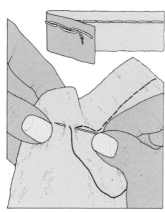

Oversewing

If your machine does not have a zigzag stitch use oversewing to finish seam edges on fabrics which fray easily.

Hold the fabric with the edge to be worked away from you. Insert the needle 3mm to 6mm from the edge and bring the thread over the edge of the fabric. Make the next stitch 6mm further on.

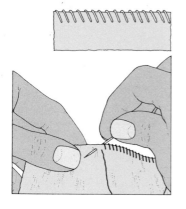

Blind hemming stitch

Blind hemming is worked on the inside fold of the hem so that the stitches are almost invisible. The thread should not be pulled taut.

Holding the work with the fold of the hem towards you as shown, take a very small stitch inside the hem fold edge, picking up a thread of the single fabric on the point of the needle before taking another stitch on the inside hem fold of the garment.

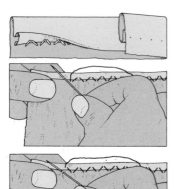

Herringbone stitch

Herringbone is used for securing hems on heavy fabrics which do not fray easily and on stretch fabrics. It is worked from left to right.

Insert the needle through the inside of the hem turning, then right and down to make a small stitch in the single fabric. Move the needle diagonally up and right and take a small stitch from right to left in the hem fold, but not through it.

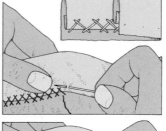
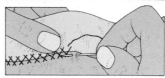

Hem stitch

Hem stitch is used for hems on medium-weight or lightweight fabrics. The stitch size will depend on the fabric. The thread should not be pulled taut or the fabric will pucker.

With the work held as shown, pick up a thread of the single fabric on the needle point and then catch a thread of the fold on the point of the needle before pulling through.

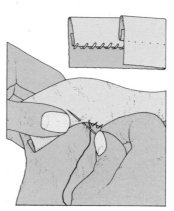

Slipstitch

Slipstitch is used for flat hemming with a turned-in edge on light- to medium-weight fabrics. The thread should not be pulled taut, and the stitches should be worked about 6mm apart.

Pick up 1 or 2 threads of the single fabric and then slide the needle through the hem fold for about 6mm. Draw the thread through.

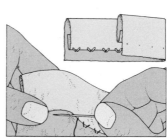

Buttonhole stitch

Buttonhole stitch is worked with the needle pointing towards you, and the fabric edge away from you.

Insert the needle into the right side of the edge of the buttonhole. Bring it out 3mm below. Loop the thread hanging from the eye of the needle from right to left under the point of the needle and draw the needle upwards to knot the thread at the buttonhole edge.

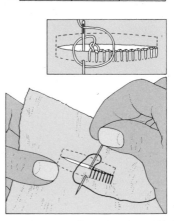

PATTERN SIZES

For most of the patterns in this book we have given three basic sizes – 10, 12 and 14. We have assumed that, on average, the measurements given in the chart are typical of these particular sizes and the patterns have been made accordingly. Compare your own body measurements with these, making a note of them and the extent to which they differ.

Many of the designs in this book have been cut intentionally large or full, so slight differences between your measurements and the figures given in the chart are of no consequence. When making jackets and tops, use the size closest to your bust size; when making skirts or trousers, use the size closest to your hip size; and when making dresses use the size nearest to your largest measurement.

The cutting line for each size is denoted on the charts by a different type of printed line – a solid black line for size 10, a solid red line for size 12 and a broken black line for size 14. In some places the cutting line is the same for all three, so the lines converge.

Seam and hem allowances *are* included on the charts – the seam allowance is usually 1.5cm, the places where it differs from this are marked on each chart.

Simple alterations in hem length will, more often than not, take care of differences in height; account for this when cutting out. Where the balance of a garment will be "thrown" by simply altering the length at the bottom, we have given a lengthening/shortening line on the chart. To make such adjustments see p. 143.

One-size patterns
A few of the patterns are one-size – the pattern given is designed to fit sizes 10, 12 and 14.

Taking body measurements

It is essential to be careful and honest when taking measurements. For greatest accuracy, stand naturally, wear your normal underclothes and have someone to help you.

Bust
Measure around the fullest part of your bust.

Waist
Measure around the natural indentation at your waist.

Hips
Measure around the fullest part of your hips – it is usually about 18–23cm below the waist.

	SIZE 10	SIZE 12	SIZE 14
Bust	83cm (32¾″)	88cm (34¾″)	93cm (36½″)
Waist	61cm (24″)	66cm (26″)	71cm (28″)
Hips	89cm (35″)	94cm (37″)	99cm (39″)

NB Imperial equivalents are to the nearest ¼ inch

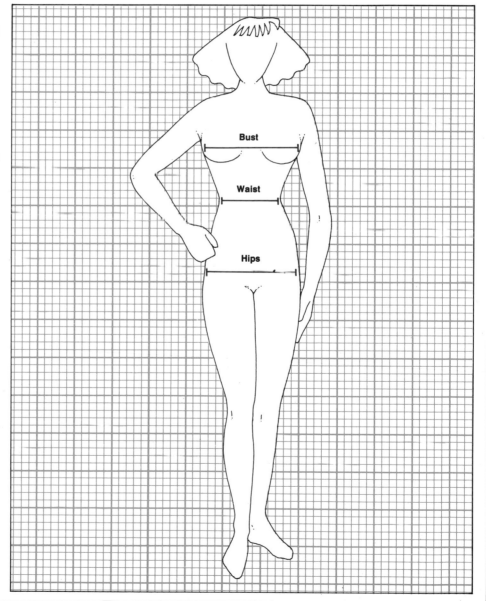

MAKING THE PATTERNS

All the patterns in this book have been given in chart form. It is easy to scale them up on to pattern paper using the following method. Make sure your pattern paper is marked in the correct scale.

REMEMBER: SCALE = 1/5
Use 1cm grid pattern paper, then
1 square on chart = 1 square on pattern paper

---

1 Count the number of pattern pieces on the chart and make a note of the total so that you can check back at the end that none have been omitted.

2 Lay your pattern paper flat, ironing out any creases with a warm iron if necessary. Use a fine felt pen or sharp soft pencil to mark the pattern paper.

3 Having decided on your particular size, study the pattern chart and work out the longest and widest dimensions of one pattern piece, using the bold lines as a rough estimate of the overall length and width. (Cut the largest pattern pieces first, as smaller pieces can be fitted into left-over paper.) Transfer these dimensions to the pattern paper and use them to draw a square or rectangle within which you know the entire pattern piece will fit. This is your initial guide within which you will then draw the pattern details.

4 Using the bold lines of the grid as a basic guide and the finer lines for the exact position, mark a cross on the pattern paper where each prominent point at the top, bottom and side edges in the pattern shape falls to establish the basic area the pattern piece occupies.

5 With these marks as your guidelines, plot the outline of the pattern piece, making a cross on the pattern paper at the exact point where the cutting line on the chart intersects the grid lines. Join the centres of the crosses to form a continuous cutting line.

6 Using a fine felt-tip pen, transfer *all* notches, balance marks, pocket points, grain lines, foldlines etc. At the same time, before you cut out a pattern piece always mark the title of the garment, which piece of pattern it is, how many pieces should be cut, and whether the pieces should be cut on the fold. *Everything* that is written or marked on the pattern chart should be transferred to your pattern piece.

7 When you are satisfied that you have transferred all marks and instructions, cut around the line of the pattern piece with all-purpose scissors (do not use your dressmaking shears for this). Following the instructions on the pattern chart, mark the seam allowances at the edges. If you have notchers, use these to indicate the

seam allowance, cutting a notch at each seam allowance marked. Otherwise mark clearly with felt pen. In general the seam allowances are 1.5cm, but occasionally they are 5mm or 1cm so check the chart instructions carefully.

8 Before you start to cut your fabric from the pattern, always check roughly that, for example, front and back pieces of a pattern are approximately the same size.

You can do this by counting the number of heavy squares on each piece or matching two seam edges which will eventually be sewn together, such as side seams.

9 Keep all pattern pieces belonging to one garment in an envelope or polythene bag, marked clearly with the name of the garment and the total number of pattern pieces.

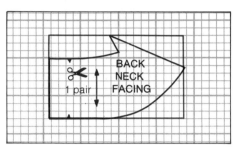

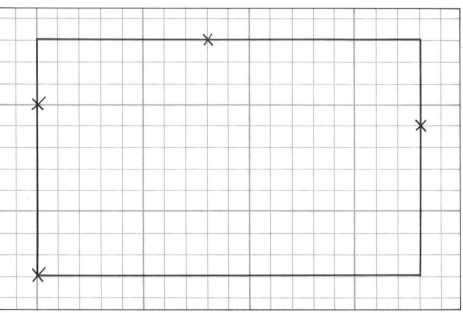

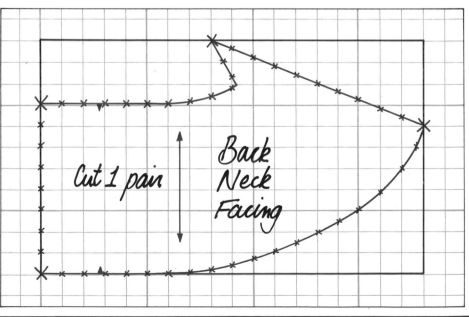

ALTERING PATTERNS TO MAKE THEM BIGGER OR SMALLER

Lengthening and shortening patterns

For many of the garments simple alterations in hem length will accommodate differences in height, or skirt length preferences. However, where the balance of a garment will be "thrown" by simply altering the length at the bottom, the pattern must be adjusted at the lengthening/shortening line. When you first start to alter patterns it is best to make the pattern twice – once to the size indicated on the chart and then again, incorporating the appropriate changes for your particular measurements. As you become more proficient you should be able to include the adjustments as you make the pattern for the first time.

Remember, if you alter a pattern, to leave enough room for "wearing" ease, and if you alter a pattern piece you will have to alter any corresponding pieces that are affected by the alteration. For example if you want to make the Wrapover Dress shorter, you will have to shorten the front facing as well as the dress front and back.

Making patterns wider or narrower

It is easier to lengthen or shorten a pattern piece than to make it wider or narrower, since in general fewer features are affected. However we have given widening/narrowing lines on most of the pants. The same principles apply as when lengthening or shortening a pattern.

How to alter a pattern

1 Choosing the standard size closest to your measurements, transfer the pattern from the chart on to pattern paper, and cut it out.

2 Place the standard pattern you have made over a new sheet of pattern paper, aligning the squares on both pieces exactly. If you are altering the length of the pattern, pin the top edge of the standard pattern to the new sheet, if you are altering the width of the pattern, pin the side edge of the standard pattern to the new sheet. When both length-wise and width-wise alterations are to be made, make length-wise alterations first.

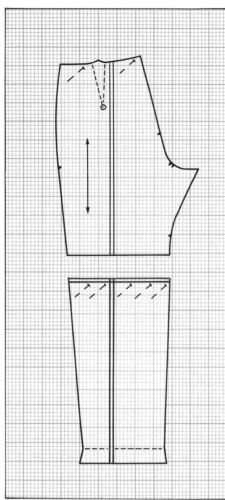

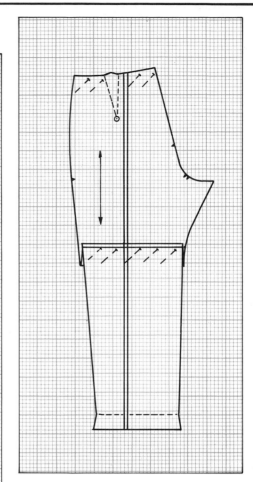

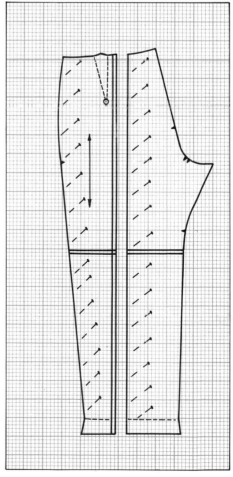

3 To make a pattern piece longer, cut the standard pattern along the horizontal lengthening/shortening line marked and pull the bottom piece downwards to accommodate the necessary alteration (see above). To make the pattern piece shorter, fold a tuck in the standard pattern along the lengthening/shortening line, making the depth of the tuck *half* of the total amount to be taken out (see right). Pin the pattern in this new position on the pattern paper below.

4 Use the same technique to alter the width of a pattern piece but make the tuck or cut the pattern *vertically* along the widening/narrowing line (see right).

5 Draw around the pattern, and where you have altered the pattern, draw in a new line, tapering between the original lines so that the new line runs smoothly into the original lines.

6 Transfer all the notches, dart positions. pocket positions, seam allowances etc. on to the new pattern. Finally cut out the new pattern piece.

CUTTING OUT
Preparing the fabric

Some materials such as indian cotton, denim and loose weave fabrics are liable to shrink the first time they are washed and so it is advisable to wash, dry and iron such fabrics before cutting out. If you are unsure whether or not your fabric will shrink, cut two small squares the same size, wash and dry one, then compare it with the unwashed square.

Stretch fabrics should be laid out flat and left to "relax" overnight, before cutting, since they may have been stored under tension when on the roll in the shop.

Laying out

Assemble all the equipment you will need for cutting: the fabric, the pattern pieces, pins, scissors, chalk, and prepare a large, clear, clean surface. It is important to have enough room to lay out the whole pattern at once, before starting to cut. Fold over part or all of the fabric if some or all of the pieces have to be cut in pairs or on a fold.

The grain line on the pattern pieces should be placed along the lengthwise grain of the fabric, providing the fabric permits. Use your short rule to help you position the pattern accurately along the grain. Position the large pattern pieces first, fitting smaller pieces into any spaces created. Ensure that pieces which need to lie on a fold do so.

Pin all the pattern pieces securely to the fabric. It is a good idea to draw around the pattern pieces with tailor's chalk, as an extra guideline, before cutting.

Laying out problem fabrics

Some fabrics, because of their design or the way in which they are made, require more careful laying out. These fabrics include those with a pile (nap), patterns running in one direction, and checks or stripes. Generally beginners should avoid such fabrics if possible because of the accuracy required in laying them out.

Laying out napped fabrics or one-way designs

If you do use a napped fabric, such as velvet or corduroy, the pile must lie the same way on every piece of the garment and the pattern pieces must therefore be laid out so that they all follow the same direction. This will take more fabric than if you were using fabric without a nap. If you are unsure of the direction of the pile, smooth the surface of the fabric with your hand. One-way designs are similarly laid out.

Laying out fabric with checks and stripes

Checks and stripes should match at the side seams, centre seams or openings, waistlines, armholes and sleeves. Position the pattern pieces carefully to make sure they match. Shift the pattern pieces so that the balance marks align on the same check or stripe. It is sensible to choose patterns without too many seams. Be careful to match the checks and stripes at the line where the seam is stitched, rather than on the edge of the seam allowance. Make any alterations to the pattern before laying out as this affects the way the design joins.

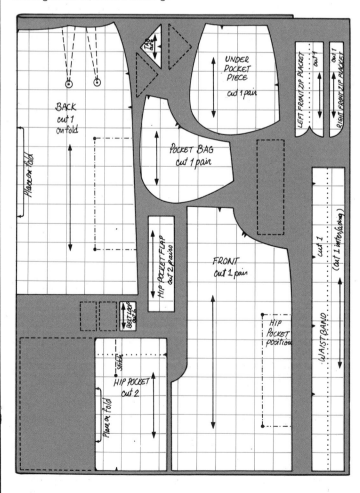

Key to construction marks

—————	**Cutting line – size 10**
—————	**Cutting line – size 12**
– – – – –	**Cutting line – size 14** The seam allowance is included in the pattern.
⟷	**Grain line** This should always run parallel to, or at right angles to the selvedge.
⌐———⌐	**Place on fold** The edge of the pattern indicated must be placed along a fold, so that a double piece of fabric is produced on cutting out. Notches, etc. should be made on both sides.
· · · · · ·	**Foldline** This marks the line along which fabric must be folded when indicated in the pattern.
▶ ▶ >	**Notches** These are used to match one part of the garment to another when making up. They are also known as balance marks.
—————	**Lengthening/shortening line** This indicates where the pattern may be lengthened or shortened (see p. 143).
‖	**Widening/narrowing line** This indicates where the pattern may be made wider or narrower (see p. 143).
◉	**Buttonhole position**
⟩	**Dart**
✁	**Cut**
CB CF	**Centre-back/Centre-front**

144

Cutting

Make sure you have pinned *all* the pattern pieces before you start cutting out. Always cut on a flat surface with sharp scissors. Open the blades wide and cut right to their points. Cut all the main pattern pieces first. Make sure that all the necessary marks are transferred to the fabric before unpinning.

Cutting checklist

1 Do you have all the pattern pieces for the design?
2 Is the material entirely flat and are all the pattern pieces straight on the grain of the fabric?
3 If the fabric has a nap are the pattern pieces lying in one direction only?
4 If the fabric is printed, are the pattern pieces arranged so that the fabric design matches when joined together?
5 If the pattern is to be used double, is it lying with the appropriate pattern edge on the fabric fold?
6 Is the fabric lying on an even surface?

Cutting bias strips

The instruction "cut 4 bias strips, xcm x ycm" frequently appears on the patterns. These are narrow strips of fabric, cut diagonally across the grain, used for finishing off curved edges of garments, such as necklines and armholes. Cut the bias strips *after* cutting out the main pattern pieces. It does not matter if you cannot cut the length of strip required in one; simply join several shorter strips together.

This method of cutting bias strips does not apply to knitted fabrics. If you wish to bind a knitted fabric, use commercial bias binding.

How to find the true bias

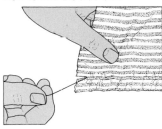

1 Make sure that one raw edge of the fabric is straight by pulling one of the cross threads. The edge should run parallel to this line.

2 Lay the fabric out flat. Fold one corner over diagonally so the straight raw edge is against the selvedge. The diagonal fold is the true bias. Cut strips of the required length parallel to this line on either side of the fold.

Joining bias strips

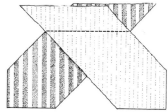

Pin the short ends, with right sides facing, matching pattern if necessary. Stitch across ends, 5mm from the edge.

NB For purposes of binding, bias strips do not always have to be cut exactly on the true bias. It is possible to cut strips slightly off the true bias, but make sure there is adequate "stretch" in the strip.

MARKING THE PIECES OF FABRIC

Always leave the pattern pinned to the fabric until all the marks on the pattern have been transferred to the material.

Cut small "V"-shaped notches at the positions marked around the edge of each piece. Mark seam allowances with chalk or by making a small "nick" at the fabric edge. Transfer all other marks (such as button positions, pleat lines and darts) on to the fabric pieces with chalk or tailor's tacks (see below).

Before you separate the cut pieces of fabric from the pattern mark the wrong side of each piece with a large tailor's chalk cross to avoid confusion when making up.

Marking with chalk

Tailor's chalk provides a quick means of marking fabric. Make sure that it brushes out of the fabric you are using without staining.

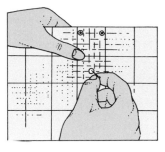
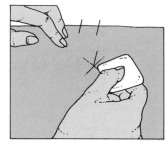

1 With pattern still in position on double or single layers of fabric after they have been cut, stab a pin through the pattern and the fabric at each symbol, so that pin emerges through other side.

2 Push the pinhead right through the pattern paper, then remove the pattern, taking care not to lift the pins from the fabric. Make chalk crosses at each pin on wrong side of each layer of fabric.

Marking with tailor's tacks

This method of marking fabric, although a little more time-consuming at first, is particularly useful for marking double layers of fabric since the stitch is duplicated through both layers.

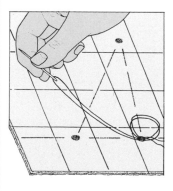
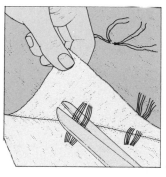

1 With a length of doubled, unknotted thread make a small stitch through the pattern and both layers of the fabric, leaving a 2.5cm end. Make another stitch at the same point and leave a 5–8cm loop and a 2.5cm end.

2 When all the symbols have been marked in this way, cut all the loops, and lift the pattern off the fabric, taking care not to pull out the thread markings. Gently separate the two layers of fabric a little and cut the threads so markings are left in both layers.

MAKING UP
Pinning and tacking

When you first start to sew pinning and tacking are essential at every stage. As you become more proficient, you may find that you prefer to take short cuts, particularly if you are working with fabric you are accustomed to. Whenever you use a fabric new to you it is advisable to go back to basics.

Having aligned seam edges and balance marks pin the seam in position. Follow the pinning line with a line of tacking stitches, removing the pins as you go. If you decide to omit tacking, take care to remove pins before the machine needle reaches them.

Seams

A seam is made when two or more pieces of fabric are joined together with a line of stitching. Seams are normally machine stitched. Make sure that the needle and thread used are appropriate for the weight and texture of the fabric (see pp. 138–9).

Because the seams of a garment have to withstand wear and tear, the beginning and end of the line of stitching should always be secured with a few reverse stitches.

Types of seams
There are several different types of seams, and the type of fabric and garment determines the one used. A flat seam can be used on most garments, the raw seam edges should always be neatened (see opposite). Although a flat seam is always made with the right sides of the fabric facing, some other seams, such as a French seam, are started with the wrong sides together.

Seam allowances
Enough fabric should always be left between the line of stitches and the fabric edge to prevent fraying. This is the seam allowance. In this book seam allowances are included in the patterns. They are usually 1.5cm on side seams, but for special features such as pockets, armholes, necklines and tabs 1cm or 5mm seam allowances are included. These are clearly indicated on the pattern charts.

Flat seam

A flat seam is the basic seam. It is used on normal weight fabrics where there is no special strain on the seam. Plain straight stitch is used to stitch the seam, unless stretch fabric is being used, in which case the seam is sewn with a narrow zigzag stitch.

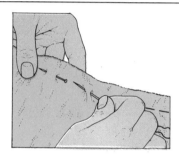

1 With the right sides of the fabric facing, pin the fabric together at intervals along the seamline.

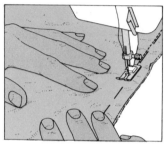

2 Tack close to the seamline and remove the pins. Then stitch along the seamline, reverse stitching a few stitches at each end.

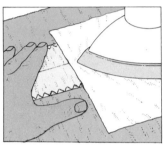

3 After removing the tacking stitches neaten the seam allowance. Press the seam open.

French seam

A French seam is generally used for fine fabrics or for those which fray easily. It is a seam within a seam and when finished should be about 7mm or less in width.

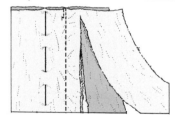

1 Place the wrong sides of the fabric together. Pin and tack in position close to the seamline. Stitch 7mm to the right of the seamline to the end of the seam. Press as stitched. Then trim the seam allowance to 3mm.

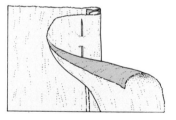

2 Press the seam open. Then turn the right sides of the fabric together. Fold on the stitch line and press. Tack in position, enclosing the seam allowance from the previous seam.

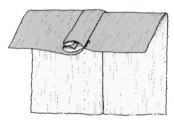

3 Stitch along the seamline and press. Remove tacking stitches.

Flat fell seam

A flat fell seam is a very strong seam which provides a neat finish for either side of the fabric and which withstands heavy wear and frequent washing. The seam can be made with right or wrong sides of fabric together.

1 With wrong (or right) sides of fabric together, pin and tack along seamline. Stitch along the seamline and press seam open. Then press both seam edges over to one side. Trim the under seam allowance to half its width.

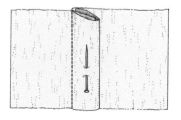

2 Turn the upper seam allowance edge evenly over the trimmed edge, press and pin into place.

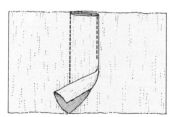

3 To flat fell neaten, edgestitch along the folded edge through all layers of fabric, removing the pins, and press as stitched.

Lapped seam

A lapped seam is used for joining sections of interfacing to avoid bulk.

Lap one edge of the fabric over the other with the seamlines directly over each other. Tack and then stitch along the seamline with a wide zigzag stitch or a straight stitch. Trim the seam edges.

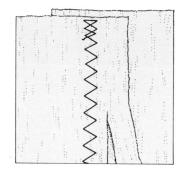

Strengthening seams

In some places, such as the underarm seam where a sleeve joins the bodice of a garment, there is considerable strain on the seam and it should be strengthened by sewing another line of stitches just inside the original seam line.

Trimming seams

The seam allowance on these patterns is usually 1.5cm and in most places it is sufficient just to neaten any raw edges. However, wherever the seam curves or where you need to eliminate any bulk, the seam allowance must be trimmed after the seam has been stitched, to leave a neat, flat seam.

Notching If the seam allowance is on the inside of a curve, cut "V"-shaped notches into it at regular intervals, almost to the stitching. This prevents puckering because it allows the fabric to overlap on the curve.

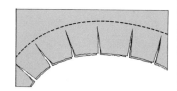

Clipping A seam allowance on the outside edge of a curve should be clipped to ease the fabric. Make small snips at frequent intervals, as close to the stitching as possible.

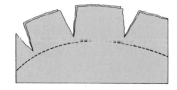

Layering Layering is used on seam allowances to eliminate bulk where you have several fabric thicknesses, such as on collars and cuffs. Trim interfacing as close to the stitching as possible. Trim the under layer to within 3mm of the stitching and the outer layer to within 6mm.

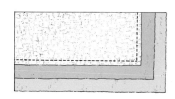

Mitring At corners of seams and where a seam meets a hem-line, the excess fabric on the corner point must be cut away before the corner can be turned neatly. Cut away the excess triangle of fabric across the corner, taking care not to cut the stitches. At hems cut a triangle of seam allowance away on either side of the seam, so that the seam allowances meet the hemline in a neat "V".

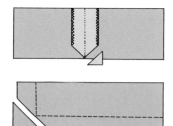

Seam finishes

Seam finishes are designed to neaten seam edges and to prevent fraying. Most straight seams are finished separately, i.e. each edge is neatened and then the seam is pressed open. Curved seams are neatened together, after being trimmed if necessary.

Zigzag-edged seam

This is a useful and quick method for finishing fabrics which fray.

Set the machine to an appropriate stitch length and width and place the edge of the seam allowance, right side up, so that the needle sews once into the fabric and once outside it. Press the seam open.

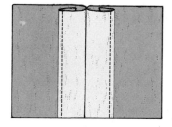

Turned under seam

This is a neat finish for light- to medium-weight, non-bulky fabrics. It is the method to use if your machine does not have a zigzag stitch.

Fold under the edge of the seam allowance by 3mm and press into position. Working on the right side, stitch close to the edge of the fold. Press the finished seam open.

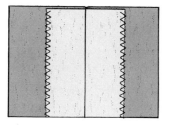

Oversewn seam

If your machine does not have a zigzag stitch, use this method on heavy-weight or bulky fabrics.

Using single thread oversew the edges of the seam allowance (see p. 140). Do not pull the thread too tight.

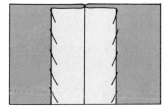

Bound seam

This provides a neat finish for an unlined jacket or coat and is particularly suitable for heavy fabrics. Use seam binding or Paris binding.

Fold the binding in half length-wise and press. Fold the binding around the seam edge and stitch close to the uppermost edge, catching in the under-neath edge.

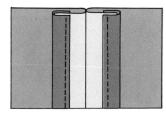

Bias bound seam

An alternative method for binding a seam. Use commercial bias binding or make your own from lightweight fabric.

Attach the binding in the same way as a bias strip is attached, omitting the understitching in step 2 (see p. 152).

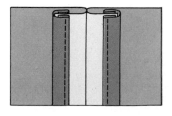

Staystitching

Staystitching is a line of machine stitches sewn around curved edges or edges cut on the cross to prevent stretching or mis-shaping while the garment is being made up. It is also used to hold garment pieces temporarily in position.

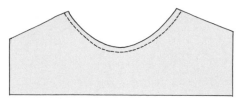

Use a long stitch length and make the line of stitching as soon as you have cut the fabric, before you start to handle it. Make your row of staystitching just within the seam allowance so that it will not show on the finished garment.

Topstitching

Topstitching is a decorative stitch made from the right side of the fabric through to the wrong side, through one or more thicknesses of fabric. It is used around collar edges, along the edges of yokes, cuffs, pleats, lapels, bindings, seams and many other features and is often combined with edgestitching. For the purposes of this book we advise you to use a short stitch to give the characteristic neat finish to all your clothes. Before topstitching, make sure that all seam allowances are pressed in the direction indicated in the pattern instructions and tacked in position if necessary. Layering seam allowances to reduce bulk will ensure that the topstitching lies flat.

Using the machine foot as a guide, stitch through the fabric keeping the stitching line parallel to the edge against which you are lining up the foot.

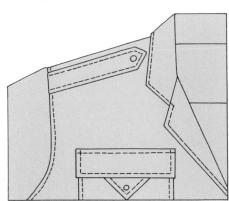

Topstitched garment

Edgestitching

Edgestitching is done on a garment where there is a fold which needs to be held firmly and neatly in position. It is decorative as well as functional and therefore must be made with a short stitch and the correct tension in both upper and lower threads. Many of the garments in this book rely on edgestitching as a method of finishing off turned in edges, particularly in the summer sections. Quite often, edgestitching takes the place of pressing, using the machine clamp to hold the fold in the material.

Turn under 5mm to the wrong side. Press if necessary. Stitch through both layers of fabric from the wrong side close to the folded edge, using a short stitch.

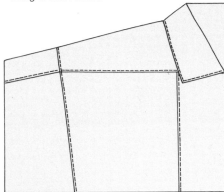

Edgestitched garment

Break stitching

At the sides of gathered skirts, and the turn of a rever, it is a good idea to "break" the line of stitching. This makes it easier to gather a long line of stitching, or allows the rever to "roll" when the under facing becomes the upper facing at the point where the rever runs into the bodice of a jacket.

Understitching

Understitching is a line of stitching around a facing used to help the facing lie flat against the garment. It is not visible from the right side of the garment, but will ensure that revers and facings are firm and prevent them from curling up. It is used in many of the garments in this book, on collars, facings and revers.

Facings

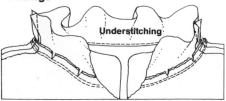

1 *After you have stitched the facing to the armhole or neck edge, press the facing and seam allowances away from the main garment, clipping them where necessary so that they lie flat. Then make a row of stitching on the facing, from the right side, close to the seam joining the neck edge or armhole edge to the facing, through pressed-back seam allowances, all the way round.*

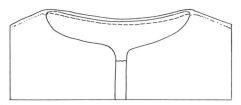

2 *Press facing and turn back against the inside of the garment.*

Revers

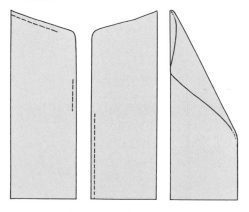

No understitching visible on finished rever

To understitch a rever use the same method of stitching as for neck facings, but because of the turn of the rever the understitching also changes sides. Start your line of understitching at the neck edge, stitching on the right side of front bodice piece around neck and down front edge of rever, through bodice and seam allowances only, close to seamline. Stitch as close to the corner as you can. Break stitching just above turn of rever, pulling threads through and tying off. Leave a gap of about 5cm and then start a new line of understitching on the facing, through rever and seam allowances, down to hem.

Fastening off ends

To fasten off ends of thread when stitching on right side of fabric (such as when topstitching), pull end of under thread gently until a loop of the top thread comes through. Pull this loop (with the help of a pin) to bring top thread through. Fasten off ends of thread by either tying together, or stitching into fabric by hand.

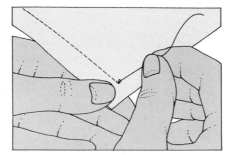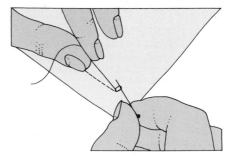

Trying on the garment as you sew

It is important to continually check the fit of the garment you are making. Make sure that when you try a garment on at any stage, you are wearing the clothes you intend to wear with the finished garment – it is pointless fitting a jacket very closely if, for example, you intend to wear a sweater underneath. To avoid unpicking machine stitches, try garments on after you have tacked seams. Then stitch the seams and try the garment on again to ensure the seam lies in the correct position.

When making a bodice section, try the garment on after you have joined the shoulder seams to make sure they are the correct length. Then try it on again after you have joined the side seams, inserted the sleeves, attached pockets and so on. Similarly with trousers and skirts – try them on as soon as you have a basic shape, checking that the degree of darting, etc is appropriate for your figure. Close-fitting garments will require more trying on than loose, full garments. Always try on a garment before hemming any edge.

Common fitting problems

Minor alterations may have to be made to your garment after the first fitting but before final stitching takes place.

Fitted skirt back too tight
If the skirt is too tight at hip level, wrinkles will appear below the waist. Release the centre back darts and then restitch them by curving them inwards to follow your own shape more accurately. The darts may also need shortening.

Shoulder seam too long
Any correction should be made at the crown of the armhole. Remove tacking stitches and re-position the armhole with the seam exactly on the shoulder top. Do not adjust the sleeve seam allowance.

Badly positioned bust dart
The point of the bust dart should be at the fullest part of the bust. If the dart point is too high re-pin from the point, keeping the widest part of the dart in its original position.

Gaping neckline
A gaping neckline can be adjusted by taking in the shoulder seams, making tucks around the neckline or taking it in at the centre back.

Pressing

Pressing is essential in all dressmaking and should be done after completing every step, such as when a seam has been made and neatened, darts have been made, collars and pockets have been turned. Pressing is done in specific areas and should not be confused with ironing where the entire surface of a garment is smoothed. Correct pressing adds a professional look to any garment as well as helping to ensure seams, darts, folds and so forth lie in the correct direction as you sew.

1 *Before starting to press, always test the heat of the iron on a small sample of the fabric you are using to make sure the iron is set at the correct temperature.*

2 *Linens and cottons require a hot iron, wools slightly cooler and synthetics a warm iron.*

3 *Always press on the wrong side of the fabric, using the toe of the iron to open out seams and corners, then lowering the iron on to that particular region. Lift the iron and apply it further up the garment, taking care not to slide it as in ironing.*

4 *Use a pressing cloth to avoid shining fabrics (use a dry cloth with a steam iron, a damp cloth with a dry iron). Silk should be pressed completely dry.*

5 *Remove all pins and tacking stitches before pressing as these will mark the fabric.*

6 *If the fabric to be pressed is very thick, such as a tweed, insert a piece of fabric between the seam allowance and the main body of the garment to prevent the seam allowance making a ridge on the right side. If you have them, use a sleeve board and tailor's ham for pressing sleeve seams and curved areas.*

EXCESS MATERIAL
Darts

Darts are used to provide fullness at the bust, hip, shoulder and elbow. They can be curved or straight, single or double pointed. Their width, length, shape and position will depend on the design and the fit of the garment.

Unless used as a decorative feature, darts are made on the wrong side of the garment. They should taper to a fine point. Slashed darts should be pressed flat. Other darts should be pressed as stitched.

How to make a dart

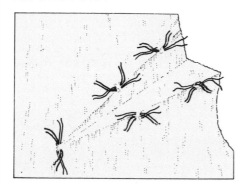

1 *Mark the dart with tailor's tacks or with chalk. Fold the dart carefully so that the markings match.*

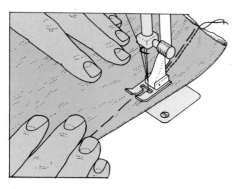

2 *Pin the dart and tack in position, starting at the seam edge and tapering the dart to a fine point. Remove any markings. Machine stitch starting at the seam edge, and finishing just beyond the point of the dart.*

Gathering

Gathering is formed by drawing up the fabric on a row of stitches. It can either be done by hand using a running stitch, or on a machine with a long stitch length. If you are hand stitching, make sure you have enough thread in your needle to complete the line of gathering.

How to gather fabric

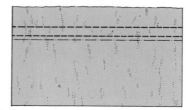

1 *Using a long stitch length and loosening the tension of the top thread, stitch just inside the seam allowance close to the seamline. Leave long thread ends, then make another row of stitches very close to the first row.*

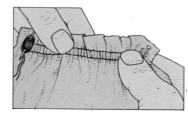

2 *Taking the under threads at each end of the rows of stitching, draw up the threads until the fabric measures the required width. Fasten threads by winding around a pin.*

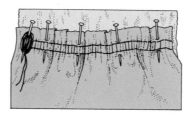

3 *Pin the gathered fabric to the ungathered fabric, with right sides together. Tack if necessary, then stitch along the seamline, with gathered fabric uppermost.*

Easing

Easing follows the same principle as gathering, but is used where one side of a seam is only slightly fuller than the other such as at a sleeve head. Whereas in a gathered seam the fabric on one side falls into a line of small irregular pleats, in an eased seam the fuller side should be smooth and moulded with no visible tucks.

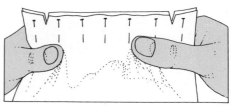

Where only slight ease is required, fullness can be controlled by pinning and bending. Bend the excess material over the shorter side in a curve and pin at even intervals, placing the pins across the seam. Remove the pins as you machine.

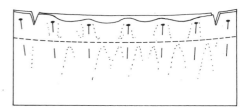

For slightly fuller amounts of fabric machine stitch with a long stitch as used for gathering, just within the seam allowance. Pull up slightly so that fullness is distributed evenly and pin against the shorter side of the seam. Stitch the seam, taking care not to stitch tucks into the fabric.

Dart finishes
Although there is usually no special finish to a dart before it is pressed, there are a few exceptions: for example deep darts, used on heavy fabrics and contour darts, used on light- to medium-weight fabrics.

Deep dart A dart which is made with a deep fold should be slashed through the fold to within 1.3cm from the point and pressed open. If the fabric frays, oversew the edges.

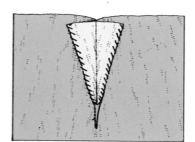

Contour darts Contour darts are pointed at each end. They should be clipped through almost to the stitching line at the widest point. A second line of stitching can be made at the curve as reinforcement.

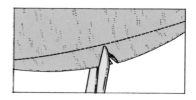

Pleats

Pleats are folds in the fabric used to control fullness. There are three ways of making pleats: knife pleats have folds lying in one direction; box pleats have two folds of equal width turning away from each other, and inverted pleats are made in exactly the same way as box pleats but on the other side of the fabric. It is essential to mark the pleats accurately, to pin or tack the pleats in position and to press them correctly.

Knife pleats

Knife pleats are used at the top of skirts and can be pressed or unpressed. They should be set so that any opening or seams in the skirt are concealed within a pleat.

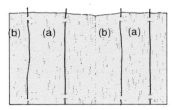

1 *Following the pattern mark the pleat positions on the fabric with tailor's tacks or chalk. Use different colours for foldlines (a) and placement lines (b).*

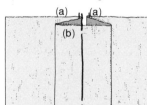

2 *With the right side uppermost, fold pleats so that (a) meets (b). Pin in position at right angles to the pleat. For unpressed pleats staystitch across the top of the pleats, along the seamline, stitching in the direction of the pleats. For pressed, or edge-stitched pleats, tack each pleat in position with a diagonal stitch.*

Box pleats

Box pleats turn away from each other on the right side of the fabric and the underfold meets in the centre on the wrong side. They are most often used singly.

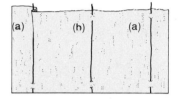

1. *Following the pattern mark the pleat position on the fabric with tailor's tacks or chalk. Use different colours for foldlines (a) and placement line (b).*

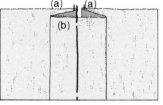

2 *With the right side uppermost fold pleat so that (a) meets (b). Pin in position at right angles to the pleat. Tack in position, if necessary.*

Inverted pleats

Inverted pleats are made in exactly the same way as box pleats, except that the inverted pleat is on the right side of the fabric, and the box pleat on the wrong side.

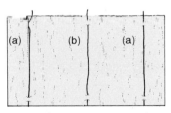

1 *Following the pattern mark the pleat position on the fabric with tailor's tacks or chalk. Use different colours for foldlines (a) and placement line (b).*

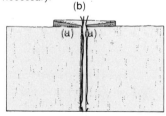

2 *With the right side uppermost fold pleat so that (a) meets (b). Pin in position at right angles to the pleat. Tack in position, if necessary.*

Stitching pleats

All pleats can be pressed or unpressed. Pressed pleats may be edgestitched. If the pleat is to be pressed to the hem, the hem must be finished first.

Edgestitched knife pleats

Edgestitch close to the fold of the pleat and finish at appropriate point. Stop at same point on each pleat. Pull threads through to wrong side and tie.

Edgestitched inverted pleats

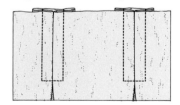

Carefully edgestitch or topstitch, pivoting at corners. Pull threads through to wrong side and tie.

Alternative method for edgestitching inverted pleats

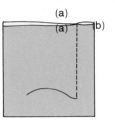

1 *Fold fabric along placement line (b), and stitch part way down foldlines (a), stitching them together.*

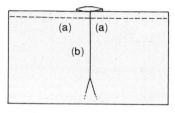

2 *Open out fabric and align placement line (b) with foldlines (a). Press. Staystitch in position.*

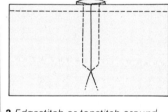

3 *Edgestitch or topstitch around stitching line.*

FACINGS AND BIAS STRIPS

Curved edges, such as necklines and armholes, are often finished off with bias strips (bindings), or facings.

Bias strips

This is a very neat way of finishing curved raw edges. For instructions on cutting a bias strip, see p. 145. Avoid placing seams of binding against seams of garment.

Attaching a bias strip

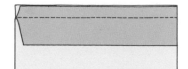  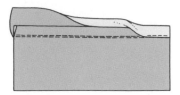

1 *Place right side of binding against right side of edge to be neatened. Tack in position and stitch 5mm from the raw edges.*

2 *Press binding and seam allowances away from garment, clipping seam allowances if necessary. Turn garment so right side is uppermost and understitch through binding and seam allowances, close to seam.*

3. *Turn 5mm to wrong side along remaining raw edge of binding and press. Pin or tack in position so entire strip is on wrong side (e.g. Vest), or half of strip is on wrong side (e.g. Ball gown). Stitch close to folded edge.*

Facings

Usually the facing is cut from a piece of the garment fabric to match the exact shape of the neckline or armhole. Take care to follow the grain indicated on the pattern. The instructions below apply to a round neckline facing, but follow the same principles when attaching an armhole facing.

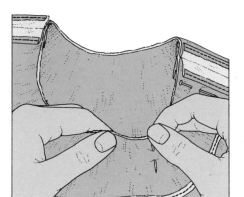 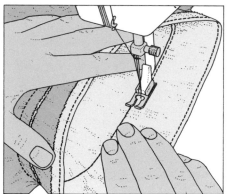 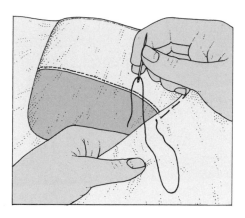

1 *Join the facing at the shoulder seams. Neaten seam edges and press open. Neaten the edge of the facing with zigzagging or by turning it under and stitching it. Pin the facing to the garment, right sides together, matching notches and shoulder seams. Stitch with short stitches around the neckline.*

2 *Trim and clip the seam allowance. Trim corners where the seams cross. Pull the facing outside the neckline. On the right side of the facing understitch around the neckline, through the facing and the seam allowances, as close to the seamline as possible, then press.*

3 *Turn the facing to the inside, rolling it under gently so that the seamline lies just to the inside of the neckline. Tack in position and press or topstitch. Catch the facing to the garment at the shoulderline seam with a few small slip stitches.*

Attaching a collar with a facing

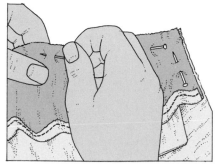 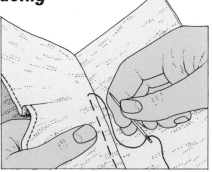 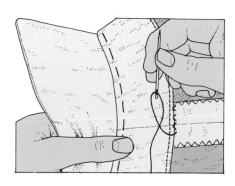

1 *Make collar according to pattern instructions. Place collar in position on the garment, underside of collar against right side of garment. Position the facing on top of the collar, right side against collar. Pin and tack through all thicknesses of fabric. Stitch along the neckline in one continuous line, reverse stitching at the beginning and end of the seam.*

2 *Trim turnings to 5mm then trim the corners and clip into the curve of the neckline, almost to the stitching line. Tack or understitch through facing and seam allowance.*

3 *To keep the facing in place, slipstitch it to the seam allowances of the shoulder seams on the garment.*

INTERFACING

An interfacing is an extra piece of fabric placed between the garment fabric and the facing. It reinforces and adds body and crispness to any faced part of the garment, preserving the shape and giving a sharper finish to the garment. It is usually used only in certain places, such as in collars, cuffs and at openings.

The type of interfacing you use will depend on the fabric and the type of garment. It should never be heavier than the garment fabric and should be compatible for cleaning purposes. Non-woven interfacing has no grain so pattern pieces may be placed in any direction, whereas woven interfacing must be cut on the same grain as pattern pieces. The garments in this book use only light- and medium-weight interfacing.

Where interfacing needs to be seamed, a lapped seam should be used (see p. 147) and then trimmed to a minimum at the seam allowances to avoid any unnecessary bulk.

Attaching interfacing

Non iron-on
Cut light- and medium-weight interfacing to the same size as the garment pieces. Attach temporarily to the wrong side of garment with large tacking stitches. It is then stitched in when the facing is machined to the garment piece. Trim interfacing very close to the seam after it has been stitched, and remove tacking stitches.

Iron-on
Depending on the thickness of the interfacing, this can either be cut the same size as the garment pieces and then trimmed close to the seamline after the garment pieces have been machined, or it can be cut the same size as the garment pieces minus the seam allowance. To attach the interfacing, place in position on the wrong side of the garment, adhesive side down. Using an iron set on medium press interfacing firmly for a few seconds. Do not use moisture, or a steam iron.

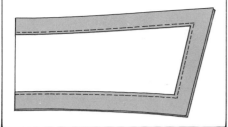

SET-IN SLEEVE

This is cut and made separately from the garment and inserted into the armhole after the bodice has been joined at the side and shoulder seams. The width and length of the sleeve can vary, but the principle of application remains the same. Make the sleeve before inserting it: join the underarm sleeve seam and finish off the cuff edge.

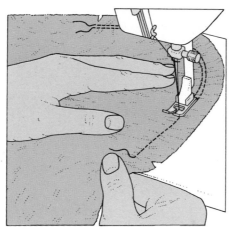

1 *To ease sleeve head, on the wrong side of the sleeve make 1 or 2 rows of gathering stitches just inside the seam allowance between the balance marks on the head of the sleeve. Turning the sleeve to the right side, slip it into the armhole, right sides facing. Align underarm seams and balance marks. Working from the inside of the sleeve, pin at the underarm and shoulder seam points and at the balance marks.*

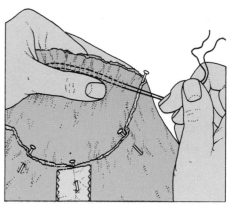

2 *Gather up the fullness in the sleeve evenly towards the shoulderline, on both sides of the shoulder seam, until it fits exactly into the armhole.*

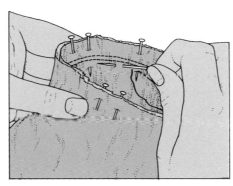

3 *Distribute the gathers evenly and pin across the seamline at close intervals and tack the sleeve in position. Fasten the gathering threads.*

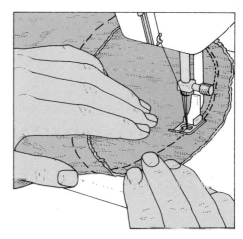

4 *From the sleeve side, stitch along the seamline starting at the underarm seam and over-lapping a few stitches at the end. Remove the gathering threads from the sleeve. Trim and grade the seam allowances and cut off the corners where the seams cross at the shoulder and underarm points. Neaten and press the seam edges.*

TURNING TABS, FLAPS AND BELTS

After you have stitched the pieces of a tab, flap or belt together, the stitched pieces must be turned through the gap in the stitching. If the pieces are sufficiently large you can manipulate the fabric through with your fingers. However, where a tab or belt, for instance, is narrow you will need to turn it with the help of a wooden spoon handle or the blunt end of a knitting needle. Starting at the narrow stitched end, pull the fabric over the handle of the spoon and then pull the outer surface of the fabric over the underneath surface until you reach the opening. Poke out the corners by gently inserting a knitting needle point inside the channel and pushing out each corner. Press the tab, flap or belt and edgestitch if necessary, catching in, or slipstitching together the sides of the opening.

FASTENINGS

Always make sure that both sides of an opening match perfectly at top and bottom before attaching the fastening. The two parts of the fastening should meet without any puckering, pulling or gaping of the fabric.

Hooks and eyes/bars

Position the hook on the under side of the overlap 3mm from the edge. Stitch both holes on the hook and the neck of the hook to keep it flat. Then position the eye or bar on the other side of the opening and stitch in place.

Press-studs

Poppers

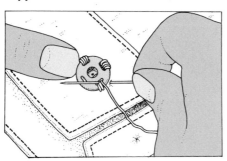

1 *To sew the socket on to the underlap make at least 4 stitches into each hole.*

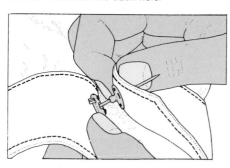

2 *To position the stud, align the two parts of the popper by putting the needle through the centres of both parts, then stitch as in step 1.*

Snap fasteners

Whether these metal studs are applied with a special tool or with a hammer, great care must be taken to position the studs correctly since it is difficult to remove them without damaging the fabric. Full instructions as to how to attach them are given on the packet. Eyelets or studs may be applied in the same way.

Buttonholes

Buttonholes can be either hand-stitched, machine-stitched or bound. Always make a test buttonhole first to check that it will fit the button. Make the buttonholes before attaching the buttons.

Marking buttonhole line

The symbol ⊙ on the pattern marks the outer edge of the buttonhole. This should have been transferred to your garment with tailor's tacks or chalk. The length of the buttonhole depends on the size of your button.
1 *Place the button next to the buttonhole mark and chalk a small cross at the other side of the button.*
2 *Using chalk or a line of tacking, mark a line between the two marks along the straight grain of the fabric, extending it a little way beyond the original buttonhole mark to allow room for the button to go through the hole.*

Hand-stitched buttonhole

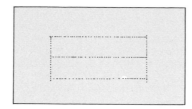

1 *Using chalk, or a short tacking stitch mark lines 3mm above and below the buttonhole line, and across the ends.*

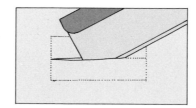

2 *Using small sharp scissors, or a razor blade, carefully slash along the buttonhole line. If the fabric frays easily, oversew the raw edges with thread to match the garment.*

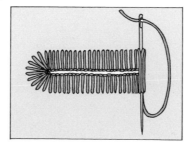

3 *Buttonhole stitch (see p. 140) around the slash, inserting the needle into the slash and bringing it out at the line of tacking stitches below. Make the stitches very close together so that a strong, secure edge is formed. At the end where the button will rest fan the stitches out, and at the other end make a bar of satin stitches, as shown.*

Bound buttonhole

1 *Mark a line with chalk or tacking across each end of the buttonhole line. Cut 2 strips of fabric on the straight grain, 12mm wide, 3cm longer than the buttonhole.*

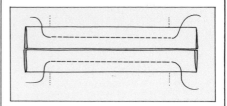

2 *Fold strips in half lengthwise, wrong sides together and press. Lay on right side of fabric, raw edges aligned with buttonhole position line. Stitch along the centre of each strip, through all thicknesses to marked lines.*

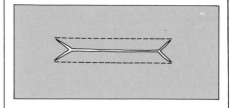

3 *Carefully slash along buttonhole line, to 5mm from marked line at each end. Turn garment to wrong side and cut diagonally into corners, just short of stitching line.*

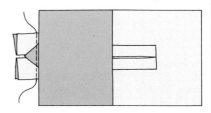

4 *Turn strips through opening to wrong side, making sure "V" shapes at each end are also turned inside. With right side of garment facing upwards, turn back edge of garment and stitch across strip ends and "V" shape. Trim ends and press carefully.*

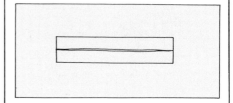

5 *The finished buttonhole. If your garment has a facing, slash facing as in step 3, directly behind the buttonhole, tuck under edges and slipstitch to back of buttonhole.*

Machine-stitched buttonhole

Some machines have a buttonhole attachment or built in mechanism so that buttonholes can be made automatically. Full instructions for setting the size of the buttonhole will be given in the booklet that accompanies the machine. Otherwise buttonholes can be machine made using zigzag stitch.

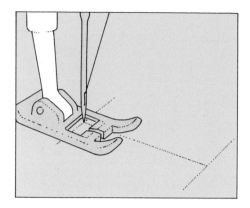

1 *Change the needle plate and foot if necessary. Set the needle position at left, the stitch length at short and the stitch width at medium. Working on the right side of the garment, centre the buttonhole line under the foot. Position the needle at one end of the marked line, on the left side.*

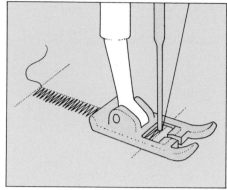

2 *Stitch slowly along the line, ending stitching with needle in the fabric next to marked line.*

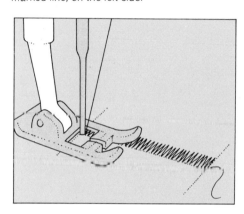

3 *Pivot the fabric on the needle so marked line is again centred under the foot. Take one stitch to bring needle to outer edge of buttonhole. Lift needle.*

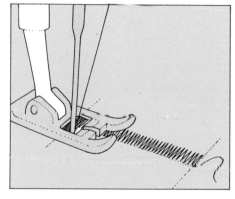

4 *Set the stitch width at wide and take 6 stitches, ending with the needle at the outside edge of the side not yet stitched. Lift needle.*

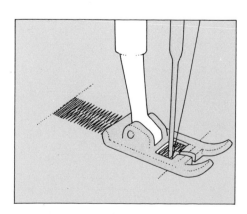

5 *Reset the stitch width to medium and stitch the second side of the buttonhole, stopping just before the end with the needle on the outside edge of the buttonhole. Lift needle.*

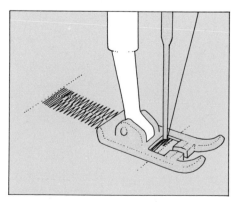

6 *Change stitch width to wide, and sew 6 more stitches. Draw threads to the underside of the garment and tie. Finally carefully slash through the centre of the buttonhole.*

Buttons

Buttons should be selected carefully to make sure they suit the weight and colour of the fabric. They should be sewn on securely with strong, matching thread, leaving enough "give" in the shank to allow the buttonhole to close under the button without puckering the fabric. Position the buttons carefully after the buttonholes have been worked. Pin the opening overlaps together, then pin through the outer edge of each buttonhole to mark the correct position for each button. Buttons are sewn on according to their construction.

Sew through buttons

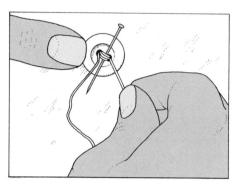

Knot the thread and make a small stitch underneath the button to hide the knot. Stitch in and out of the holes over a pin. Remove pin and wind the thread tightly around the under threads to make a shank. Fasten off securely on the wrong side of the garment.

Shank buttons

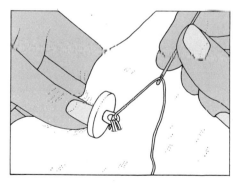

Place the button at right angles to the fabric and stitch through the loop of the shank and the garment several times. Fasten off securely on the wrong side of the garment.

Reinforcing buttons

Depending on the fabric used, the point where a button or snap fastener is attached to a garment may need to be reinforced. Use small squares of non-woven interfacing or a piece of cotton tape or seam binding. When you attach the button or stud place the reinforcing fabric on the inside of the garment directly under the button or stud, and attach the button or stud through all layers.

Zips

Zips can be put in by hand or machine and can be centred, displaced or lapped. Use the centred method for back or centre openings, the lapped method for side or centre openings and the displaced method for jeans style front opening trousers or skirts. Hand–sewn zips look more professional on tailored garments or thick fabric. Zips should be inserted before attaching the waistband or facing so that the tape ends are concealed between the waistband or facing and the garment.

Check list

1 Always insert zips into flat, pressed seams.

2 Finish off all seams before inserting the zip.

3 Make sure the hang of the garment is perfect before inserting the zip.

4 Try to pin and stitch from the bottom of the zip upwards.

5 The head of the zip should be placed just below the seam allowance of the top of the garment.

6 Use a zip foot when machine stitching.

7 Shorten long zips at the bottom by overstitching coils 2.5cm below the desired length. Cut off the excess.

Centred zip

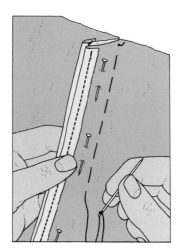

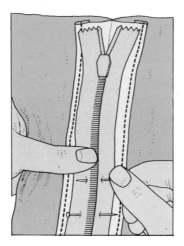

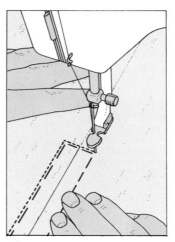

1 Stitch the seam, leaving an opening for the zip the length of the zip teeth. Neaten seam allowances and press open so the foldline forms the fitting line for the zip. Pin and tack along the foldlines. Mark the end of the opening with a pin.

2 Place the zip in position with the teeth centred over the seam, and pin from the bottom of the zip upwards. The pins should be at right angles to the zip, alternating in direction. Tack 6mm from zip teeth. Remove pins.

3 Turn to right side of garment and starting at the bottom of the zip, stitch up one side of the zip, then return to the bottom of the zip and stitch up the other side. Remove tacking and press.

Hand – sewn zip

Follow the instructions for inserting a centred zip or a lapped zip, but instead of machining zip in sew in by hand using elongated back stitch, so that the stitches on the right side of the garment are very short and barely visible. Do not pull the thread too tight. If the fabric is particularly thick, work a second set of stitches, placing them in between the first set of stitches.

Lapped zip

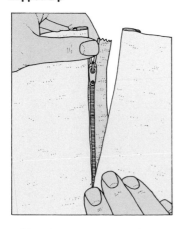

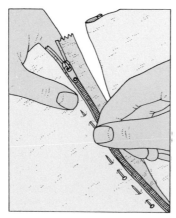

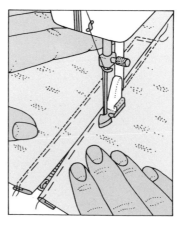

1 Stitch the seam, leaving an opening for the zip the length of the zip teeth. Neaten seam allowances, press the seam open, also press the overlapping section of the opening.

2 From the right side of the garment, position the zip under the seam. Pin and tack the unpressed edge close to the zip teeth. Lap the opposite seam allowance over the zip teeth, making sure they are completely covered. Pin and tack.

3 Stitch from the bottom of the zip upwards. Remove tacking.

Displaced zip

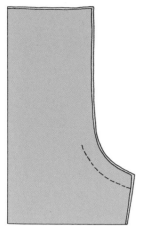

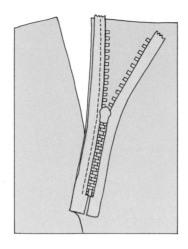

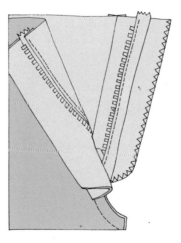

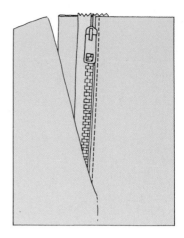

1 *If making trousers, sew under-crotch seam up to point marking bottom of zip opening. If making a skirt sew the front seam to this point. Steps 2–8 are written for inserting a displaced zip into a pair of trousers. The same principles apply when inserting a displaced zip into a skirt front.*

2 *With right side of fabric uppermost, place the zip face down on the left front (leg) piece, so that the zip tape aligns with the opening edge of the leg front. Tack zip in position down this edge following seamline, leaving other side of the zip free. Using zipper foot, stitch tacked side in position, opening zip for ease.*

3 *Press double-folded zip placket along foldline, wrong sides together. Place in position over stitched zip so that all raw edges lie along front opening edge and fold faces towards outside leg. Tack in position along original stitching line and stitch through all thicknesses. Neaten all seam allowances together.*

4 *Turn so that placket and trouser front lie flat with seam allowances facing towards outside leg. Press, then stitch on trouser front down length of zip, close to original seam.*

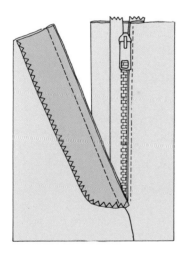

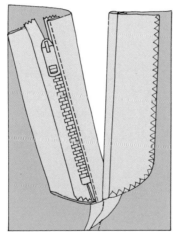

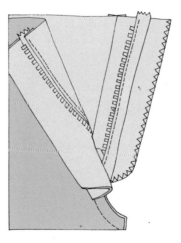

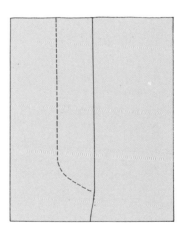

5 *Neaten the long curved edge of the single zip placket. With right sides together and aligning raw edges at front opening edge, tack this placket to right trousers front opening edge, allowing a 5mm seam allowance. Stitch.*

6 *Turn so wrong side of garment is uppermost. Press seam allowances towards centre and turn placket to wrong side of trousers front. Following seam-line of under-crotch seam, press fold at front opening in position so that the seam between placket and trousers front lies slightly in from fold edge on inside.*

7 *Close zip and place trousers flat so that both fronts face upwards and zip also lies flat, facing upwards. Position free zip tape under right front, over-lapping right front opening over left front opening so zip is completely concealed. The right front opening edge should join the under-crotch seam neatly so that the entire opening lies flat. Place a pin through all thicknesses at bottom of opening to hold all layers in position. Feeling through fabric, pin free zip tape to single placket and trousers front, taking care not to pin through to left placket underneath. Then open the zip and tack the zip tape to the single placket only, in exactly the same position, but tacking so that your stitches do not come through to the trousers front. Stitch close to zip teeth, then press*

8 *Tack single placket to right trousers front, just inside neatened curved edge, from top of trousers round to point at bottom of opening. On right side of fabric, topstitch through right trousers front and placket, using tacking line as a guide and stitching from top edge to bottom of zip. Take care not to catch the double placket underneath. Pull threads through at bottom and tie. Turn to wrong side and with zip closed stitch across lower ends of left and right plackets to hold both together. Trim placket ends and neaten together.*

HEMS

A neat, level hem is essential for a professional finish to any garment. Having taken trouble to ensure the correct fit and hang of your garment you must choose the most appropriate method for finishing the hem. The actual shape of the skirt, as well as the type and weight of the fabric, will help determine which method you use. In the patterns in the book instructions are given for the most suitable way of hemming garments when made in the fabrics illustrated. If you choose to make a garment in a different fabric you may want to choose a different method of hemming which is more appropriate to that particular fabric. It is best to finish off hems by hand if an invisible finish on the right side of the garment is required.

Before marking the hem, make sure that the garment fits perfectly and hangs correctly. Any adjustment to the rest of the garment will affect the fall of the hem and therefore the look of the entire garment. If a lining is attached to the skirt the two hems should be measured and marked separately.

Marking the hemline

Before measuring the hem length, take into account the shoes, belts etc, you intend to wear with the garment and allow for the way these affect the hem length. If possible find someone to mark the hem for you.

Using your metre stick, measure an even distance from the floor, and mark the position of the final hem length above the raw hem edge with chalk. Move the ruler around the hem to take into account the hang of the skirt at every point. For longer skirts, stand on a stool.

Fold the hem at the chalk line, pin, and then tack, 5mm in, all the way around bottom of hem. Press from wrong side to sharpen hem fold. Cut away surplus fabric so that the hem is the same depth all the way round. Trim any seam allowances within the hem at side seams, back seam etc, to 5mm.

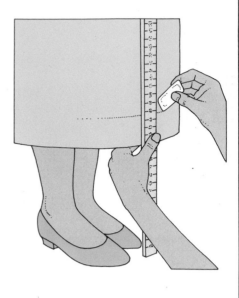

Machine-stitched hem

Machine-stitched hems are useful because they can be sewn quickly and they provide a strong finish to a hem edge. Because machine stitched hems are sewn from the wrong side through to the right, take care to sew neatly and evenly, always making sure you have enough thread in your bobbin to form a continuous line of stitching.

1 Having established the correct length of your hem, and allowing 1.5cm for the turn-up of the hem, trim away surplus material. Fold under 5mm to wrong side and stitch.

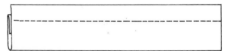

2 Turn under a further centimetre, pin or tack in position if necessary and stitch close to the first folded edge through to the right side.

3 Use a short stitch length and ensure that the stitching line runs parallel to the hem edge, as this line of stitching will be seen from the outside of the garment. Remove pins or tacking and press hem.

Slipstitched hem

This is suitable for garments which are frequently laundered and for linings. It provides a firm, neat hem which is invisible from the right side.

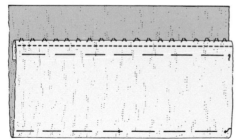

Fold under 5mm to wrong side along the raw edge of the hem and stitch. Fold up required depth of hem to wrong side. Pin in position, matching seams and distributing any fullness evenly. Tack if necessary. Slipstitch folded edge of hem (see p. 140). Remove pins or tacking and press hem.

Herringbone hem

This is suitable for loosely-woven or knitted fabrics.

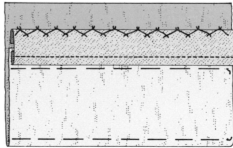

Neaten the raw hem edge with zigzag stitch or bias binding. Fold up required depth of hem to wrong side, and pin in position matching seams. Tack if necessary. Herringbone stitch around finished edge (see p. 140). Remove pins or tacking and press hem.

Zigzag hem

This is suitable for knitted fabrics and bulky wools if you do not want to bind the hem.

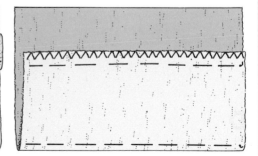

Neaten the raw hem edge with zigzag stitch, trimming away any straying threads. Fold up required depth of hem to wrong side and pin in position, matching seams. Tack if necessary. Hem stitch or slipstitch the zigzagged edge (see p. 140). Remove pins or tacking and press hem.

Index

Acknowledgements

I would like to express my gratitude to the many people who have helped with this book. For their support, advice and hard work I would like to thank Bridget Harris, Denise Brown, Melanie Miller, Debbie Lee and Amy Carroll and especially Margaret Watkins and Rod Parker.

Flat photography
Ian O'Leary

Illustrators
Kuo Kang Chen
John Hutchinson

Fashion photography
Roger Eaton

Make-up
Louise Constad
at Laraine Ashton
using Elizabeth Arden

Hair
Wendy Sadd
at Simon Rattan

Pattern grading
Ron Klein

Typesetting
Chambers Wallace

Reproduction
Reprocolor International

Dorling Kindersley would like to thank **The Singer Company** for the loan of a *2010* Singer sewing machine; the following companies for lending props: **Talisman** for jewellery, **Mulberry Co.** for accessories, **Bertie Shoes** for shoes and **The Button Box** for buttons; Michelle Walker and Clare Lissaman. The author would also like to thank The Cotton Institute for their advice, and all the fabric suppliers.

Pattern paper
Additional pattern paper is available by mail order at £1.50 per pack of 5 sheets (includes p&p). Send a cheque or postal order to: Dorling Kindersley Ltd. (Dept. MP), 9 Henrietta Street, Covent Garden, London WC2E 8PS. (Applies to U.K. and Republic of Ireland only.)